HV 91 .W476 1993

Welfare system reform

Welfare System Reform

Recent Titles in
Studies in Social Welfare Policies and Programs

WELFARE SYSTEM REFORM

Coordinating Federal, State, and
Local Public Assistance
Programs

Edited by
EDWARD T. JENNINGS, JR.
and
NEAL S. ZANK

Foreword by
JOHN A. GARTLAND

STUDIES IN SOCIAL WELFARE POLICIES AND PROGRAMS,
NUMBER 16

Greenwood Press
Westport, Connecticut • London

Library of Congress Cataloging-in-Publication Data

Welfare system reform : coordinating federal, state, and local public
  assistance programs / edited by Edward T. Jennings, Jr. and Neal S.
  Zank ; foreword by John A. Gartland.
       p.   cm. — (Studies in social welfare policies and programs,
  ISSN 8755–5360 ; no. 16)
    Includes bibliographical references and index.
    ISBN 0–313–28485–7 (alk. paper)
    1. Public welfare—United States.   2. Federal aid to public
  welfare—United States.   I. Jennings, Edward T.
  II. Zank, Neal S.   III. Series.
  HV91.W476   1993
  361.973—dc20   92–21361

British Library Cataloguing in Publication Data is available.

Library of Congress Catalog Card Number: 92–21361
ISBN: 0–313–28485–7
ISSN: 8755–5360

First published in 1993

Greenwood Press, 88 Post Road West, Westport, CT 06881
An imprint of Greenwood Publishing Group, Inc.

Printed in the United States of America

The paper used in this book complies with the
Permanent Paper Standard issued by the National
Information Standards Organization (Z39.48–1984).

10 9 8 7 6 5 4 3 2 1

Contents

Abbreviations

AFDC	Aid to Families with Dependent Children
CETA	Concentrated Employment and Training Act
DOL	Department of Labor
E & T	Employment and Training
EOP	Executive Office of the President
FNS	Food and Nutrition Service
FS	Food Stamps
FSA	Family Support Act
FSET	Food Stamps Employment and Training
GAO	General Accounting Office
HHS	Department of Health and Human Services
HUD	Department of Housing and Urban Development
JOBS	Job Opportunities and Basic Skills
JTPA	Job Training Partnership Act
LIOB	Low Income Opportunity Board
LIOWG	Low Income Opportunity Working Group
MDRC	Manpower Demonstration Research Corporation
MIG	Manpower Institutional Grant
NCEP	National Commission for Employment Policy
NGA	National Governors' Association
NJETC	New Jersey Employment and Training Commission
OEO	Office of Economic Opportunity
OMB	Office of Management and Budget
OTA	Office of Technology Assessment

PIC	Private Industry Council
SJTCC	State Job Training Coordinating Council
SPOC	Single Point of Contact
SSI	Supplemental Security Income
TAG	Technical Assistance and Training
USDA	U.S. Department of Agriculture
WIC	Women, Infants, and Children
WIN	Work Incentive program

Foreword

This book represents the culmination of a two-year project sponsored by the National Commission for Employment Policy to increase the public dialogue on the nation's public assistance system and to recommend approaches for improving coordination in that system. Although the commission's primary concern is with employment and training, the broad scope of this project was necessary because employment and training programs and associated coordination issues must be looked at within the larger framework of all federal public assistance programs.

Approximately two years ago, the commission became aware that the efficient provision of employment and training services was hampered by a number of coordination and eligibility criteria problems. To address these problems, the commission instituted a multiphase project to examine the state of coordination in employment and training programs. During the course of the project, the commission heard from approximately 200 people involved at all levels of the public assistance system: those who develop nationwide policies in Washington, D.C., those who coordinate assistance programs in the states, and those who deliver services at the local level.

The information collected by the commission helped to paint a picture of an uncoordinated $200 billion public assistance system overloaded with regulations, procedures, definitions, and terminology. The canvas was crowded with varying funding formulas, administrative provisions, eligibility criteria, planning and operating timetables, bureaucratic territoriality, and conflicting regulations.

In the fall of 1991, letters containing the commission's recommendations on coordination were sent to President Bush and the Congress. These recommendations are available in a commission special report, *Coordinating Federal Assistance Programs for the Economically Disadvantaged: Recommendations and Background Materials* (October 1991).

As a result of the commission's efforts to call attention to the coordination problem, we hope that policymakers and legislators, program designers and service providers, and analysts and academics will pay greater attention to the issues surrounding the coordination of public assistance programs. This attention should lead to policy and program improvements that will result in more efficient and effective service delivery with lower costs, more reasonable access to a streamlined and comprehensive range of potential services, and a better use of hard-earned tax dollars.

John A. Gartland
Chairman
National Commission for Employment Policy

Preface

This book, which addresses "the coordination problem," is based on papers prepared for the National Commission for Employment Policy's coordination project described in the Foreword. We have sought to provide relevant, timely, and useful information to those interested or involved in the administration or reform of the nation's public assistance programs.

The commission relied on three seminars—promoted under the title "Improving Coordination in Government-Sponsored Public Assistance Programs"—to address national-, state-, and local-level coordination issues and to hear the ideas, views, and frustrations of participants in the public assistance system. These participants ranged from subcabinet officials in Washington to service providers in local communities.

The seminar on national-level coordination issues was held in Washington, D.C., on March 27, 1991. The approximately eighty participants included senior White House and executive branch officials, agency staff, congressional staff, public policy experts, academics, state and local government officials, and representatives of interest groups involved in administering, analyzing, critiquing, or overseeing public assistance programs.

The seminar on state-level coordination issues was held in San Antonio, Texas, on May 6, 1991. The primary participants were the chairs of the State Job Training Coordinating Councils from approximately thirty states, who are in key positions in their states to influence state-level coordination issues. Other attendees included local and state government officials and public policy experts.

The final seminar, focusing on local issues in coordination, was held on July 14, 1991, in San Diego, California. Approximately thirty representatives of local governments and local implementing agencies from nine states participated in the seminar.

Following the conferences, we decided that the conference papers might be of interest to a broader population that did not attend the conference. Our attempt to expand and enhance the conference discussions resulted in a book that differs from the original conferences in three significant ways: (1) the revised conference papers presented here benefit from the interactions and discussions during the conferences; (2) three chapters provide original research not presented at the conferences; and (3) we have removed or explained as much technical language as possible so that the nontechnical reader will be able to understand the primary issues and the possible solutions presented in the book.

We owe thanks to several people for their contribution to this book. First, we wish to thank commission chairman John C. Gartland and commission director Barbara C. McQuown for taking this rather original and experimental approach to disseminating the findings of the public policy process. We would also like to thank Sharronne Queen of the commission staff for her assistance in preparing portions of the manuscript. We also thank Angie Hoskins of the Martin School of Public Administration at the University of Kentucky for secretarial assistance. Charles Hardin provided invaluable assistance on the index. Of course, we appreciate the efforts of our contributors and thank them for the time they spent in painstakingly revising their original conference presentations.

The findings and recommendations presented in this book are solely those of the editors and contributors and not those of the National Commission for Employment Policy or the University of Kentucky.

Part I

INTRODUCTION

Chapter 1

The Coordination Challenge

Edward T. Jennings, Jr. and Neal S. Zank

Coordination was *the* issue of American social policy in 1991. National commissions identified the proliferation of uncoordinated programs as the source of severe problems affecting the well-being of children, infant mortality, and the delivery of public assistance and job training services. Other reports pointed out the critical need to coordinate foster care and adult illiteracy programs. Several national conferences brought the coordination issue to the attention of policymakers and program administrators, offering a variety of suggestions to improve service delivery and bring coherence to policy.

Nowhere is the coordination problem more evident than in the vast array of public assistance programs. The federal government administers seventy-five programs to provide assistance to the economically disadvantaged (National Commission for Employment Policy, 1991). These programs offer many forms of assistance: direct financial aid; assistance for medical care, food, housing, and energy; education, training, and employment services; and other services. They account for more than $200 billion in assistance expenditures (Burke, 1989). Only 25 percent of the expenditures for these programs is in cash; the remainder is in the form of noncash benefits, such as food stamps, payments for medical care, and housing. These programs are supplemented by a variety of state, local, and private initiatives.

The primary objective of these programs has been to meet the basic needs of the economically disadvantaged. The three ways followed historically to accomplish this objective have been (1) transferring income to the poor to provide a minimum standard of living, (2) providing the poor with in-kind benefits that will enable them to reach a minimum standard of living, and (3) providing the poor with the services and tools that will enable them to become self-supporting and reach, on their own, a minimum standard of living (Advisory Commission on Intergovernmental Relations, 1987).

These programs and the agencies that administer them are organized around administrative features and legislative oversight responsibilities. They lack a comprehensive orientation toward either services or clients. The public assistance system is not structured to deliver services in a manner that is recipient-friendly or that, at least, takes into account the total needs of the recipient. Each program is supported by its own bureaucracy, rules, and constituency. This type of dispersion exists at the federal, state, and local levels.

From the perspective of the individual seeking support, the prospect can be particularly daunting. Few programs are wholly self-contained; most deal with only part of an individual's or family's needs. Many recipients continue to have trouble determining just what services are available to them, much less taking advantage of the full range of opportunities. Nor is the system structured to deliver all services of a particular type in a systematic manner.

The multitude of regulations, procedures, definitions, and terms used in federal public assistance programs has contributed to an assistance system that is fragmented, uncoordinated, and difficult to administer. Many who work in the public assistance delivery system and many who wish to benefit from it see the system as inefficient, costly, and confusing. State and local program administrators and implementers find the paperwork requirements burdensome and the differing program mandates difficult to administer. Program recipients or beneficiaries find the programs to be arbitrary and duplicative in their requirements, difficult to understand, and hard to access. Of course, taxpayers find the programs to be wasteful and inefficient (U.S. Office of Management and Budget, 1980; Low Income Opportunity Working Group, 1986).

The fragmented design of the current public assistance system also means problems for aid recipients who move from one program to another. The possibilities include a lack of coverage, interruption of assistance, or falling through the cracks as one loses one's eligibility for one program and becomes eligible for another. Potential clients, typically with children in tow, bounce from agency to agency and travel from one end of town to the other in order to negotiate these systems.

The current operating practices also have high costs. Agencies perform redundant or overlapping tasks, offering similar services to the same target groups of beneficiaries. Layers of unnecessary bureaucracy move excessive paperwork. Computer systems do not communicate with each other. Commitment of funds to these administrative activities means fewer dollars allocated for aiding the disadvantaged.

A solution to part of this problem, at least, is improving coordination among these programs and the agencies that manage them. With the federal government supporting seventy-five different public assistance programs, it is not hard to see why coordination would be a frequent and frustrating concern. Although the programs have varied purposes and use diverse means to pursue objectives involving multiple constituencies, there is often considerable overlap of goals, methods, and clientele. Progress on the integration of human services has been intermittent at best, since efforts were made to generate such integration in the early 1970s (Agranoff, 1991; Mikulecky, 1974; Yessian, 1991). Even though requirements for coordination have become a standard feature of statutory law, the number of programs proliferates and linkages become more tenuous.

For program administrators and service providers, coordination should mean more efficient and effective resource management and service delivery, potentially lower costs by utilization of improved procedures and realization of economies of scale in service delivery, access to a broad range of information, and easier evaluation of programs. Coordination also provides a means to more effectively link together the different parts of the system to work more effectively. Eligibility conflicts would be removed, and intake procedures would be simplified. The recipient is presented with a seamless or integrated set of services that meets his or her needs, without the encumbrances presented by different documentation requirements, funding streams, and agencies. In simple terms, coordination is a way of reducing the waste associated with unnecessary duplication of services and providing easier or more reasonable access to a streamlined, more comprehensive range of potential services.

It is difficult to get some participants in the system to consider changing the system because they see the cure as being worse than the disease. Change is costly, in one way or another, and decision makers do not always see the benefits that will follow change. Unfortunately, they do not understand that their part of the system affects the rest of the system. Although change in the measurements or definitions of eligibility standards at the federal level may not result in cost savings in Washington, the positive effects of such change would be felt throughout the system. Much of the "innovation" at the local level, designed in reality to cope with the administrative problems created in Washington, would not be necessary and real savings in both dollars and productivity could be realized.

Therefore, changes at the federal level would serve, in effect, as catalysts for total systemic change. As one state job training administrator said, if federal and state leaders could sit down and discuss legislative barriers to coordination and change definitions or programs so that people are better served "it would be a visible demonstration of how the federal partner is doing more than providing lip service."

This book is intended to stimulate thinking about approaches to dealing with the substance of public assistance policy as it bears on coordination issues, organizational arrangements for policy development and delivery, and processes for building linkages between disparate but related programs. It does not attempt to determine the appropriate definition of need or the necessary level of benefits. Its focus is on process, not funding.

THE CONTEXT FOR CHANGE

Of course, the coordination problem does not exist in a vacuum. Rather, it exists within the context of (1) broader demands for reform of the welfare system; (2) extraordinary pressure on federal, state, and local government budgets; (3) increased demands for accountability in public programs; and (4) increased international economic competition.

There is strong public pressure to reform public welfare systems—pressure that has grown despite the adoption of major welfare reform legislation in the Family Support Act of 1988. Policy prescriptions from the Right have ranged from requiring welfare recipients to work to reducing incentives that work against a strong family structure. Solutions from the Left have included more adequate welfare allowances and improving the poor's access to jobs and a broad range of services. The one point on which both sides agree is that the current system must be made more effective and efficient and coordination among programs must improve.

This public pressure is a product, in part, of broader public concerns about government taxing and spending. With the federal deficit at an all time high and state and local governments raising taxes while cutting services, there is widespread belief that government has to find ways to pursue its goals more effectively while spending less. The social service arena is one target of this concern. Discovering internal inefficiencies and reducing operating costs through coordination are ways of achieving these goals.

Demands for accountability in federal and state programs have also been a topic of public concern. Over the past twenty years, elected officials, the public, and interest groups have increasingly challenged public programs to demonstrate their effectiveness. Opinion polls and recent elections demonstrate that the public finds the status quo unacceptable. Among other things, this demand for accountability has led to the setting of performance standards in legislation, the growth of program evaluation, and the increased activity of the U.S. General Accounting Office and its state counterparts. Demands for increased public scrutiny, increased legislative oversight, and administrative reform incorporate the failure to adequately coordinate the public assistance system.

These multiple pressures have come as the United States is attempting to solve its economic problems in an increasingly competitive international economic environment. Although there are many reasons for America's economic difficulties, a variety of studies suggest that we suffer because of the low educational attainment and skill levels of significant parts of the population. Improvements in the systems of public assistance are critical if the United States is to meet this challenge.

This context of public pressure, demands for accountability and effectiveness, the need to control government spending, and international economic competition highlights the compelling need for coordination. We now turn our attention to describing how widespread the coordination problem is.

THE PROBLEM IS WIDESPREAD

Unfortunately, the coordination problem is found throughout the public assistance network. Most social service program areas confront similar administrative and institutional obstacles. The examples below illustrate some of these problems.

Look at job training. It has been estimated that there are forty-five federal programs that have an employment and training focus or a significant skills training component, with funding of approximately $20 billion (U.S. General Accounting Office, 1989). Responsibility for these forty-five programs is spread across dozens of congressional committees and six cabinet departments.

Major job training programs are administered by three agencies. The Department of Labor's Employment and Training Administration administers the Job Training Partnership Act (JTPA), the employment service, and several other programs. The Administration for Children and Families of the Department of Health and Human Services (HHS) administers the Job Opportunities and Basic Skills (JOBS) program. The Food and Nutrition Service (FNS) of the U.S. Department of Agriculture (USDA) administers an Employment and Training (E&T) program as a component of the Food Stamps program.

Congressional turf issues arise here as well. The JOBS program falls under the jurisdiction of the Finance and Ways and Means committees. Food Stamps Employment and Training oversight is maintained by the two agriculture committees. JTPA and many other job training services are the province of the Senate Labor and Human Resources and the House Education and Labor committees.

A multitude of program differences exist across the entire range of employment and training and vocational education programs funded by the federal government. For example, some programs, such as JTPA, are 100 percent federally funded, while others, such as JOBS, require a match between federal and state funding.

The problems go beyond employment and training programs. A recent article in *Policy Review* (Bishop, 1991) reported on the maze of programs addressing adult literacy. A 1986 report by the Federal Interagency Committee on Education identified fourteen different agencies administering seventy-nine different literacy and literacy-related programs. The five main agencies that administered adult literacy programs were the Departments of Defense, Education, Health and Human Services, Justice, and Labor. According to the article, only the Defense and Justice departments used adequate methods or techniques for measuring program success. Few of these programs could even state accurately or completely how much they spent on adult education.

Even programs addressing the problem of foster care for children are not immune. The *Congressional Quarterly* identified fifteen major programs providing such services. These programs, which do not include Aid to Families with Dependent Children (AFDC) or Social Service Block Grants, total approximately $2.4 billion. In addition, congressional oversight is divided among a host of committees: Finance and Labor and Human Resources in the Senate, Ways and Means and Education and Labor in the House. On top of this are the subcommittees and appropriations committees. Apparently, the split jurisdiction and associated turf battles held up legislation for months in the 101st Congress while the committees fought over various child welfare approaches (Rovner, 1991).

Relief from the coordination problem will not be found in other child welfare programs. The federal government provides child care assistance for working mothers through more than twenty separate programs, spread over at least five cabinet departments (HHS, USDA, Treasury, HUD, and Labor). The size of these programs ranges from the $2 billion Head Start program to the $1 million grant programs providing miscellaneous services (Ooms, 1989).

At the state level, the agency administering the Title XX Social Service Block Grant child care program is sometimes different from the agency administering the JOBS child care program. Each program has different eligibility criteria, funding streams, and other requirements. Related early childhood education programs, such as Head Start, may be located in yet a third agency and have their own rules, regulations, and eligibility criteria (Ooms, 1991).

The numbers are even more startling in federal infant mortality programs. One reviewer identified ninety-three federal programs administered by twenty federal agencies addressing issues related to infant mortality. Almost $9 billion in federal and state funds are used to combat infant mortality through prenatal and neonatal care. The range of programs and agencies underscores the difficulty of providing comprehensive services to mothers and babies. USDA administers the Special Supplemental Feeding Program for Women, Infants, and Children, the Public Health Service administers the Maternal and Child Health grant program, and the Health Care Financing Administration operates Medicaid. Each program has its own eligibility standards, different from the others (Singh, 1990).

The National Commission to Prevent Infant Mortality, in its April 1991 report, *One-Stop Shopping: The Road to Healthy Mothers and Children*, identified part of the problem of programs designed for women and infants. It reported that Medicaid, the Women, Infants, and Children (WIC) nutrition programs, and other programs established to serve women and children operate on completely different tracks.

> They have different application processes, eligibility requirements, and terminologies. Each is designed to treat a specific symptom, not an entire person. . . . As the size of government and the number of programs have increased over the years, so has the fragmentation between these programs, both vertically—between the federal, state, and local levels, and horizontally—between administering agencies and service providers. As a result, programs are administered by multiple agencies, which use multiple funding streams, as well as different definitions, terminology, and factors for determining eligibility and benefits. (9–10)

The commission referred to the delivery system as an obstacle course (National Commission to Prevent Infant Mortality, 1991).

The National Commission on Children found a complex array of programs providing support and assistance to families with severe problems. To its dismay, however, the commission found that these programs seldom meet the needs of the families. As the commission put it, "Service providers in separate programs serving the same family rarely confer or work to reinforce one another's efforts. . . . As a result, families seeking assistance often encounter a service delivery system that is confusing, difficult to navigate, and indifferent to their concerns" (National Commission on Children, 1991: 79).

HOW THE COORDINATION PROBLEM DEVELOPED

Until the 1930s, local governments in the United States were responsible for the administration of most public welfare activities. Federal activities were limited to emergency relief efforts and only a few states had initiated active programs. The change in economic conditions brought about by the Great Depression in 1929 provided the justification sought by social reformers who were looking to establish a federal role in public welfare. A new system of federal grants was initiated to stimulate the creation of basic welfare programs in every state under minimal national standards and to share in supporting these programs (Dawson and Gray, 1971; Elazar, 1972).

As the decades passed, responsibility for initiating, operating, and financing these programs shifted to the states and, mostly, the federal government. With the War on Poverty of the 1960s, the federal presence in public assistance expanded rapidly. New programs, such as Food Stamps, were initiated and eligibility for older programs, such as Aid to Families with Dependent Children (AFDC), was extended. The federal government expanded its role as an initiator of programs as well as a policy innovator willing to apply various forms of pressure to states and localities in order to get them to conform to federal expectations. This federal expansion took place for a variety of reasons, including (1) the desire on the part of advocates for the poor to obtain better and more secure assistance for the poor and (2) state and local government urging that the federal government create new programs for the poor and assume more of the costs of these assistance programs (Advisory Commission on Inter-governmental Relations, 1987; U.S. General Accounting Office, 1987a).

During this period, the White House relied on a single office to coordinate public assistance programs. From 1964 through 1975, the Office of Economic Opportunity (OEO) was authorized to coordinate both new and old poverty programs. OEO, however, was never able to establish itself as an effective force for coordination.

The "new" welfare system of the 1960s had strong elements of both centralization and decentralization. While federal action expanded, so did that of states and localities. The federal efforts brought increased funding, support for a wider array of activities, and a growing body of rules and regulations. Within this framework, there was considerable variability of state and local program design and administration. State and local governments complained of rigid rules and regulations, endless documentation requirements, and unresponsiveness to local conditions (Dawson and Gray, 1971; Butler, 1987; Jennings et al., 1986; Walker, 1981; Wright, 1978).

Public assistance programs experienced sizeable spending increases throughout the 1970s, although structural changes occurred only in the early part of the decade. The Nixon administration used numerous grant programs and differing program approaches to produce structural changes. The Department of Health, Education, and Welfare carried out experiments in services integration. Two of the objectives of these experiments were coordinating the delivery of services and the rational allocation of resources at the local level in order to be responsive to local needs. Among the approaches encouraged were the consolidation of programs and the simplification of administrative procedures (Conlan, 1988).

Although welfare reform received serious discussion in the Carter administration, little action on coordination took place in the late 1970s. In December 1978, the Carter administration initiated an interagency Eligibility Simplification Project to make recommendations on the simplification of client eligibility criteria among major public assistance programs. The project's completion in October 1980, shortly before the election, precluded any direct action on the report's recommendations by that administration.

Thinking on public assistance issues changed somewhat in the 1980s. The Reagan administration proposed a broad welfare reform program based on several considerations: targeting aid to the "truly needy"; reducing fraud, waste, and abuse; promoting competition (e.g., through vouchers); and eliminating programs believed to be ineffective (e.g., the Comprehensive Employment Training Act program). Eligibility standards were tightened in some programs, stronger work requirements were authorized by law, and some progress was made in improving program administration (through the requirement that all states establish income and eligibility verification systems for the major welfare programs).

For the most part, the federal government tried to lessen its role in program design and implementation. In reality, the intergovernmental system for the administration of public assistance programs that evolved in the 1980s was composed of federal programs shaped increasingly by planning and operational decisions made by state and local agencies.

Important changes instituted in the 1980s included a series of welfare initiatives that culminated in the Family Support Act of 1988 and the consolidation of many programs into block grants. In response to these initiatives, many governors and states adopted new management and policy approaches. These approaches entailed overhauling their welfare programs, attracting high-quality administrators, and experimenting with new approaches for designing, managing, and administering these programs.

Some argued that differences between states called for maximum state discretion in designing certain welfare programs, although many states looked to the federal government for leadership on the integration of these services and programs (Elazar, 1972; U.S. General Accounting Office, 1988). States differed in their capacity to implement programs, the administrative structures they had in place for coordination, and the level of funding they had available. In addition, the labor market and characteristics of welfare recipients differed among states. Many believe that only state and local providers can offer services tailored to local needs.

The extent of federal or state involvement in a particular program ranges from determining program guidelines, to administering the program, to just providing a resource transfer to implementing jurisdictions. For most public assistance programs (such as AFDC, Food Stamps, and Medicaid), management or administrative guidelines are determined by the federal government and the program is administered or implemented by state and local governments. Functions such as program formulation, setting eligibility criteria, determining benefits, and administration may be performed at either the federal or state level, depending on the program. The federal government generally oversees the transfer of funds and audits their use, but rarely interferes with program operations. In many instances, the states determine the extent to which they will be involved. A state may elect to have the program administered centrally (state administered) or locally (state supervised).

In contrast, this federal-state administrative network does not apply to programs for most elderly or disabled persons, whose Supplemental Security Income (SSI) cash assistance is typically administered through Social Security Administration district and branch offices. The transfer of these programs to federal administration occurred in the 1970s as part of an effort to develop uniform, national standards for the treatment of these recipients. Although these federal offices do not administer the Food Stamp program, they do perform some joint processing of applications. These same offices, of course, directly administer the Old Age, Survivors, and Disability Insurance programs.

The Reagan administration also initiated a White House review of welfare policy in 1986, which led to a new national strategy to reform public assistance, presented in the report *Up from Dependency* (Low Income Opportunity Working Group, 1986). This strategy focused on welfare reform through state-sponsored demonstrations of innovations in public assistance programs, with the aim of reducing dependency.

The strategy was implemented at the federal level in 1987 by the establishment of the Low Income Opportunity Board (LIOB). LIOB, a subsidiary unit of the White House Office of Policy Development, was created to serve as a single point of contact for states wishing to obtain waivers from federal statutes and regulations that frustrated innovative welfare reform at the state and local level. The Economic Empowerment Task Force replaced the LIOB in 1990.

Coordination was also a central feature of some of the legislation enacted in the 1980s. The innovative Job Training Partnership Act (JTPA) of 1982 emphasized coordination between state governments and the business community through the use of state job training coordinating councils, as well as between JTPA programs and other programs for employment, training, and human resource development. The Family Support Act of 1988, the major piece of welfare reform legislation during the past decade, contained guidance to the executive branch on coordinating welfare programs, the Job Opportunities and Basic Skills (JOBS) program, and other employment and training activities at the state and local level. Coordination mandates were also included in education and food aid legislation.

ELEMENTS OF THE COORDINATION PROBLEM

The coordination problem, as it has evolved, is easy to identify: too many administrative agencies providing too many assistance programs under the oversight of too many congressional committees. The problem is composed primarily of five elements.

Like so many other things, the problem starts at the top. The absence of presidential leadership in this area has been damaging. In recent years, domestic policy discussions about welfare reform have addressed the question of who receives assistance under what conditions; however, not enough attention has been paid to how programs are run and how benefits are dispensed. Presidential influence has rarely penetrated the web created by the existing uncoordinated system.

At a time when agencies are fighting for every budget dollar that they can, it is easy for cabinet and subcabinet officials and political appointees to avoid coordinating with their peers if they believe that their budgets might be reduced or if they fail to see how their efforts will benefit from such coordination. White House policy coordinating agencies have yet to lead the way in this battle.

Government agencies are the second element of the problem. These agencies are hamstrung by budgets and procedures. They do not cooperate enough, let alone coordinate enough. Joint policy making between agencies sharing similar goals rarely, if ever, exists. Within the public assistance system, there are many overlaps—in mandates, in targets, in services provided. This diversity has resulted in a costly system that is composed of conflicting or overlapping administrative and regulatory provisions; funding disparities and different funding streams; and differing eligibility criteria, planning and operating timetables, and definitions and terminologies.

The lack of coordination at the federal level is also an obstacle to the states' ability to pursue program integration. Surveys indicate that many states believe that the sheer number of agencies, organizations, and congressional committees involved in administering and overseeing public assistance programs makes coordination extremely difficult. Almost all of the respondents to a 1987 General Accounting Office survey of states' views believed that federal efforts to make uniform definitions, terminology, and eligibility requirements would help state efforts to achieve service integration (U.S. General Accounting Office, 1987b).

The jurisdictional issues associated with congressional committees represent a third and special element of the problem. Since congressional oversight most often occurs through the committee structure, the effectiveness of committee work is the most important task in assuring proper congressional oversight over public assistance programs. Currently, jurisdiction for the initiation and review of antipoverty policy is split among a number of different committees. This splintered structure of decision making is an obstacle to effective program implementation because it does not allow the committees to consider the full scope of all related policies, programs, and needs. In addition, the division of responsibility on Capital Hill leads to multiple points of access for members of Congress, interest groups, affected publics, and the executive branch, as well as multiple opportunities for enhanced coordination.

Even some members of Congress accept the fact that they are part of the problem. Speaking in July 1991 to a government conference called "Making the Connection: Coordinating Education and Training for a Skilled Workforce," Representative Steve Gunderson focused on the education and training component of the public assistance system and complained that the structure of Congress itself impedes coordination because too many committees have jurisdiction over those issues. He cited the different committees with jurisdiction over the JTPA and JOBS programs. He went one step further when he described the House Education and Labor Committee's effort to establish state human investment councils in the Carl D. Perkins Vocational and Applied Technology Act reauthorization bill that would coordinate vocational education, JTPA, adult education, and Wagner-Peyser programs. That effort fell somewhat short of the mark when "JOBS wasn't included because that would have put the bill in the jurisdiction of Ways and Means, which could have held up the bill."

The state and local problem is the fourth element that inhibits coordination within the public assistance system. On the one hand, state and local input into the project design and rule making process is usually absent. State and local governments are often not well-served by their representatives in Washington and rarely have the time to participate in the federal regulatory process. And too many programs are designed in ways that inhibit state and local flexibility in the implementation of programs. Only state and local service providers can offer a responsive set of services tailored to local needs. Federal efforts often discourage or, at a minimum, serve as barriers to state and local innovation.

On the other hand, state and local governments are a big part of the problem. In order to increase beneficiary access and improve program administration, it is imperative to overcome state and local barriers to coordination, such as bureaucratic territoriality, different philosophical perspectives on the causes of and solutions to poverty, conflicting federal and state regulations and reporting requirements governing different programs, overlapping but not identical goals and performance measures, and administrative differences in operating procedures for processing clients, contracting, and reporting. A variety of coordination techniques are available; not all are being used.

The fifth and final element of the coordination problem is eligibility criteria. The variety of poverty levels as well as the array of eligibility criteria for federal assistance programs have made implementation difficult for state and local governments and for potential aid recipients. Operating rules of the various governmental levels involved in running the programs also vary by program and state.

Federal assistance programs utilize a variety of methods to determine whether a person is eligible for benefits. Although the eligibility criteria for an individual program are related in some rational way to the purpose of that program, when considered as a system the differences in eligibility criteria for the different programs multiply administrative burdens upon both recipients and program staff. They make a generally user-unfriendly system even more complicated and confusing. A major problem in addressing systemic reform and in streamlining policies and procedures is that many of the eligibility rules and procedures are set by statute rather than by administrative action.

More than 80 percent of the states responding to a 1987 GAO study of states' views on coordination indicated that different programs using different definitions, terminology, and eligibility requirements concerning a client's financial status and other factors (e.g., definition of household) served as very great or great obstacles to coordination (U.S. General Accounting Office, 1987b). A state health and social service agency official testified recently before Congress that his state has managed to integrate AFDC and Food Stamps regulations, but that it would have been more helpful if these regulations had been integrated by the federal government before they were transmitted to the states.

Three factors are generally employed to determine program eligibility: the poverty level, income eligibility standards, and definitions of "assistance units."

The federal government employs several different eligibility measures. These are often based on measures of poverty. However, different poverty measures are often used for administrative, legislative, or programmatic purposes. A 1986 Domestic Policy Council welfare reform review discovered that seven of the fifty-nine programs that it examined used 100 percent of the poverty income guidelines to determine eligibility, while twenty programs set limits at some multiple of those guidelines (such as 130% or 185%). The remaining programs used such measures as the median income of a state or county, a state-determined eligibility level or standard of need, or some other measure (Low Income Opportunity Working Group, 1986).

The two major issues with respect to income eligibility criteria are how the income eligibility requirements are defined and how income levels are determined. It has been reported that variations in income maximums themselves, especially what is counted as income and what is not (exclusions or disregards), create the worst problems of the public assistance system. Sometimes only cash income is considered, other times in-kind or noncash benefits are added to cash. Also, some programs count the income of other family members when they determine eligibility levels, while others do not.

As a general rule, programs with substantial monthly benefits (AFDC, SSI, and Medicaid) have detailed rules about what must be counted as income and what must be disregarded. For example, the value limit of an automobile is $1,500 for AFDC, $4,500 for Food Stamps, and $1,500 for Medicaid.

These programs also tend to have the lowest income eligibility levels, generally limit eligibility to those with "cash" income below the official poverty line, and require recipients to document their income and report income changes to the welfare agency. In contrast, smaller programs generally have less strict standards and require less documentation (Low Income Opportunity Working Group, 1986).

The coverage of a program depends on who is included in the assistance unit as well as on the income eligibility levels themselves. Depending upon the particular program, the assistance unit may be defined as a family, household, individual, or couple.

Although the Food Stamp and AFDC programs are both designed to assist low-income households, the programs' standards for determining which household members are eligible to participate differ considerably. The Food Stamp program's household definition generally encompasses all household members who prepare and eat meals together, but AFDC uses the family, which generally includes only dependent children, their siblings, and their parents or other caretaker relatives as the eligibility unit. The income of a member of a household could be included in determining Food Stamp eligibility if that person prepares and eats meals with household members but is not responsible for dependent children. The AFDC program does not assume so wide a responsibility of all household members for each other as is assumed by Food Stamps, so the household member may not qualify for AFDC eligibility.

The end result of conflicting eligibility criteria is predictable: restricted access among those who are eligible. Potential recipients are so intimidated by the prospect of documenting their eligibility in this program maze that they never apply at all. Others make it part of the way through the process only to drop out before their frustration prevents them from successfully demonstrating their eligibility for all of the programs for which they qualify.

HOW THE BOOK IS STRUCTURED

The remainder of this book is broken into four parts. Distinguished academics, public policy experts, and practitioners contributed the chapters that make up Parts II, III, and IV.

Part II identifies the issues and institutions involved in coordinating public assistance programs at the level of the federal government. Part III focuses on the primary roles of the state government in coordination, namely, planning and organizing. It also presents information on coordination mechanisms and their application to particular programs. Part IV presents the local perspective on coordination issues in different areas of public assistance—job training, at-risk youth, housing and integrated services—as well as an analysis of local-level implementation of the JOBS program.

Part V offers the editors' conclusions about the public assistance system and our recommendations for improving coordination in the system.

REFERENCES

Advisory Commission on Intergovernmental Relations. 1987. Docket Book, Ninety-Third Meeting. June 5.

Agranoff, Robert. 1991. "Human Services Integration: Past and Present Challenges in Public Administration." *Public Administration Review* 51 (November/December): 533–42.

Bishop, Meredith. 1991. "Why Johnny's Dad Can't Read, The Elusive Goal of Universal Adult Literacy." *Policy Review* (Winter): 19–25.

Burke, Vee. 1989. *Cash and Noncash Benefits for Persons With Limited Income: Eligibility Rules, Recipient and Expenditure Data, FY 1986–88.* CRS Report 89–595 EPW. Congressional Research Service, Library of Congress. October 24.

Butler, Stuart. 1987. "Power to the People." *Policy Review* 40 (Spring): 3–8.

Conlan, Timothy. 1988. *The New Federalism: Intergovernmental Reform from Nixon to Reagan.* Washington, D.C.: The Brookings Institution.

Dawson, Richard E., and Virginia Gray. 1971. "State Welfare Policies." In *Politics in the American States, A Comparative Analysis,* 2d ed., edited by Herbert Jacob and Kenneth N. Vines. Boston: Little, Brown and Company.

Elazar, Daniel. 1972. *American Federalism, A View from the States.* 2d ed. New York: Thomas Y. Crowell Company.

Jennings, Edward T., Jr., Dale Krane, Alex Pattakos, and B. J. Reed, eds. 1986. *From Nation to States: The Small Cities Community Development Block Grant Program.* Albany: State University of New York Press.

Jennings, Edward T., Jr. 1989. *Job Training Coordination: Issues and Approaches.* Report prepared for the Missouri Division of Job Development and Training. Columbia: Department of Public Administration, University of Missouri-Columbia. June.

Low Income Opportunity Working Group. 1986. *Up From Dependency, A New National Public Assistance Strategy.* Report to the President by the Domestic Policy Council. Also, Supplements 1, 4, and 5.

Mikulecky, Thomas J. 1974. *Human Services Integration.* Washington, D.C.: American Society for Public Administration.

Nathan, Richard P. et al. 1987. *Reagan and the States.* Princeton, N.J.: Princeton University Press.

National Commission for Employment Policy. 1991. "Background Paper on Federal Public Assistance Programs: Coordination and Eligibility Issues." Washington, D. C. February 20.

National Commission on Children. 1991. *Beyond Rhetoric: A New American Agenda for Children and Families.* Washington, D.C.

National Commission to Prevent Infant Mortality. 1991. *One-Stop Shopping: The Road to Healthy Mothers and Children.* Washington, D.C.

Ooms, Theodora. 1989. "Federal Child Care Policy: Current and Proposed." Background paper. Family Impact Seminar. Washington, D.C. April 28.

————. 1991. "Child Care in the 101st Congress: What Was Achieved and How Will It Work?" Background paper. Family Impact Seminar. Washington, D.C. January 25.

Rovner, Julie. 1991. "Children in Crisis Overwhelm Foster-Care Programs." *Congressional Quarterly* (March 30): 795–800.

Singh, Harmeet K. D. 1990. "Stork Reality: Why America's Infants Are Dying." *Policy Review* (Spring): 56–59.

U.S. General Accounting Office. 1987a. *Welfare: Issues to Consider in Assessing Proposals for Reform.* HRD–87–51BR. February.

————. 1987b. *Welfare Simplification: States' Views on Coordinating Services for Low-Income Families.* HRD–87–110FS. July.

————. 1988. *Welfare: Expert Panels' Insights on Major Reform Proposals.* HRD–88–59. February.

————. 1989. U.S. General Accounting Office. *Training Programs: Information on Fiscal Years 1989 and 1990 Appropriations.* HRD 89–71FS. April.

U.S. Department of Health, Education, and Welfare. 1976. *The Measure of Poverty. Technical Paper II: Administrative and Legislative Uses of the Terms "Poverty," "Low-Income," and Other Related Items.* Poverty Studies Task Force. September.

U.S. Office of Management and Budget. 1980. *Eligibility Simplification Project.* October.

Walker, David B. 1981. *Toward a Theory of Functioning Federalism.* Cambridge, Mass.: Winthrop Publishers.

Wright, Deil S. 1978. *Understanding Intergovernmental Relations: Public Policy and Participant Perspectives in Local, State, and National Government.* North Scituate, Mass.: Duxbury Press.

Yessian, Mark R. 1991. *Services Integration: A Twenty Year Retrospective.* Washington, D.C.: U.S. Department of Health and Human Services, Office of the Inspector General.

Part II

THE FEDERAL ROLE

The public assistance system is a set of programs, activities, and institutional arenas for decision making and action. It consists of congressional committees, the White House, executive branch agencies, and executive and legislative entities of state and local government that provide the service delivery capacity for much of the federal public assistance programs. In 1991, it included seventy-five federal public assistance programs and countless state and local efforts that sometimes interact with the federally supported initiatives and often provide models for national policy. Part II addresses institutional, statutory, and regulatory aspects of policy development and implementation at the federal level that affect coordination issues.

The White House and Executive Office of the President (EOP), as Kevin R. Hopkins discusses in Chapter 2, are capable of playing a crucial role in fostering coordination, and they can do this in several ways. The most important way is by using the prestige and visibility of the president to support initiatives to enhance program coordination. As the nation's leader, the president is in a unique position to set the agenda for policy making. Presidents can set the terms of public debate and give considerable impetus to certain proposals by lending their endorsement. The importance of presidential leadership cannot be overemphasized. Study after study has suggested that leadership involvement is crucial to successful coordination efforts.

Beyond this agenda-setting and attention-focusing activity, Hopkins suggests several steps that can be taken by the president or the White House to support coordination, such as (1) intensifying the use of interagency working groups to resolve interagency disputes or reduce variations in important components of public assistance programs and (2) expanding the authority and capacity of White House policy-coordinating agencies to improve program coordination and enhance the opportunity for states to implement innovative ideas.

As James Gimpel documents in Chapter 3, responsibility for different aspects of public assistance policy is dispersed primarily among eleven congressional committees and numerous subcommittees. With responsibility divided not only among substantive authorizing committees but also between those committees and the appropriations committees, there are multiple points of access for members of Congress, interest groups, affected publics, and the executive branch. This arrangement not only assures the participation of diverse concerns and viewpoints in policy making, but also ensures a significant degree of insularity in policy development because of congressional norms and procedures.

Simply put, different committees have responsibility for different programs that affect the same people. Programs overlap not only in their target groups, but also in the problems they address. There is no requirement that these interrelationships among programs receive careful consideration in congressional deliberations. In fact, the fragmentation of authority among committees and the strong claims to jurisdiction by the committees stand as effective barriers to consideration of programmatic linkages. Any change in the structure or processes of Congress threatens the power of affected committee members, interest groups, and public agencies. Gimpel attempts to guide us through these congressional pathways.

The responsibility for public assistance programs is divided among numerous executive agencies. This division both creates the need for coordination and stands as a hindrance to it. Each agency's attention to its own needs, priorities, and mission colors its view of the relationship between its own programs and those lodged elsewhere. Coordination is normally a low priority because the agency has its own action agenda to pursue. When agencies seek coordination, they seek it on their own terms in keeping with their perception of public purpose.

As Lawrence Neil Bailis points out in Chapter 4, a range of existing mechanisms can continue to provide support for coordination efforts. These include meetings of cabinet secretaries and high-level staff; jointly sponsored conferences; coordination in technical assistance efforts; reorganization; ad hoc efforts to address specific barriers to coordination; and interagency task forces and committees. Bailis explains the benefits and shortcomings of these and other administrative reforms.

The previous three chapters addressed some of the organizational and institutional obstacles in coordination. Another roadblock to coordination is presented by the vast array of federally supported programs, with their competing definitions, rules, and regulations. Organizational sponsors are augmented by separate state and local initiatives. Organizational diversity can be even greater at the state and local level than at the national level. Frequently it seems no one is in command.

Beyond the problems of command and control, state and local administrators often report difficulties that originate in provisions of federal statutes and regulations. In Chapter 5, Christopher T. King identifies several distinct areas in which changes in federal policy might foster improved coordination. Most important, perhaps, is the matter of eligibility rules and definitions, including the income level that is deemed to demonstrate need and the treatment of different resources in determining income. It has been raised as a problem by state administrators who find that the labyrinth of rules and definitions hinders efforts to institute one-stop eligibility determination and integrated case management.

Many state administrators of public assistance programs have suggested that technical issues are the most significant barrier to coordination. Although these differences do not prohibit coordination, they make it more difficult. Where possible, reductions in these differences would make the job easier for those who promote effectiveness through coordinated services. King suggests approaches to minimize those differences.

Chapter 2

The Presidency and the Coordination of Public Assistance

Kevin R. Hopkins

A number of approaches are employed at the level of the White House or the Executive Office of the President (EOP) to minimize problems arising from the lack of coordination among public assistance programs in the executive branch of the federal government. Among these approaches are legislative and administrative mandates for agencies to consult with each other, link their programs, and jointly review their activities; interagency working groups which consider issues that cross agency lines; reorganization efforts aimed at eliminating overlap or duplication among programs; and the involvement of White House coordinating agencies and the president himself. These initiatives have made varying degrees of headway in streamlining and improving the coordination of public assistance programs. Yet, many serious problems remain.

WHY BE CONCERNED ABOUT COORDINATION?

Imagine the difficulty of preparing one's income tax return—perhaps the most grueling task many of us face during the entire year. As hard as it is to collect and organize the relevant tax information for one or two family members, think how difficult—even impossible—it would be if you had to compile the tax and income information for seventy-five family members.

Now imagine that each of these seventy-five family members lived in different parts of the country, were paid by seventy-five different employers and used seventy-five different filing and accounting systems, and you have some idea of the challenge involved in coordinating the seventy-five public assistance programs that are part of the federal government's safety net for the economically disadvantaged.

Within the public assistance system, coordination is lacking in a number of key areas: differing client intake and case-management procedures; administratively and geographically diverse program application sites; varying eligibility criteria; and fragmented budgetary and oversight responsibility vested in a multitude of federal agencies and congressional committees.

Why should the White House be concerned about the lack of coordination among public assistance programs? A number of reasons are worth stating explicitly:

- Lack of coordination often produces overlapping and duplicative administrative structures, resulting in the unnecessary expenditure of program funds on administrative functions that could be better allocated to directly assisting the poor

- Lack of coordination makes it difficult for lawmakers and executive branch officials to assess the relative cost effectiveness of the various programs, and to identify gaps in coverage or assistance

- The profusion of programs creates an administrative maze that state governments seeking to improve program coordination or to implement innovative service delivery approaches find difficult and, at times, nearly impossible to negotiate

- The diversity of public assistance programs makes it hard for potential program beneficiaries to apply for and collect the public assistance to which the law entitles them

- The program maze makes it very difficult to demonstrate to taxpayers that the funds for the programs are achieving their objectives and are being spent in the most cost effective way possible

The most harmful consequence of the current, fragmented public assistance system—and the main reason we should be concerned with this lack of coordination—is that such a system makes it difficult, if not impossible, to achieve the objective of promoting true financial self-sufficiency among the poor.

Consider for a moment what would happen if a far-reaching, public assistance streamlining program was proposed on a nationwide scale. A look at the politics of what would be involved makes the answer obvious. The members of the Senate Finance and the House Ways and Means committees would no doubt leap in with a denunciation of the plan because it would do away with Aid to Families with Dependent Children (AFDC). The Agriculture Department and scores of farm organizations would protest the abolition of Food Stamps. Health service providers and medical associations would decry the elimination of Medicaid. Public housing developers would dig deep into their political war chests to ensure that no politician voted to put an end to public housing. And longtime advocates of traditional public assistance programs would deliver the coup de grâce by branding the plan as only one more attempt to shred the social safety net.

This would be the likely result of such a reform effort because every existing public assistance program has an entrenched and powerful constituency. It is a constituency composed not so much of the assistance recipients themselves—who, after all, only want to make sure they have enough money to live, and to live as well as they can. Rather, the most persistent support for these programs comes from what has been termed the "iron triangle" of political interests for whom these programs constitute political power and financial wherewithal—the federal executive branch departments and agencies that administer the programs, the congressional committees that oversee them, and the private firms that deliver the services or benefits.

Against this array of forces, attempts at improving the coordination and efficiency of existing programs can go only so far, no matter how well-intentioned. Eventually, these efforts will run head-on into the steel wall of resistance of an agency that refuses to let its budget be cut in the name of streamlining, of a congressional committee that refuses to cede jurisdiction over a program in the name of coordination, of the service provider that refuses to relinquish its multimillion-dollar management fee in the name of administrative efficiency. Such people and the organizations they represent do not necessarily act this way out of bad intent or callousness to the poor. They are merely protecting their own self-interest—as humans and their institutions are wont to do.

The problem is, the self-interest of members of this "iron triangle" often conflicts with the self-interest and self-sufficiency of the poor people and families that public assistance programs are intended to serve. All too often, in permitting government agencies, congressional committees or service providers to protect their own power and economic health, our society winds up sacrificing the autonomy and financial well-being of the poor themselves.

These are among the very problems that ongoing coordination efforts are designed to remedy. Still, there are a number of steps the White House could take directly to speed this process along.

THE WHITE HOUSE ROLE IN COORDINATION:
WHAT NEEDS TO BE DONE

The increased complexity of, and interrelatedness with, the public assistance system calls for an important White House role in interagency policy coordination. The historical record on White House coordination of public assistance issues and programs is spotty.

From 1964 through 1975, administration welfare policies were pursued through the Office of Economic Opportunity (OEO). The Carter administration initiated an interagency Eligibility Simplification Project to recommend simplifications of client eligibility criteria among major public assistance programs. The project's completion in October 1980, shortly before the 1980 election, precluded any direct action on the report's recommendations by that administration (U.S. Office of Management and Budget, 1980).

The Reagan administration initiated a White House review of welfare policy in 1986. Managed by the Low Income Opportunity Working Group (LIOWG) of the Domestic Policy Council, this review led to the publication of *Up from Dependency*, which was presented as a new national public assistance strategy. The strategy that grew out of that review was welfare reform through state-sponsored, locally-controlled demonstrations of innovations in public assistance programs with the aim of reducing dependency (Low Income Opportunity Working Group, 1986).

In 1987, the White House Office of Policy Development's Low Income Opportunity Board (LIOB) helped to bridge a gap that existed between the federal government and the states for programs that serve the economically disadvantaged. The LIOB was composed of the Office of Management and Budget (OMB) and the departments and agencies that administer programs for the economically disadvantaged, including the Departments of Agriculture, Education, Health and Human Services, Housing and Urban Development, Interior, Justice, and Labor.

Prior to the Low Income Opportunity Board's creation, state efforts to obtain waivers from many programs were sporadic and quite limited. For those states that did attempt such changes, it could take years to design a new program and gain the necessary federal approvals. The LIOB expedited welfare reform by providing one-stop shopping to states, allowing them to try new approaches to welfare and to treat the myriad programs as a system. The LIOB acted as a single point of contact for states wishing to obtain waivers from federal statutes and regulations that frustrated innovative welfare reform at the state and local level.

Instead of dealing with the many federal welfare programs and agencies in a piecemeal manner, a state applied to the Low Income Opportunity

Board for waivers on a broad range of programs at one time. LIOB then assisted the state in its efforts to obtain the required waivers from the appropriate federal agencies. Most of the state-sponsored, locally-controlled demonstrations of innovations in public assistance programs reviewed by the LIOB during its first two years were for the AFDC, Food Stamp, Medicaid, and Child Support Enforcement programs.

LIOB helped states launch many different kinds of experiments to restructure their welfare systems. For example, a Wisconsin "learnfare" program that linked AFDC benefits with high school attendance by children in the family and a New Jersey plan to turn hundreds of welfare beneficiaries into family day care providers (thereby increasing day care services while reducing the welfare roles) are two examples of the types of programs implemented as a result of LIOB actions. Among the benefits of the LIOB system was that under its principle of cost neutrality the savings from a change in one program could be used to offset increased spending in another, as long as there was no net increase in federal cost. Thirteen state projects had been authorized through the LIOB as of mid-1990. It is important to keep in mind that these changes were administrative, not substantive, reforms, and therefore did not change the direct-aid concept that underlies welfare (Hopkins, 1988).

Beyond its one-stop shopping function, the LIOB's other stated functions included identifying major problems (present and prospective) in public assistance programs; working with agencies and outside groups in reviewing policy alternatives with respect to public assistance matters; and monitoring the implementation of approved public assistance policies.

In late 1990, the LIOB was replaced by the Economic Empowerment Task Force. The task force was intended to build on the Low Income Opportunity Board's work by pursuing new initiatives to promote enhanced coordination.

ACTION RECOMMENDATIONS

To assist state governments that are attempting to improve public assistance coordination or to develop innovative public assistance approaches, the White House could expand the authority and mission of the Economic Empowerment Task Force, giving it additional authority to do the following:

- Systematically review and coordinate all public assistance programs serving the economically disadvantaged

- Develop a policy-making framework for formulating a common definition of, and standard for measuring, poverty; reducing conflicts and duplications among agencies and departments; eliminating unnecessary administrative requirements related to public assistance programs; and making more uniform the financial and nonfinancial eligibility requirements pertinent to these programs

- Grant broad waivers or exemptions from federal rules that establish state procedures for implementing public assistance programs (with the waivers or exemptions being left in force for a limited period of time and accompanied by careful monitoring of state compliance); thereafter, the task force could work with OMB to codify the waivers or exemptions into standard operating procedures (where they were governed by administrative rules), or to prepare proposed legislation (where they were controlled by statute)

- Create a federal-level information clearinghouse that would enable states to more readily share their program innovations with other states, and to learn from each other's successes and failures

- Direct federal agencies to fund systematic evaluation studies of state-level public assistance experiments

- Develop a uniform reporting system to track the implementation and outcomes of state-level public assistance innovations

One idea currently being examined is "empowerment opportunity areas." Empowerment opportunity areas are geographic concentrations of poor people or target groups that would be eligible to receive special waivers from federal public assistance program requirements. In 1991, the Bush administration provided support for a project on integrated services for children and families. This project is exploring how federal social welfare programs could be restructured to provide a more integrated approach to the problems of disadvantaged children and families.

The White House, situated at the pinnacle of the federal executive branch's policy-making machinery, clearly could take the lead in encouraging and expanding many of the administrative reforms just described. It could do so in a variety of ways.

The White House plays a pivotal role, for instance, in creating or defining the missions of the numerous interagency working groups that are a regular part of executive branch policy-making operations. When a coordination problem among agencies or departments resulting from disparate administrative regulations is identified, the White House and Executive Office of the President staff could ensure that this issue is placed on the agenda of the appropriate interagency working group. Or, to the extent the issue does not fall within the purview of any existing working group, the White House and EOP could create a new group designed for this or a suitably broader purpose. It might even make sense, for the sake of policy-making coordination, to create a single interagency working group whose sole responsibility is the coordination and streamlining of federal public assistance programs.

In any case, once a particular coordination issue or collection of issues is assigned to a working group, the EOP staff could carefully monitor the process to make sure that the matter received prompt and diligent consideration. Then, when necessary, they could ensure that any outstanding questions were brought to the appropriate cabinet-level policy council for decision.

Beyond this case-by-case approach to interagency coordination, the Office of Management and Budget theoretically promotes improved public assistance coordination through its regular budget review and regulatory review processes. To amplify this role in its annual budget review, for example, OMB could examine the progress of the respective agencies in improving coordination and in streamlining their public assistance programs, and could make selected changes in these programs and their associated regulations a part of their passback requests. Alternatively, OMB could establish within its ongoing regulatory review procedures a mission dedicated exclusively to enhancing public assistance coordination.

When coordination problems cannot be resolved administratively, the White House domestic policy office and OMB could jointly draft legislation to make the necessary changes. Then, in conjunction with agency and departmental congressional relations staffs, the White House Congressional Affairs Office could work closely with the appropriate congressional committees and key senators and members of Congress to ensure quick, favorable action.

Finally, the White House could bolster the prospects of its own creative public assistance ideas, like economic empowerment areas, by vigorously advocating these ideas among the public, social service professionals, and political leaders.

Steps like these would go a long way toward improving the coordination of government-sponsored public assistance programs.

In addition, the White House has an even more important role to play in this arena. To achieve a real revolution in our approach to public assistance requires the creation of a countervailing political movement more powerful than the self-interested political forces of the members of the "iron triangle." The White House alone has the ability to build this kind of political constituency. But to succeed, the advocacy of genuine empowerment for the poor must reach all the way to the president himself.

Political leaders of all ideological stripes now concede that many of our country's most pressing domestic problems—drugs, crime, poverty, poor academic performance among youth, illiteracy, and the deterioration of our cities—will remain with us until and unless the poor are able to take greater charge of their own lives and see some hope for a better life in so doing. The president should use his immense political skills to persuade the Congress and the American people to support the liberation of the poor families who continue to inhabit our cities and towns, mired in a poverty that, to many, must seem inescapable.

REFERENCES

Hopkins, Kevin R. 1988. "Social Welfare Policy: A Failure of Vision." In *Assessing the Reagan Years*, edited by David Boaz. Washington, D.C.: The Cato Institute.
Low Income Opportunity Working Group. 1986. *Up From Dependency, A New National Public Assistance Strategy*. Report to the President by the Domestic Policy Council. Also, Supplements 1, 4, and 5.
U.S. Office of Management and Budget. 1980. *Eligibility Simplification Project*. October.

Chapter 3

Congress and the Coordination of Public Assistance

James Gimpel

Reducing poverty while reducing the cost of public assistance has been of some concern on Capitol Hill almost from the time sweeping public assistance legislation was enacted in the Social Security Act of 1935. In that seminal legislation, these concerns were expressed by the incorporation of titles to provide both noncontributory public assistance in the form of Aid to Dependent Children (Title IV) and an extension of a vocational rehabilitation program to put the unemployed back to work.

Today, with mounting deficits and record relief rolls, the concern for putting the poor back to work is more intense than ever. It is not a concern stimulated only by the fiscal crisis of the federal government. There is widespread, bipartisan consensus among members of Congress and their staff that empowering the poor through literacy and job training is the right thing to do. The central issue, then, is not whether empowerment is a good and proper goal. It is whether this goal is being accomplished. If not, how do we adjust in order to move in the right direction? Prosperity alone is no antidote for poverty, as the 1980s demonstrated.

This chapter addresses the issue of the role of Congress and congressional oversight in the implementation of welfare and work policies. One of the main reasons we have been unable to resolve our most pressing social problems is that there are fundamental flaws in the current institutional construction of House and Senate committee jurisdictions. Furthermore, congressional staff often lack the experience to exercise competent policy judgments in their areas of responsibility. Laws are written and standards are set at the top, with no sensitivity to program implementation. There are other problems, to be sure, but the failure to exercise intelligent oversight stands as an obstacle to both accountable government and programmatic efficiency.

THE NATURE OF CONGRESSIONAL OVERSIGHT

The comptroller general, head of the U.S. General Accounting Office, has defined congressional oversight as the "process by which the Congress learns about the implementation, results, effectiveness and adequacy of its past legislative work, including the policies implicit in laws and the programs and activities carried out under laws" (Congressional Research Service, 1989). Implementation, results, effectiveness, and adequacy are the operative terms. By this definition, Congress is responsible for evaluating program performance; investigating instances of poor administration, waste, dishonesty, and fraud; and assessing agency or individual ability to manage and accomplish program objectives. In addition, Congress is charged with the task of ensuring that executive policies reflect the public interest.

Oversight is carried out in several settings and scrutiny is generally reactive rather than proactive. Most committees are generally advocacy oriented—actually inclined to give most bureaus a pass without much scrutiny (Aberbach, 1990; Foreman, 1988). Under ordinary circumstances, members do not go out looking to harass an agency unless they have an ideological axe to grind.

From the perspective of program administrators, the generally reactive nature of Congress's investigative scrutiny is a good thing. It means that Congress is not out to micromanage the agency on a daily basis. However, the reactive nature of oversight also has a negative side. Members and staff rarely venture out to learn about a program and its implementation. They are usually interested in program administration only if they hear complaints about a particular bureau's waste, inefficiency, or incompetence. This would be fine, if, in response to such cases, members and staff did not take upon themselves the tasks of directing program administration and creating new initiatives out of whole cloth. Congressional actors should not be expected to learn everything about program administration. But staff and members often legislate, boss, and bully, as if they do know something about program administration, when often they do not (National Academy of Public Administration, 1992).

THE SETTINGS FOR OVERSIGHT

Individual letters from constituents are enough to rouse initial interest in scrutinizing a program. A constituent raises a complaint about the administration of a program of which she is a client, and the member calls the agency's attention to the issue. The bureaucracy responds to these complaints on a case-by-case basis, and usually the matter is resolved with dispatch.

More formally, congressional oversight takes place in the agency and program reauthorization and appropriations process. Programs regularly come up for reauthorization before the relevant legislative committee—sometimes annually, other times biannually. At the reauthorization hearings, agency officials appear to report on the effectiveness of their programs and answer any questions members may have. Clients of the program are sometimes called to testify, as are outside experts who may be doing relevant research on some major aspect of the program.

At the reauthorization markup, where the text of legislative bills is actually reviewed and voted out to the floor, members often recommend major changes in a program by offering amendments that must be voted upon by the full committee. Funding levels are recommended in this process, although relevant appropriations subcommittees actually decide the level of funding.

Finally, oversight of administration takes place in the now familiar setting of investigative hearings of scandals. The savings and loan debacle, the recent problems at HUD, and the sale of arms to the Nicaraguan contras are familiar examples where Congress reacted by launching an exhaustive oversight investigation followed by passage of a flurry of new legislative initiatives and regulations designed to prevent such problems from ever happening again.

Hearings, of whatever kind, are often designed more to draw media attention than to solve substantive problems (Foreman, 1988). The first panel called before the Senate Labor and Human Resources Committee often consists of three or four "hard-luck cases." These individuals are frequently screened ahead of time and "scripted" by majority leadership staff. The questions aimed at this panel are designed to provide the chairperson with soundbites and anecdotes to support already decided views about the way welfare or labor programs should work. Leading questions are common. Indeed, hearings before the most ideological committees, such as the Labor and Judiciary committees, are orchestrated to make partisan points. Most minds are made up well in advance.

If the questioning is pointed enough, sometimes press coverage is generated on a topic. Surprisingly enough, agencies take congressional inquiries seriously, no matter how shallow they may be. Committees have just enough power, and members just enough ambition, to be effective. Consequently, programs are often changed or redirected. These changes, however, are often in response to problems that are staged and/or hyped, not real. Given the structure of congressional committees, comprehensive, thoughtful reconsideration of a program area is next to impossible.

OVERLAPPING JURISDICTIONS AS A BARRIER TO EFFECTIVE OVERSIGHT

Since congressional oversight most often occurs through the committee structure, improving the effectiveness of committee work is the most important way to improve Congressional oversight of federal programs. Jurisdiction for the initiation and review of antipoverty policy is split among a number of different committees that tend to reflect broad policy areas rather than the needs and interests of program clients. These interests are not served by some arbitrary textbook segmentation of government operations. Poverty is a problem that has many facets, but for program purposes poverty afflicts individual clients and families. The committee system requires reform to adequately assess and anticipate the clients' needs.

It is hard to argue that the current jurisdictional arrangements are responsive to the broader public or the client interest of the programs. Major responsibility for job training and welfare policy in the Senate is delegated to the Committee on Labor and Human Resources. In the House, responsibility for work incentive and welfare programs is delegated primarily to the Education and Labor Committee. But these committees do not have exclusive jurisdiction.

In fact, the world of antipoverty policy is complex and bewildering at the top. The Senate and House committees on Agriculture, for instance, are responsible for the Food Stamp program as well as nutrition programs, such as school lunches and Women, Infants, and Children (WIC). The Senate and House committees on Banking, Housing, and Urban Affairs are responsible for public housing. The two committees on Energy and Commerce have jurisdiction on various issues relating to public health. The House and Senate committees on Government Operations claim jurisdiction on all program implementation issues, including intergovernmental relationships between the federal, state, and local governments. The two Veterans Affairs committees address issues of vocational rehabilitation, education, and other benefits for veterans. The House Ways and Means Committee and the Senate Finance Committee are responsible for reviewing all proposals manipulating the tax code, as well as social security and work incentive programs. There is also an astonishing number of subcommittees that exercise jurisdiction in the area of antipoverty and entitlement policy. In total, the House currently has 192 committees and subcommittees in all legislative areas and the Senate has 118.

There were attempts to streamline the committee system in the 1970s. Many of the proposed reforms made sense, but few were adopted. A number of committees were slated for abolition, but in the House none was ultimately eliminated. The most-needed reforms were not even proposed, such as the rotation of committee members in order that interests would not entrench themselves around particular assignments (Rieselbach, 1986). Committee chairs and staff were naturally quite fearful that they would lose power. In the Senate, the number of committees was pared down some, but with no discernible impact on the formulation of entitlement and poverty policy.

This redundant morass of House and Senate panels is an obstacle to effective program implementation. Programs fail to meet the demand for coordination because they are not considered by the same set of policymakers at one place and at one time. It is a mistake to assume, as many congressional bureaucrats do, that coordination problems exist only because of problems at the administrative level. Indeed, implementation failure is built right into the statutory design of some programs.

Take, for instance, the hard-to-serve population groups that seem to be missed by programs like those under the Job Training Partnership Act (JTPA). If job-training programs originate out of one committee, while welfare, education, and nutrition programs are the creation of another, what guarantee is there that programs will operate to address the disadvantaged person's need for comprehensive services? Given current institutional design, it is no surprise that eligibility criteria for these programs are inconsistent and the programs cannot work together. To amplify the point, this administrative chaos exists not just at the delivery site or in program administration, but begins in Congress where responsibility for the fate of America's underprivileged is diffused in a committee structure in need of reform.

A major step to reform the process would be to delegate responsibility for public assistance programs for noncontributors to a single Committee on Public Assistance in each chamber. All food and nutrition programs, job training, housing, health and welfare programs targeted at the poor and disabled would be the responsibility of this committee. This makes the committee system reflect the clientele of the programs it is supposed to review.

For constitutional reasons, issues relating to the tax treatment of the poor and the spending for these programs would still have to be directed through the House Ways and Means Committee and the Senate Finance Committee, but eliminating overlapping jurisdictions would provide for a more accountable system in which decisions affecting poverty and entitlement policy would be traceable to one panel.

It may not make sense to treat all veterans as a separate and distinct class. Many veterans are disabled and some are impoverished. In these cases, their needs are similar to those of other citizens in the poverty population, and they can be served by the same programs. True, veterans benefits go beyond the traditional forms of public assistance, with the extension of such "middle-class entitlements" as housing and education benefits, but there is no reason to have a *full* committee to design policies in these areas. The veterans affairs panel could easily be a subcommittee of the proposed Committee on Public Assistance.

A much less sweeping reform would be to create an intrachamber conference committee structure to work out the details in statutory design that will facilitate the coordination of government programs. Selected members of panels legislating in the area of human resource policy would meet to consider how alterations in a program's design would influence other programs serving the same clients. If the consequence of a particular housing policy is to encourage displacement and residential mobility in the poverty population, this has significant implications for those who are delivering other services to that population.

Currently, conference committees function only to resolve differences between versions of a bill following passage of the legislation in each chamber. An intrachamber conference committee could be appointed to work out differences following a bill's exit from the committee system, but prior to consideration on the floor. This could create added delay, but the point of the reforms proposed here is to introduce a measure of comprehensiveness to the consideration of a proposal through institutional design. With that end in mind, speed is not necessarily a virtue.

Another modest reform would be to require issuance of a public assistance impact statement for each congressionally-authored institutional reform or adjustment in federal assistance programs. The committee staff should be required to write the report, fully justifying the reform and explaining its impact on implementation of the program, its consequences for the implementation of other assistance programs, and its anticipated effect on clients of the program. This process would force reluctant and understudied congressional staff to carefully consider the implications of their legislative action, something they rarely do, and almost never do well.

For changes made in program administration without congressional approval, Congress should require such a statement from the secretary of the relevant department of government.

STAFF INEXPERIENCE AS A BARRIER TO EFFECTIVE OVERSIGHT

Improved staff work would go far in making government programs more efficient and responsible. In Congress, many important policy decisions ultimately fall to staff, especially committee staff. The members themselves have so many demands on their time that they rarely focus on substantive issues of policy. The weakness of the system is the lack of personnel who understand how statutory design influences program implementation. In addition, committee staff have almost no time, little money, and often no will to conduct their own independent investigations and evaluations. Important details of implementation and administration go ignored because of crowded hearing schedules and the demand to establish a record for political purposes.

Theories of representation and accountability inform us that eventually this inattentiveness will have consequences, but by the time past ignorance is finally recognized, those who first put the shortsighted programs in place are long since gone and cannot be held publicly accountable. It takes time to determine whether a program will succeed. The solution? Ensure that programs are designed at the outset in anticipation of as many things that can go wrong as can reasonably be determined. That takes expertise and a willingness to interact with the executive branch agencies.

The argument is not that committee members and staff are unintelligent or unskilled, although sometimes that is true. Rather, committee members and staff lack experience and contact with the programs as they are implemented in the field. They also lack experience with previous programs that have been tried and found lacking. To paraphrase Pressman and Wildavsky (1973: 137), divorced from history and problems of implementation at the delivery site, committee staff and members "may think great thoughts together. But they have trouble imagining the sequence of events that will bring their ideas to fruition." So, instead, incredibly high standards are set and the details of implementation are delegated to the bureaucracy. As the National Commission for Employment Policy has pointed out, the result is that Hispanics cannot take advantage of job training programs because they are not enrolled in some other public assistance program (1990). Or, the hard to employ are ignored by job training programs in order to meet the short-term political demand for instant and measurable success.

In a book that is now more than twenty years old, Theodore Lowi (1969) argues that federal welfare programs began failing most decisively when Congress decided to delegate rule making to bureaucrats and granted broad discretion down the line. In other words, once the regulations were deemed too complicated for Congressional authorship, members and staff turned to an even more bureaucratically insular group, the executive agencies, where there may be more expertise, but where there is much less accountability to the public. Rather than abdicating its role as regulator, Congress should have sought the staff expertise to write the rules. Because Congress is a democratic institution, the appropriate balance would have been struck between having a representative, politically responsive institution, and one that has the expertise to regulate in the public interest.

Ultimately, the key is to make the difficulties of implementing and coordinating programs like JTPA and Aid to Families with Dependent Children (AFDC) part of the initial formulation and subsequent revision of policy. As a practical step, this is done by providing federal social service agencies with the wherewithal to educate congressional staff by taking them to the field, frequently, to obtain the necessary exposure to the issues at the delivery site.

Staff of the Armed Services Committee are escorted virtually on demand to whatever site it is they wish to visit, near or far. All of their expenses are paid by the relevant branch of the military. By contrast, when members of the Labor and Human Resources staff wish to visit the site of a nearby drug treatment and prevention center, along with agency officials from the Department of Health and Human Services (HHS), they have to use committee funds because HHS has no such budget. The committee funds do not cover all expenses of the field research. The attitude seems to be that field investigation is not important in the social service areas. All relevant issues can be dealt with in hearings or in telephone conversations.

I propose, therefore, that social service agencies be provided a limited budget directed at educating congressional staff and members by getting them to field operations. The additional funding should not be given directly to the committees because many times the committee staff and members do not realize the need to undertake this form of field activity. Fieldwork takes effort and many Capitol Hill bureaucrats are comfortable with just staying in their offices and exercising "oversight" over the telephone.

To extend this recommendation, official program evaluation arms of the government—such as the General Accounting Office (GAO) and the Office of Technology Assessment (OTA)—should provide congressional staff with the opportunity to see firsthand the problems and issues of implementation identified in their reports to Congress.

GAO reports often obscure the significance and magnitude of the implementation and coordination problems they identify. Perhaps intimidated by its nonpartisan charter, GAO seems inclined to weaken its recommendations rather than step on the toes of someone important or powerful. The key to such an agency's survival, so it is thought, is to take the risk-averse approach and sound wishy-washy. Of course, GAO should be nonpartisan. Objectivity is an indispensable standard of evaluation. What GAO could do is go beyond its reports and hearing testimony to actually take congressional staff to the field and offer them clear, on-site cases of waste, fraud, duplication, and abuse.

CONCLUSION

Policies such as the ones recommended in this chapter may go far to remedy the lack of staff experience and sensitivity to the implementation of federal programs. In addition, these changes could open needed channels of communication between Congress and the executive branch in an era of divided government, when such cooperation is sadly lacking, but badly needed. Except for the proposal to consolidate the jurisdiction for antipoverty policy into one committee, the recommendations are fairly modest and would encounter less political resistance than something "radical" like nonpartisan merit hiring. The goal of professionalization is not nonpartisanship, but experience and the ability to determine what works, what doesn't, and why.

REFERENCES

Aberbach, Joel. 1990. *Keeping a Watchful Eye*. Washington, D.C.: Brookings Institution.
Congressional Research Service. 1989. *Congressional Oversight Manual*. Washington, D.C.: Library of Congress.
Davidson, Roger. 1989. "Two Avenues of Change: House and Senate Committee Reorganization." In *Congress Reconsidered*, 4th ed., edited by Bruce Oppenheimer and Lawrence Dodd. Washington, D.C.: Congressional Quarterly Press.
———. 1990. "The Legislative Reorganization Act of 1946." *Legislative Studies Quarterly* 15, no. 3 (August).
Foreman, Christopher. 1988. *Signals from the Hill*. New Haven, Conn.: Yale University Press.
Lowi, Theodore. 1969. *The End of Liberalism*. New York: W. W. Norton & Co.
National Academy of Public Administration. 1992. *Beyond Distrust: Building Bridges Between Congress and the Executive*. Washington, D.C.
National Commission for Employment Policy. 1988. *Serving AFDC Recipients: Initial Findings on the Role of Performance Standards*. Washington, D.C. May.
———. 1988. *JTPA Performance Standards: Effects on Clients, Services and Costs*. Washington, D.C. September.
———. 1990. *Training Hispanics: Implications for the JTPA System*. Report No. 27. Washington, D.C. January.

Ornstein, Norman, Thomas Mann, and Michael Malbin. 1989. *Vital Statistics on Congress, 1987–1988*. Washington, D.C.: Congressional Quarterly Press.

Parris, Judith H. 1979. "The Senate Reorganizes Its Committees, 1977." *Political Science Quarterly* 94 (Summer).

Pressman, Jeffrey, and Aaron Wildavsky. 1973. *Implementation*. Berkeley and Los Angeles: University of California Press.

Rieselbach, Leroy. 1986. *Congressional Reform*. Washington, D.C.: Congressional Quarterly Press.

Chapter 4

Coordination Among Administrative Agencies

Lawrence Neil Bailis

This chapter analyzes actions that federal officials can take to promote coordination among public assistance programs at all levels of government. In particular, it focuses on changes in the structure and functioning of the relevant federal agencies that are most likely to promote these results. Two conclusions are advanced in this chapter. First, a good deal of progress in enhancing coordination is possible at the federal level without *any* fundamental changes in the way federal agencies do business among themselves. Second, it would be more productive to pursue relatively modest changes like creation of an independent interagency commission to promote coordination than it would be to try to bring about major reorganization at the federal level.

Although most examples in this chapter address welfare employment program issues, the analyses and conclusions are, for the most part, generalizable to other aspects of public assistance programs where coordination is needed, including coordination among income maintenance programs and between these programs and others.

GOALS OF COORDINATION

It is widely agreed that coordination should be seen as a means to an end, not an end in and of itself. Therefore, it would be helpful to review the goals that people hope to achieve through enhanced federal-level coordination:

- Eliminating duplication of effort and otherwise improving the efficiency with which programs are administered at the federal level, yielding savings for taxpayers
- Increasing the likelihood that barriers to coordination at the state and local level are identified and remedied through legislation or regulatory activities, thereby promoting greater program quality, effectiveness, and efficiency at the service delivery level

POTENTIAL ACTIONS TO PROMOTE COORDINATION

As noted in numerous publications and public discussions of the issues, many low-income American families receive income-conditioned public assistance through programs administered by three different agencies—Aid to Families with Dependent Children (AFDC) administered by the Department of Health and Human Services (HHS), food stamps administered by the U.S. Department of Agriculture (USDA), and Section 8 housing certificates administered by the Department of Housing and Urban Development (HUD).

Their needs for education and training can be met through programs administered by at least four federal agencies—Job Training Partnership Act (JTPA) programs administered by the Department of Labor (DOL), the Job Opportunities and Basic Skills (JOBS) program administered by Health and Human Services, a variety of adult and vocational education programs administered by the Education Department, and the Food Stamp Employment and Training (FSET) program administered by USDA. A wide range of programs for the homeless funded by the Stewart B. McKinney Homeless Assistance Act of 1987 and administered by Labor, Health and Human Services, Education, and Housing and Urban Development can also come into play.

Each of these programs must carry out the same functions of eligibility determination and provision of benefits and services. Each federal agency interprets legislation, promulgates regulations and administrative guidelines, and monitors state and local program activity to make sure that the legislation and regulations are adhered to. Each devotes attention to changes in programs funded through other agencies to determine what impact, if any, they may have on their own programs. Logic suggests that if these programs were better coordinated at the federal level, duplication of effort would be reduced and administrative efficiency increased at the federal level. There would be increased opportunities to uncover and rectify problems in coordination among the programs that are manifested at the state and local levels.

At the most ambitious level, enhanced coordination might involve a major metamorphosis—a redistribution of functions among the federal agencies in which one agency was responsible for income maintenance, another for employment and training, and so forth. For example, the Food Stamp Employment and Training program, JTPA, and JOBS programs could be brought under a single organizational roof. At a more modest level, formal and informal efforts could be made to get the policymakers and administrators of each of these programs to work more closely together to identify areas of overlap and duplication and to work to eliminate them.

In both of these cases, administrative cost savings at any level of government will only be possible if (1) planned reorganizations can be translated into reality, and (2) the realignment either results in a more efficient structure at the federal level or helps to bring duplication and inefficiency to light at the state and local levels and makes it easier to eliminate them through changes in law or regulations.

Both the literature and conversations with officials of public assistance and related programs at various levels of government suggest that federal executive branch agencies can promote state- and local-level coordination by increasing the incentives to coordinate and, then, getting out of the way. In particular, this approach might include such things as:

- Identifying barriers to state and local coordination that result from inconsistencies or conflicts in goals, purposes, administrative procedures, funding cycles, and taking steps to eliminate them

- Providing funding and other financial or nonfinancial incentives to state and local agencies that engage in coordination

- Providing state and local officials with the flexibility to modify or ignore federal-level barriers to improve interagency collaboration as discussed later in this chapter

- Providing information on the benefits of coordination

These steps are consistent with the report of the JTPA Advisory Committee (1989) which indicated that "Experience suggests that (the federal government) cannot mandate or guarantee meaningful collaboration, but the Department of Health and Human Services, Department of Labor, and Department of Education can promote coordinated planning (at the state and local levels) and remove barriers to coordination (at the state and local levels)" (43).

REORGANIZING THE MAJOR CABINET-LEVEL DEPARTMENTS

Reorganization is one of the traditional responses to coordination problems. As noted earlier in this chapter, it would seem logical to try to reorganize the federal government so that all programs that relate to a given function are located in a single agency, for example, having one agency, such as the Department of Health and Human Services, administer all income maintenance programs, and another, such as the Department of Labor, provide all employment-related education and training.

Shifting the responsibility for all employment programs for public assistance recipients, including JOBS and the Food Stamp Employment and Training program, to the Department of Labor's Employment and Training Administration would increase the opportunity for the staff of the secretary and assistant secretary of labor to engage in high-level policy reviews that would highlight inconsistencies among key elements of these programs, such as definitions, reporting requirements, funding cycles, and so forth, and then allow them to take action to overcome these inconsistencies.

On the other hand, if the JOBS program proves to be both more effective and politically attractive than programs administered by the Department of Labor, it might make sense to shift authority for other training programs for disadvantaged Americans to HHS, giving an assistant secretary of that agency the same opportunities that were given the assistant secretary of labor in the previous case.

However attractive it may seem, there are at least three potential pitfalls associated with this kind of approach. On a theoretical level, reorganization to increase linkages among some programs may well lead to a weakening of ties among others. Consolidation of responsibility for JOBS, JTPA, the Food Stamp Employment and Training program, and vocational education within a given department might result in improved coordination among these programs, but it could also result in a decrease in coordination between these programs and income maintenance aspects of the AFDC program that would remain at Health and Human Services and the Food Stamp program at USDA. Similarly, if a new agency were created to handle all income maintenance programs, it would still face the need to coordinate with the service programs in HHS and the employment programs at the Department of Labor and elsewhere.

More practically, the opportunity to promote administrative simplification and cost savings would be diminished if the basic elements of each program remained intact in legislation that is developed by different congressional subcommittees and committees. For example, there are notable differences in many of the elements of the employment and training programs that are currently under the aegis of the Department of Labor, and there is little reason to believe that bringing additional programs under the DOL umbrella would have more effect. The October 1989 Report of the JTPA Advisory Committee listed six roadblocks to better linkages among the programs that are currently administered by DOL's Employment and Training Administration: (1) differing eligibility requirements; (2) incompatible program timetables; (3) significant variations in requirements concerning allowable expenditures; (4) differences in reporting requirements; (5) differing provisions concerning levels of review and communications through state, regional, and national levels; and, (6) in the case of long-established programs, adherence to traditional administrative practices that are resistant to change. This list is not very different from the ones that are now frequently compiled to list barriers to better coordination of welfare employment programs that are under the aegis of different federal departments.

Finally, it would take a considerable amount of time, energy, and political capital to bring together a coalition that is powerful enough to pass the legislation needed to enact this kind of reorganization. The current organization of public assistance programs is at least in part a reflection of congressional committee jurisdictions and the desires of powerful interest groups, as discussed in Chapter 3. Changing this situation would probably require strong presidential leadership and, even with this leadership, is no simple task.

Why not create umbrella superagencies instead of merely shuffling the responsibilities of the existing agencies? Logic suggests that if all relevant functions were under a single secretary it would be easier to resolve differences among programs. Creation of such an umbrella agency or agencies at the federal level would require the same extraordinary amounts of time and political resources to pass the needed legislation as would be needed for the less broad-based reorganizations.

In sum, devoting scarce resources of time and energy to promote major reorganization of the agencies responsible for public assistance programs can only be justified if they are likely to produce the desired results.

ACHIEVING COORDINATION BY IMPROVING PROCESSES AND PROCEDURES

Federal executive agencies can do a great deal to improve coordination that does not involve *any* formal efforts to reorganize or create ambitious new coordinating mechanisms at the federal level. More specifically, each federal agency that administers one or more public assistance programs can promote greater efficiency in federal-level program administration by building on existing, written interagency agreements and less formal coordination efforts that provide for high visibility meetings of secretaries and high-level staff, where verbal commitments to support coordination are made; jointly sponsored conferences on specific topics; coordination in technical assistance efforts, such as the current efforts to bring the three federal agencies together to oversee selected aspects of the JOBS program; and ongoing ad hoc efforts to deal with specific barriers to coordination by developing common definitions, planning cycles, and so forth. The first three of these kinds of efforts are likely to promote the fourth because they provide an institutional basis and a forum whereby staff from different federal agencies can get together to learn more about possible duplication and discuss ways to streamline program administration.

Similarly, federal public assistance agency officials can do a great deal to promote increased coordination at the state and local levels without major institutional changes. They can promote changes in federal legislation that (1) increase flexibility for state and local counterpart agency officials to administer programs by creating new waiver authority where it does not exist and expanding this kind of authority where it does; (2) strengthen the financial and nonfinancial incentives to coordinate at the state and local levels; and (3) create or strengthen central coordinating bodies at the state and local level, such as state job training coordinating councils and local private industry councils.

Agency officials can use the regulatory process to further these objectives wherever possible by reviewing their audit and review procedures to ensure that innovators will not be worse off for having taken chances. Officials can do this by providing "hold harmless" commitments for performance standards for projects involving ambitious coordination or by making assurances that certain kinds of coordination activities will be considered acceptable in audits.

Federal administrators can increase awareness of the problems facing state and local officials' efforts to coordinate by hiring policymakers and senior administrators with operational experience at the state and local level, by making field visits to state and local agencies to discuss barriers to coordination and steps that can be taken to overcome them, and by conducting research that addresses state- and local-level coordination issues. They can provide support, public recognition, and encouragement for officials in state and local counterpart agencies for efforts to coordinate with other programs.

The effectiveness of many of these steps could be strengthened by institutionalized joint planning among different federal agencies, and coordination efforts could be quite fruitful if they were to continue on an agency-specific ad hoc basis as they now do. In essence, there can be considerable progress in promoting coordination through the quiet un-dramatic activities that go on every day among policymakers and opera-tional staff in Washington.

However, it would probably be unwise to rely solely on these kinds of activities to overcome the severe challenges to coordination that characterize many aspects of public assistance programs in the 1990s. Although states and localities can increase the likelihood that these kinds of activities will happen by continuing to pressure the federal agencies with whom they deal, it is unlikely that the fundamental discontinuities among these programs can be resolved through the above-discussed, largely ad hoc activities.

ACHIEVING COORDINATION THROUGH A NEW INSTITUTIONAL APPROACH

Students of public administration often restate the aphorism that "where you stand [on an issue] depends on where you sit [in a given agency]." This line of thought suggests that it is likely that staff of a given federal department will devote first priority to the interests of their own agency and therefore expect people in other agencies to coordinate with *them*. Only sustained leadership and encouragement from the highest levels of a federal department are likely to overcome this tendency among members of interagency work groups.

Recent experience suggests, however, that we need an approach that is more permanent than the person at the top of a federal department. The recent efforts of the Departments of Health and Human Services, Labor, and Education to coordinate their efforts to implement the Job Opportuni-ties and Basic Skills program provide a good example of the strengths and weaknesses of approaches that are based on personal commitments and not institutional links. In November 1989, the secretaries of the three agencies signed an interagency agreement to cooperate in the implemen-tation of the welfare employment JOBS program. Representatives of each agency have been meeting regularly since that time, primarily around a jointly funded technical assistance effort. This shared technical assistance effort has, in turn, provided a forum in which broader interagency coordi-nation issues can be raised, addressed, and, hopefully, resolved.

However, two of the three secretaries that signed this agreement are no longer in office, and their collaborative effort does not seem to have altered the broad differences in perspective that the agencies bring to employment programs. The ongoing collaboration around a JOBS technical assistance contract did not avoid at least some duplication of effort in the planning for a major conference on coordination of vocational-technical education, adult education, JTPA, and JOBS programs that was held in the summer of 1991. Nor did it promote widespread changes in the ways that programs relate to each other on the state and local levels. Most important, it has not yet produced any ideas that will reduce administrative costs at the federal level or many tangible changes in legislation, regulations, program policy, and regulatory frameworks.

Both the literature and common sense tell us that permanent change is unlikely, at best, in large bureaucracies unless there are organized advocates for change. Efforts based on the commitments of one or two key officials rarely maintain their momentum after the founding generation of initiators moves on to other responsibilities unless there is some institutional mechanism to carry on.

Therefore, in order to increase the likelihood that current federal-level efforts to promote coordination are continued—if not accelerated—it would be helpful to go beyond the personal commitments of key agency staff and build an institutional capacity to promote coordination, one or more structures whose staff are committed to the perspective of "the whole client" and the goals of improved service, and not the perspectives and goals of individual federal agencies.

In recent years, as discussed in Chapter 2, several interagency bodies dealing with programs for low-income Americans have been set up as part of the White House staff. The Low Income Opportunity Board was created in 1987 and replaced by the Economic Empowerment Task Force in 1990. Although these bodies have the standing to play a major coordinating role, they have been criticized by some as being too political to be seen as neutral conveners or advocates for improved efficiency. However, there are many other less political models that are worthy of further consideration in this regard. In the case of welfare employment programs, at least three models are available.

Model A is a nine-member, independent Interagency Welfare Employment Commission headed by designees of the secretaries of HHS, DOL, Department of Education (ED), and USDA and representatives of state and local government and other interested groups. It would be important that the chair of the group not be permanently identified with any of the federal agencies. Therefore, the group might adopt a rotating chair, or might pick its chairperson from the nonfederal commissioners.

The commission's responsibilities would focus on the policy level, including an ongoing mandate to identify (1) the overlapping and duplication of effort among federal, state, and local public assistance and related programs; (2) the benefits that would accrue to improved coordination among federal, state, and local agencies; (3) the barriers to improved coordination at all levels of government; and (4) the concrete steps that the Congress and the federal agencies could take to overcome them. Ideally, the commission would have resources of its own that would permit it to go beyond report writing and thus have a more direct impact on service delivery. One way to accomplish this would be to provide funding to the commission that could be subcontracted to federal, state, or local agencies engaged in promising approaches to coordinated service delivery. Another might be to give the commission sign-off authority to approve coordination plans prepared by various agencies.

Model B is a two-year independent study commission funded by HHS, DOL, ED, and USDA that would be overseen by representatives of high officials in the four agencies and staffed by an existing, widely respected group, such as the National Research Council or National Academy of Public Administration. Its role would be to review interagency coordination experience in human services at the federal and state levels in the United States and other industrialized countries in order to define and assess alternatives to the current divisions of responsibilities among the federal agencies, and the likely impact of these changes on program administration at the federal, state, and local levels.

Model C is an expansion of the role of existing bodies, such as the National Commission for Employment Policy, to incorporate some ongoing responsibilities in the area of interagency coordination. One role of such a group might be to convene operational-level staff, rather than policymakers, from the affected federal agencies, their state and local counterparts, and other interested parties in order to (1) examine specific technical coordination problems, such as incompatible funding cycles, and (2) develop ideas of correcting them through technical amendments to existing legislation or regulatory action.

The specific type of coordinating body that is created is less important than the overall objective of creating an institution whose staff are not beholden to any of the major federal agencies and who can, therefore, act as neutral conveners for meetings and conferences to address coordination and as vigorous lobbyists to agency policymakers to promote increased efficiency of federal program administration as well as better coordination at the state and local levels.

Care would have to be taken to ensure that the staff of these bodies do not intrude on the ongoing, day-to-day operational responsibilities of the federal agencies and do not succeed in taking on functions that are currently assigned to the individual agencies. This interagency approach should be far less controversial than a major federal-level reorganization, should engender far less opposition, and should, therefore, be far less costly to implement.

CONCLUSION

Despite the successes that have been achieved in promoting coordination among the federal agencies that administer public assistance programs in recent years, it is clear that much more can and should be done. A good deal can be accomplished without *any* changes in the formal relationships among the relevant federal agencies doing business with each other. Beyond this, a relatively modest effort to create, fund, and staff one or more interagency coordinating bodies represents the most promising new direction in which to go. The political cost would be relatively low and the potential benefits would be significant.

Efforts to reorganize and reassign programs from one agency to another represent a gamble. They can bear fruit if they are backed by the president and a coalition powerful enough to enact them, and if the leadership of the reorganized agencies has the political will and the influence to bring about changes that will harmonize the administration of the programs under their bailiwick.

Reasonable people differ about the likelihood that these conditions can be met in the near future for any meaningful restructuring of administrative responsibilities. Whatever one's judgment in this regard, it is important not to put all of our coordination "eggs" in the reorganization "basket." Reorganization proposals may take years to enact and still more time to result in needed changes—or they may fail, leaving the status quo even more firmly entrenched.

The need to be cautious about embarking on reorganization approaches was noted in a recently published critique of the HHS service integration efforts of the 1970s and 1980s. As noted in Kusserow (1991):

The HEW SI [service integration] agenda of the 1970s sought far-reaching institutional reforms in the human services system. Many of the initiatives developed were comprehensive ones, spanning categorical programs areas, seeking new lines of authority. . . . Although it is possible that long-term gains may justify such expansive efforts, the prospects for generating and sustaining the necessary political, programmatic, and financial support are not good. The chances of success appear to be much greater if policy-makers pursue more modest objectives, stressing incremental, near term gains. (8)

It is important to recognize that there is much that can be accomplished in terms of promoting coordination with relatively little expenditure of political capital. The relatively easily attainable aspects of the agenda for change outlined in this chapter should be pursued regardless of any strategic decision of whether or not to go forward with ambitious reorganization schemes.

REFERENCES

Bailis, Lawrence Neil. 1989. *An Assessment of the JTPA Role in State and Local Coordination Activities: Report on the Literature Review.* Submitted to the Employment and Training Administration, U.S. Department of Labor. Washington, D.C. January.

Job Training Partnership Act Advisory Committee. 1989. *Working Capital: Coordinated Human Investment Directions for the 90s.* Washington, D.C.: Department of Labor. October.

Johnston, Janet. 1987. *The Job Training Partnership Act.* Washington, D.C.: National Commission for Employment Policy.

Kusserow, Richard P. 1991. *Services Integration: A Twenty Year Retrospective.* Washington, D.C.: U.S. Department of Health and Human Services Office of Inspector General.

Levitan, Sar, and Frank Gallo. 1988. *A Second Chance: Training for Jobs.* Kalamazoo, Mich.: Upjohn Institute.

Trutko, John, Lawrence Neil Bailis, Burt Barnow, et al. 1990. *An Assessment of the JTPA Role in State and Local Coordination Activities: Final Report.* James Bell Associates, Inc.

Chapter 5

Federal Policy Changes to Enhance State and Local Coordination

Christopher T. King

Eligibility criteria for public assistance and related programs for the economically disadvantaged in this country vary widely, despite the fact that most of them are designed ostensibly to achieve the same basic goal—alleviating poverty for individuals and their families (National Commission for Employment Policy, 1991). Such variation almost inevitably leads to conflicts and helps to create the potential for program duplication. This is hardly a new problem. Volumes have been written about it, and select committees and task forces have devoted hours of otherwise productive time trying in vain to solve it (Barth et al., 1974; Low Income Opportunity Working Group, 1986; Job Training Partnership Act Advisory Committee, 1989).

This chapter neither revisits the details of these programs and their conflicting provisions nor provides a definitive guide to a land free of programmatic conflict and duplication. Instead, it attempts to stimulate discussion among policymakers, including state job training coordinating council (SJTCC) chairs and staff, many of whom are seasoned veterans of the process, about strategies for resolving conflicts between these criteria and for promoting program coordination. The chapter begins by offering some general considerations and suggesting a menu of possible federal and state strategies. It concludes with some brief observations about the nature of coordination and efforts needed to promote it.

GENERAL CONSIDERATIONS

The reasons for the existence of major eligibility and related conflicts in these programs have been meticulously detailed elsewhere (National Commission for Employment Policy, 1991). Programs emanate from different committees in Congress and are designed to accomplish different and specific program objectives. They have differing needs for regional or local variation in their eligibility criteria, and, once legislated, are housed in federal agencies with different guiding philosophies and administrative approaches. These differences lead to restricted access for those who are eligible. Some individuals are so intimidated by the prospect of documenting their eligibility in this program maze that they never apply at all. Others make it part of the way through the maze only to drop out before completing it, their energy and determination having failed them before they could successfully demonstrate their eligibility for all of the programs.

These conflicts also result in increased costs for both program staff and clients who do participate. It takes an enormous amount of staff time and energy—not to mention reams of paper and computer space—to handle the complexities of conflicting program eligibility. A concomitant administrative effort is called for at all levels to monitor and audit the application of these criteria. Some states implementing client-friendly initiatives for human service delivery have documented the toll exacted by the more traditional program approaches (Michigan Job Training Coordinating Council, 1989; Texas State Job Training Coordinating Council, 1990). Potential clients, typically with children in tow, bounce from agency to agency, traveling from one end of town to the other negotiating these systems. The flip side of increased cost is that fewer eligible people are served.

There are other, less obvious, costs. Recent ethnographic research on poor families suggests that there are adverse intergenerational effects as well (Lein, 1991). Even the very young children of welfare mothers learn how to "work the system." Children find out early on what they should and should not say to caseworkers, and just how to shield their parents and siblings from the impact of the puzzling rules they encounter. These perverse and possibly long-lasting behaviors unfortunately make perfect sense for surviving in a hostile world. Naturally, the public also is affected by stories circulating about these conflicting provisions, finding ready confirmation of the view that public programs truly are bureaucratic nightmares with little sensitivity to the needs of poor people. Finally, to the extent that program staff are drained by their efforts to cope with or circumvent these conflicts, program effectiveness suffers for those lucky enough to actually become participants. There is ample justification for eliminating unnecessary conflicts in eligibility criteria and related provisions and for fashioning strategies to promote program coordination.

CONFLICT RESOLUTION AND COORDINATION STRATEGIES

There are a host of possible strategies for resolving conflicts and promoting program coordination. A number of these are presented and discussed here. Both federal and state strategies are examined with an eye towards the Job Training Partnership Act (JTPA) and related programs.

The Do-Nothing Strategy

From the federal perspective, the easiest and least expensive course is to pursue what might be termed the *do-nothing strategy*, which has certainly been the strategy of choice for some time. As earlier chapters indicate, there is little appetite for change where it is needed most—in the Congress and the executive branch. The do-nothing strategy simply acknowledges this and essentially leaves the current cost structure intact. State and local staff and their clients would continue to bear the brunt of the conflicting program provisions. It might be noted that this strategy is in line with the 1980s version of the New Federalism, in which programs dealing with the disadvantaged were typically told to "ask your governor" instead of running to Washington for solutions to problems.

The Minimalist Strategy

A second broad approach might be called the *minimalist strategy*. This strategy also accepts the fact that there is currently little federal support for making substantive changes in eligibility criteria or other provisions of these programs. However, it envisions doing more than standing by and watching the wreck-in-progress. Although it does not attempt to modify the statutory language or the administrative rules, it does take the mildly proactive federal posture of supporting and nurturing state and local efforts to better cope with the differing legislative provisions and administrative rules governing the programs.

Increasingly, states and some cities (e.g., New York City, Corpus Christi, Texas) have pursued fresh approaches to service delivery for the disadvantaged. Michigan developed the Opportunity Card, which is shaped like a credit card and allows agency assistance staff to access client information from a computerized database. Pennsylvania initiated a Single Point of Contact demonstration; and Maryland, New Jersey, New York, and Texas either implemented or planned initiatives with a similar focus. This is by no means a complete list. Each of these efforts attempts to ease the burdens associated with client eligibility for and access to programs, as well as to facilitate effective program participation. In general, these initiatives have not tried to change the basic criteria governing program eligibility. What they have done is rationalize or streamline the process of applying and documenting eligibility for the programs so that—from the client's perspective at least—the systems become virtually seamless (Levitan et al., 1989).

Considerable state and local resources have been expended on these initiatives. Without making the costly commitment to change policies and restructure programs, the Congress and executive branch could invest relatively modest federal resources (e.g., matching funds or challenge grants) to bolster state and local efforts. The momentum already exists and may well be increasing. It may be an opportunity for the federal government to get an inexpensive ride on initiatives that would yield long-term returns in the form of higher participation, improved access, and lower administrative costs. Depending on the breadth and scope of these initiatives, the White House's Economic Empowerment Task Force, which replaced the Low Income Opportunity Board in late 1990, may need to be involved at some point.

Another minimalist strategy would be for Congress and the federal agencies to encourage states and localities to rationalize eligibility and bolster their efforts to collaborate more. There are many avenues for doing so. Examples include the use of preambles in program regulations to reinforce the federal intent to coordinate, as well as inserting stronger language in the numerous technical assistance guides (TAGs) issued by federal agencies each year to guide policy making and program operations at the state and local level. Of course, such efforts may not be all that successful if the targets perceive that their persuaders are lobbing stones from glass houses.

Although neither of these strategies envisions any substantial federal commitment, whether of agency staff, time, or resources, going further necessarily entails greater expenditures of both. The strategies described below would require varying levels of federal investment. Administrative strategies are described first, followed by legislative approaches. A miscellaneous set rounds out the menu of coordination strategies.

Administrative Strategies

Administrative strategies seek to identify those areas where the responsible agencies have discretion under existing law to change the criteria for determining and documenting program eligibility or to induce more effective collaboration with related programs through other means. Effective administrative strategies might address common terms and definitions, documentation requirements, and performance standards.

Conflicting terms and definitions among programs are among the more frustrating dimensions for program administrators, staff, and clients. Reading or functioning levels that render a person illiterate for one program do not necessarily do so for another, a phenomenon that contributed to the creation of a cabinet-level literacy task force (National Commission for Employment Policy, 1991). Income for one program is not always income for another. In fact, a common source of friction between JTPA and both Food Stamp and Aid to Families with Dependent Children (AFDC) programs is that enrolling recipients in on-the-job training (OJT) programs, which has often produced desirable net post-program earnings for these groups, provides them with immediate income but typically leaves them ineligible for further assistance. Where possible, the parent federal agencies should be able to develop common terms and definitions for use in their programs, and they should do so with the long-run interests of their clients firmly in mind. Clients should not be penalized for doing what is clearly advantageous for them and for society over the long term. Unfortunately, many of the terms and definitions are legislatively based rather than administratively based.

The JTPA legislation states that AFDC recipients are categorically eligible for participation. However, states and localities have not uniformly followed this provision. Instead, they have become entangled in lengthy debates over their possible fiscal liability for any mistakes in eligibility certification. Many states have required AFDC recipients to repeat the entire eligibility process, which means full documentation. Federal rule changes might be able to smooth the way toward resolving this documentation and eligibility issue and others of a similar nature.

Documentation practices also vary widely from state to state within programs, creating very different coverage. An important example of this phenomenon is the AFDC-Unemployed Parent (UP) program, especially now that it is available in all states. Each state has enormous discretion in determining what it will accept from applicants as documentation of quarters of work in order to establish program eligibility. States such as West Virginia tend to rely heavily on unemployment insurance (UI)-covered employment documentation, which is relatively easy given the degree of unionization, UI coverage, and resulting support from the state employment security agency; similar policies in the Carolinas have resulted in very low AFDC-UP take-up rates. Other states (e.g., Missouri) have taken a proactive approach, allowing eligibility workers to phone employers directly for nonwritten verification of employment. Changes in federal legislation might produce more consistent coverage across all states.

Programs for the disadvantaged now routinely include provisions for performance standards and supporting data collection and measurement systems. Increasingly these are outcome-oriented. JTPA was the first to have a comprehensive federal-state system, complete with performance incentives and sanctions (King, 1988). However, Food Stamp Employment and Training, the Family Support Act's Job Opportunities and Basic Skills (JOBS) program, and the Carl D. Perkins Vocational and Applied Technology Act (1990) programs all contain provisions that are broadly similar. They even contain language mandating or encouraging coordination of such standards, ostensibly reducing the effort any one program must make to get the others to come to the coordination table. Yet, all of these programs contain broad areas of discretion over such factors as the specific measures and standards, the time period for measurement, and the nature of the adjustment system for differences in state and local conditions, among others. With a concerted administrative strategy, federal rules could play a significant role in bringing these systems together. The way in which performance is measured and rewarded has the potential for an enormous impact on interprogram coordination.

Unfortunately, in recent years Congress has reduced state and local discretion in the area of program eligibility and resource targeting, so that administrative strategies may offer less potential relative to other approaches. Alongside JTPA and the recently amended Perkins Act, the Family Support Act (FSA) and JOBS are remarkably prescriptive in most areas, including eligibility and targeting. With only limited study, it should be possible to identify areas that hold out the best potential for concerted administrative action to enhance program coordination.

Note that states and localities actually responsible for program implementation are on the receiving end of very separate federal agency rule making. Unfortunately, it is unusual to have any significant degree of coordination in the development of program regulations at the federal level. The Office of Management and Budget (OMB) would seem to be the logical choice to assist in this regard. However, OMB has its own problems internally. It performs both budget and management-reporting functions that could benefit from more coordination. And, it is common for individuals from different sections within OMB to put their own imprimatur on such program features as reporting requirements and standards, leaving federal agency staff to take the heat from governors, local officials, and program operators for the resulting conflicts. Still, lacking OMB interest, federal agencies could invite the active participation of their counterparts in the process, especially in vital areas such as eligibility documentation, performance standards, and others.

Legislative Strategies

The following strategies envision legislative action to change eligibility, documentation, and other program provisions. This is not to say that all such changes are of the same order of magnitude. Some are relatively minor yet still would need legislative action because the particular provision or requirement is imbedded in law rather than regulation.

A number of programs for the disadvantaged cut through the complexities of the eligibility process to a large extent by making recipients and participants in related programs categorically eligible for services. Currently, Food Stamp and AFDC recipients are categorically eligible for JTPA; AFDC recipients are eligible for Medicaid; and Food Stamp eligibles gain eligibility for their children in school breakfast and lunch programs (National Commission for Employment Policy, 1991). Practical problems with categorical eligibility persist at the operations level. Without taking on the excruciating task of developing a full-blown national consensus on the meaning and definition of poverty and bringing much of the authorizing legislation into line, there might be a simpler, far less elegant solution: cast a broad, albeit clumsy, safety net by cross-referencing eligibility for as many programs as possible.

A cost-benefit analysis of existing eligibility and documentation provisions and rules might be revealing. The marginal benefits of adding eligibility provisions and rules beyond those for basic programs such as AFDC and Food Stamps must be small, while the marginal costs (e.g., increased record keeping, staff time, monitoring, and auditing responsibilities) at all levels are likely to be substantial. At the least, it should be possible to amend the various provisions to maximize their shared elements and to minimize associated documentation requirements.

One approach to promoting coordination in job training programs historically has been the use of set-asides—pots of money specifically designated for coordinated efforts by related programs and agencies. One of the best known of these is the education coordination set-aside (Section 123) in Title II-A of JTPA. The fundamental premise behind such set-asides is that coordination costs: Greater coordination can be expected if these costs are at least partially offset. While set-asides have been effective in some instances, a recent review of the literature suggests that their record is mixed and that more research is needed to identify the conditions under which they work best (Bailis, 1989). One of the difficulties has been that set-asides often have been viewed as a guaranteed source of funding whether or not interprogram coordination actually occurred. It is worth noting that the Department of Labor's 1991 legislative proposal would have eliminated the JTPA education set-aside completely in favor of provisions requiring governors to prepare and submit a plan for a new State Linkages and Coordination Program (proposed as Part C of Title II-A). Neither the House nor the Senate thought much of that proposal. In May 1992, a conference committee was busy working out differences between the JTPA amendments that passed the House (HR 3033, October 1991) and the Senate (S 2055, April 1992); both versions essentially retain the current education set-aside.

A preferred strategy would be to offer financial incentives only for coordination results. The Comprehensive Employment and Training Act (CETA) of 1973, which preceded JTPA, contained incentives for areas that would consolidate their program boundaries in order to offer services more along labor market lines. In addition, under JTPA, governors may use 6 percent of their state's Title II-A funding in part to reward greater service to hard-to-serve groups. These groups have included welfare recipients and JOBS participants. As amended by JTPA in 1982, the Wagner-Peyser Act, which authorizes the labor exchange system, also contains language (Section 7b) allowing states to reward coordinated programs. Whether such incentives would be productive on a wider scale is uncertain, but coordination activity should be given a boost by the offer of financial rewards in these times of increasingly tight state budgets.

Another approach that has surfaced in policy discussions recently is the creation of so-called human investment councils (Job Training Partnership Act Advisory Council, 1989; King, 1988). Unsuccessful 1990 House versions of the Perkins and JTPA amendments contained provisions for such councils, as did the Department of Labor's 1991 JTPA package. Proposals have called for broad-based councils to be established at the federal and state levels to foster coordinated program approaches in such key functions as planning, operations, and oversight. The JTPA conference committee was dealing with different language involving such councils in May 1992: the House version (HR 3033) allowed states to establish State Human Resource Investment Councils, while the Senate version (S 2055) contained no reference to them. It is worth noting that JTPA allows governors to use their state job training coordinating councils to serve similar functions for the employment service and welfare employment programs. A few governors have capitalized on this opportunity for their states, including those of New Jersey, Oregon, and Washington. If councils were established focusing only on planning (e.g., common terms and definitions, approaches and cycles) and performance (e.g., similar standards and structures for rewards and sanctions), interprogram coordination could be enhanced considerably.

Miscellaneous Strategies

Three others strategies outlined below do not fit neatly into the preceding categories. Within agencies, the inspector general (IG) and program staffs function so independently that state and local programs often are driven to pursue unduly conservative approaches—especially for documenting eligibility—to avoid the possibility of disallowed costs because of serving ineligible participants. To a great extent this is the intent and a natural outcome of their respective roles. However, there is room for much improvement.

This problem worsened in the 1980s. Under the New Federalism, states were given far less federal direction and guidance and took on increasing responsibility for developing program policies, while IGs continued to bring a more singular national view to their task. The current situation of JTPA throughout the country offers a prime example of this problem.

JTPA was passed in late 1982, giving governors major new responsibilities in such important areas as performance standards and incentives, procurement, and programs for dislocated workers. Well into 1986, the response given by the Employment and Training (E & T) administration to state JTPA staff asking for guidance on these matters was typically a three-word reply: Ask your governor. This has not kept the IG from second-guessing the governors, particularly in procurement matters, the use of dislocated workers' monies, and the like. In fact, significant portions of the more prescriptive procurement language contained in both Senate and House versions of the JTPA amendments in conference in 1992 appear to have been drafted more in response to IG than authorizing committee concerns.

Barriers to effective program coordination typically include such factors as not speaking the other's language and not understanding the nature of their philosophy, special delivery system requirements, or performance expectations. One demonstrated way of surmounting this barrier is to promote the use of joint technical assistance and training (TAT) where state and local (and even federal) staff from related programs are brought together to hear simultaneously the same messages and receive the same kinds of training and assistance. Not coincidentally, these staff share common issues and problems and build lasting personal relationships that are probably the underlying basis for real coordination and collaboration over time. Stories about the good old days—from the early Work Incentive (WIN) program that was jointly administered and featured teams of case managers from welfare and the employment service—are still being fondly recalled. Under the Department of Labor's Manpower Institutional Grant (MIG) program, which was discontinued in the early 1980s, existing and potential staff from programs such as CETA, WIN, and vocational education were often included in joint education and training. The TAT project, which is part of JOBS and jointly sponsored by the federal Departments of Health and Human Services, Labor, and Education, is a wonderful example of this strategy.

Another avenue could be pursued on the federal level, even by small programs, by taking advantage of recent technological developments and the widespread use of computers. Again, without trying to resolve conflicts in program eligibility criteria, the development of expert-systems eligibility software, compatible with a wide range of hardware, should be well within reach. Such a system was successfully instituted in Wisconsin several years ago, when technology was considerably less friendly. A multiagency effort could be launched to design, develop, and implement this software. A national technical assistance and training project should accompany this as well. Such public-domain software, coupled with some simplification in data and documentation requirements, could help state and local programs cope more effectively and efficiently with conflicting criteria, while reducing client burden and facilitating program access.

CONCLUSION

A recent Ford Foundation report opened with the following statement: "Social welfare policy in the United States must be fundamentally reformed and modernized. Economic, demographic and social conditions have changed, but our social policies have not adapted to these changes" (Common Good, 1989: 1).

The need for action to promote greater coordination among programs serving the disadvantaged is very real, especially at the national level. There are substantial costs associated with conflicting eligibility and other program provisions, and most typically they are borne by program staff at the state and local level and by the clients and their families. Many conflicts can be traced back to federal regulations, legislative language, and congressional committee structures. It is not asking too much for key policymakers to reach agreement on these issues. Numerous strategies are available. At the same time, those who have studied coordination over the years caution that expectations should be kept reasonably low (Bailis, 1989).

The key federal actors may be unwilling to get their own houses completely in order, although recent developments, including the joint technical assistance and training project for JOBS, are encouraging. However, the least they can do is to provide a modicum of assistance to those who are suffering daily from their messiness. On the cheap side, they could support existing state and local efforts to provide one-stop shopping and to design and operate seamless services; or, they could develop and disseminate multiprogram eligibility software via a national TAT project. On the more costly side, Congress, the White House, and the key federal agencies could commit their energies and resources to housecleaning on a grand scale, designing a more rational, cohesive system of programs for the disadvantaged.

It might be helpful to conclude by offering a few relatively soft observations about coordination, drawn largely from the experiences of researchers conducting a rigorous, multiyear evaluation of welfare-to-work program coordination at the state and local level in Texas (Gula and King, 1990).

People matter. After all, organizations don't coordinate—people do. The best examples of coordination tend to be where people from different programs know and trust each other. This should come as no surprise, yet it often seems to.

Limited resource availability promotes coordination. As the literature suggests, areas where resources are constrained tend to pitch in to deliver services in a more collaborative manner. Clearly, this should not be taken as the be-all and end-all advice for policy development regarding coordination. Ultimately, it could lead to wholesale reductions in resources for programs serving the disadvantaged despite the fact that each effort currently is only reaching a tiny fraction of those eligible.

Effective organizational coordination must occur at all levels. Formal agreements between agency heads, assistant secretaries, and program managers are all well and good, but if frontline staff have not gotten the message, real day-to-day coordination between programs is unlikely to take place.

Measuring effective coordination is difficult. Self-assessments, descriptions in coordination plans, and other traditional means inadequately measure effective coordination. This problem is made worse because some of the best coordinated programs often appear to meet or communicate infrequently on a formal basis: They have achieved a level of trust and familiarity where issues and problems can be handled by a simple phone call or a handwritten note. Probably the best indicator of coordinated service delivery is an abundance of "credit-sharing" rather than "blame-finding" among key program actors.

Finally, based on recent findings from this Texas multiyear coordination evaluation (King et al., 1991), the good news is that coordination efforts, despite their costs, bear the desired fruit. Substate areas of Texas with more coordinated approaches to service delivery for welfare recipients exhibit greater service levels to hard-to-serve welfare clients, more intensive program treatments, better immediate job placement rates, and higher postprogram employment and earnings levels, even allowing for the differing local population and economic circumstances. These preliminary findings offer support and encouragement to policymakers and program staff at all levels. They should keep striving for better service delivery for disadvantaged and other populations in need of assistance. Despite the undeniable, often considerable costs involved with program coordination, it is well worth the effort.

REFERENCES

Bailis, Lawrence Neil. 1989. *An Assessment of the JTPA Role in State and Local Coordination Activities: Report on the Literature Review.* Submitted to the Employment and Training Administration, U. S. Department of Labor. Washington, D.C. January.

Barth, Michael C., George J. Carcagno, and John L. Palmer. 1974. "Toward an Effective Income Support System: Problems, Prospects, and Choices." Madison: Institute for Research on Poverty, University of Wisconsin-Madison.

Common Good. 1989. *The Common Good: Social Welfare and the American Future-Policy Recommendations of the Executive Panel.* New York: Ford Foundation Project on Social Welfare and the American Future. May.

Gula, Annette, and Christopher T. King. 1990. *Welfare-to-Work Program Coordination in Texas: Report on the Initial Site Visit.* Austin: Center for the Study of Human Resources, The University of Texas at Austin. December.

Job Training Partnership Act Advisory Committee. 1989. *Working Capital: Coordinated Human Investment Directions for the 90s.* Washington, D.C.: U.S. Department of Labor. October.

King, Christopher. 1988. *Cross-Cutting Performance Issues in Human Resource Programs.* National Commission for Employment Policy Research Report 88–12. Washington, D.C.: National Commission for Employment Policy. August.

King, Christopher, Annette Gula, and Deanna T. Schexnayder. 1991. "The Effects of Program Coordination in Texas Welfare-Employment Programs: Preliminary Results." Paper presented to the 13th Annual APPAM Research Conference. Bethesda, Md.

Lein, Laura. 1991. "The Role of Food Programs in the Lives of Persistently Poor Children." Manuscript. Austin: School of Social Work and Department of Anthropology, The University of Texas at Austin.

Levitan, Sar, Garth Mangum, and Marion Pines. 1989. "A Proper Inheritance: Investing in the Self-Sufficiency of Poor Families." Washington, D.C.: The George Washington University, Center for Social Policy Studies. July.

Low Income Opportunity Working Group. 1986. *Up From Dependency: A New National Public Assistance Strategy.* Report to the President by the Domestic Policy Council.

Michigan Job Training Coordinating Council. 1989. *Creating a Human Investment System.* March.

National Commission for Employment Policy. 1990. *Training Hispanics: Implications for the JTPA System.* Report No. 27. Washington, D.C. January.

————. 1991. "Background Paper on Federal Public Assistance Programs: Coordination and Eligibility Issues." Washington, D.C. February 20.

Shapiro, Isaac, and Robert Greenstein. 1988. "Holes in the Safety Nets: Poverty Programs and Policies in the States—National Overview." Washington, D.C.: Center on Budget and Policy Priorities. April.

Texas State Job Training Coordinating Council. 1990. *Creating a Human Investment System in Texas: No Wrong Door.* Austin: Texas Department of Commerce.

THE STATE ROLE

Improving the coordination of public assistance programs at the state level requires dealing with features of the programs themselves and making changes in institutional arrangements for decision making and action. The chapters in Part III examine efforts to improve state-level coordination through (1) the use of various tools of coordination, (2) planning processes that provide the opportunity to develop coherent approaches to service delivery, (3) the reorganization of state service delivery systems, (4) the incorporation of incentives in national legislation, (5) the response to coordination mandates incorporated in national legislation, and (6) state action to generate federal action to facilitate state and local efforts.

The delivery of human services is carried out by a mixture of state, local, and regional agencies that varies from state to state. Whatever the state does in terms of planning for human resource development and organizing itself to facilitate that development will have little meaning unless it affects and supports the actual delivery of services. In recent years, considerable attention has been given to the question of how service delivery can be coordinated in a way that will enhance the system and reduce burdens on clients. These deliberations have given rise to proposals for case management, integrated data systems, consolidated application forms, and one-stop shopping, among other things.

In Chapter 6, Edward T. Jennings, Jr. identifies the approaches states use to coordinate employment and training programs. He uses survey data to examine the extent to which those approaches are used and the attitudes of state administrators about various coordination tools and techniques.

Federal legislation over the past decade has recognized the need for planning if resources are to be put to productive use and has incorporated planning requirements in important federal initiatives, such as the Job Training Partnership Act (JTPA) and the Job Opportunities and Basic Skills (JOBS) program under the Family Support Act. Indeed, the state job training coordinating councils (SJTCCs) were created to both plan and coordinate state efforts in employment and training.

Although strategic planning processes provide a framework for developing consolidated human resource development approaches, organizational arrangements can inhibit efforts to make sense of service delivery and facilitate program activities. States have very diverse organizational arrangements for the delivery of human services. Those arrangements are a product of the history of policy and organizational development in each state and reflect political compromises, the accretion of programs over time to respond to specific needs, and constitutional mandates. Although there is no one best way to organize for the delivery of human services, it is clear that the fragmentation of human service delivery among multiple competing agencies often stands as a barrier to the effectiveness and efficiency of programs.

As demonstrated by William Tracy, Kathleen Wimer, and Edward T. Jennings, Jr. in Chapter 7, New Jersey and Connecticut have found that attention to strategic planning and organizational concerns is crucial in the effort to develop enhanced and coordinated human resource investment efforts. Planning in these states provides the means for developing policies that target resources on high priority objectives and coordinate the many agencies and programs that contribute to human resource development.

A major public policy concern is the flexibility at the state and local level in the implementation of job training programs rather than centralization at the national level. Many believe that the responsiveness of assistance programs to local needs is enhanced if they are designed at the state or local level, instead of at the federal level. In Chapter 8, Robert G. Ainsworth and Barbara B. Oakley examine the issues and controversy surrounding the education-coordination set-aside in Section 123 of the Job Training Partnership Act (JTPA).

At least 80 percent of the set-aside funds must be used to provide education and training services to JTPA-eligible participants through cooperative agreements between education and JTPA agencies. Although not more than 20 percent of the set-aside may be used for coordination of education and training services, the authors' research shows that states use the 20 percent portion of the set-aside for a variety of education and training activities. These funds allow the states flexibility in establishing criteria for designing coordination activities that include other relevant employment and training programs.

The Family Support Act (FSA), the most significant public assistance legislation of the 1980s, created a new job training program that would complement other efforts to meet widespread employment and training needs. Its basic thrust was to reduce the dependence of the poor on public assistance and enable them to meet their own needs. In Chapter 9, Edward T. Jennings, Jr. and Dale Krane discuss coordination issues raised by the implementation of the Job Opportunities and Basic Skills program of FSA.

Jennings and Krane examine state-level efforts to implement JOBS. They analyze implementation efforts in eight states, giving particular attention to coordination concerns. They identify diverse arrangements in the eight states for delivery of JOBS program components and report disagreement among administrators about how effective the coordination of JOBS has been. They also find mixed results with respect to the degree to which JOBS has been effectively coordinated with other programs and raise questions about whether JOBS programs are taking full advantage of the preexisting JTPA system.

Although state and local governments are often the unwelcome recipients of federal mandates, they are also in a position to shape the content of those mandates. They can do this through their reactions to the mandates, but they can also do it through conscious efforts to shape legislation and regulatory policy. As Dale Krane points out in Chapter 10, states and localities have numerous avenues they can pursue and tools they can use to shape federal policy in ways that are responsive to their needs and interests. In addition, they often provide the source of ideas for federal policy.

As Krane indicates, states have to make a series of choices in developing a strategy to pursue in efforts to influence federal policy. Should they follow a public or behind-the-scenes path; should they focus on elected or administrative officials; are they concerned about the substantive content or the credibility of policy? The strategies and tactics that will be appropriate and successful for states and localities will depend upon their objectives. Individual subnational governments that seek waivers and special grants can work through congressional delegations and with specific agencies of the national government. Groups of governments can work through their Washington-based public interest groups that have developed a substantial capacity to deliver the state and local message to the national government.

Chapter 6

Patterns and Perceptions of Employment and Training Coordination in the States

Edward T. Jennings, Jr.

Since the 1960s, efforts have been made to coordinate employment and training programs in state and local communities to bring together diverse resources and activities to address problems of chronic unemployment and underemployment. These efforts culminated in the Job Training Partnership Act (JTPA) of 1982, which required the creation in each state of a state job training coordinating council (SJTCC) to develop the biennial Governor's Special Services and Coordination Plan and oversee the development of coordinated employment and training activities.

This chapter documents the array of approaches that states have developed to pursue coordination and analyzes the attitudes of state officials about the tools in use. It proceeds by (1) briefly reviewing federal requirements for state coordination of employment and training programs, (2) identifying the coordination tools used by the states and classifying those approaches, (3) identifying the extent to which states use the approaches, and (4) analyzing the distribution of opinions of state officials responsible for employment and training-related programs. Data are taken from official state documents, such as the Governor's Special Services and Coordination Plan, and surveys of state officials conducted in 1989 and 1990.

FEDERAL REQUIREMENTS FOR EMPLOYMENT AND TRAINING COORDINATION

The Job Training Partnership Act includes numerous provisions intended to enhance coordination efforts. First, it creates the state job training coordinating councils and gives them several coordination responsibilities: (1) developing the Governor's Special Services and Coordination Plan, which identifies state-level coordination activities and provides standards for the coordination of programs by the service delivery areas (SDAs) and their private industry councils (PICs); (2) approving SDA plans as being in conformity with state coordination goals; (3) using funds from three state set-asides to encourage coordination efforts; (4) approving program plans of local employment service offices; (5) reviewing state employment service and vocational education plans.

A second provision of JTPA designed to enhance coordination is the sharing of power between local elected officials and the private industry councils created under JTPA. These private industry councils contain a majority of employer representatives, but also include representatives of local education agencies, the public employment service, labor unions, rehabilitation agencies, community-based organizations, and economic development agencies. This membership composition is one way of encouraging coordination. Each PIC prepares a biennial training plan that, among other things, specifies how JTPA activities will be coordinated with other employment-related programs.

A third JTPA provision aimed at enhancing coordination is the 8 percent set-aside to be spent on cooperative programs with state education agencies. A fourth provision requires SJTCCs to review the plans of all state agencies providing employment, training, and related services, and provide comments to the governor, the state legislature, state agencies, and appropriate federal agencies on the relevance and effectiveness of employment and training and related service delivery systems. Yet another provision requires SJTCCs to identify, in coordination with appropriate agencies, the employment, training, and vocational education needs of the state, and assess the extent to which employment, training, vocational education, rehabilitation services, public assistance, economic development, and other federal, state, and local programs and services represent a consistent, integrated, and coordinated approach to meeting such needs.

Thus, the Job Training Partnership Act provides diverse tools and authorizations for state councils and administrative agencies, operating under the governor, to coordinate employment and training activities. This coordination imperative is magnified by requirements that the state employment service and state education agency coordinate activities supported by the Wagner-Peyser Act, the Carl D. Perkins Vocational and Applied Technology Act, and the Adult Education Act with employment and training activities under JTPA. The Perkins Act provides, for example, that the state vocational education plan describe methods for the joint planning and coordination of programs carried out under the act with programs conducted under JTPA, the Adult Education Act, Title I of the Elementary and Secondary Education Act of 1965 as amended by Chapter 1 of the Education Consolidation and Improvement Act of 1981, the Education of the Handicapped Act, and the Rehabilitation Act of 1973.

The Wagner-Peyser Act requires the state employment service to develop jointly with each appropriate SDA and the chief elected official or officials of the service delivery area plans for implementing the Wagner-Peyser Act. Such plans have to take into account proposals developed jointly with the appropriate private industry council, and they have to be transmitted to the state job training council for determination that the plans have been jointly agreed to and that the plans are consistent with the governor's coordination and special services plan under JTPA. The Wagner-Peyser Act further authorizes the expenditure of funds to develop linkages among services funded under it and related federal or state legislation.

The Family Support Act, a 1988 law that alters provisions of the Aid to Families with Dependent Children (AFDC) program, provided for creation of the Job Opportunities and Basic Skills (JOBS) program, a major welfare-to-work effort. That legislation established a number of requirements for coordination of employment and training programs. It requires (1) the governor to assure that JOBS activities are coordinated with JTPA and other employment and training programs; (2) submission of the state JOBS plan to the SJTCC for its review and comment, with those comments to be forwarded to the governor; (3) consultation by the state agency administering the JOBS program with the state education agency and the agency that administers employment and training programs to ensure coordinated delivery of JOBS services with JTPA, the federal Adult Education Act, and Perkins Act activities; (4) consultation of the U.S. secretary of health and human services (HHS) with the secretaries of education and labor to coordinate programs at the national level and support state and local coordination efforts.

COORDINATION TOOLS AND STRATEGIES

The multitude of legislative coordination requirements leaves open the question of just what approaches the states and localities would follow to produce coordination. Legislative enactments deliberately leave great discretion in the hands of states and local areas to devise coordination approaches appropriate to varying conditions. Responding to that freedom, states and localities have created a diverse array of coordination approaches, tools, and techniques. Some of these tools involve processes for creating coordination; others involve specific arrangements of program elements.

Several studies have documented a variety of tools and strategies available to states and localities in their attempts to develop coordinated systems of employment and training programs. Burbridge and Nightingale (1989), for example, identified six configurations of organizational roles and responsibilities that are used at the local level to coordinate welfare programs with employment and training programs. Organizational models incorporating the roles and responsibilities are supplemented by a range of linkages and mechanisms for coordination, including (1) reviewing program planning documents, (2) using task forces, advisory groups, committees, and meetings, (3) nonfinancial agreements, (4) financial contracts providing services in exchange for funding, (5) drawing financial resources from different program pots to serve certain populations, and (6) integrating programs administratively or operationally.

In another study, Grubb et al. (1990) identified various patterns of coordination of vocational education with employment and training programs. They found eight models of coordination revolving around contractual arrangements, the allocation of functions among institutions, and other arrangements.

Trutko, Bailis, Barnow, and French (1989) examined the role of coordination in enhancing JTPA effectiveness and efficiency. They specify diverse approaches to coordination, suggesting that those approaches can be distinguished in terms of (1) top down versus bottom up, (2) broad scope versus narrow scope, and (3) their degree of integration.

Finally, the National Commission for Employment Policy (1991) has identified an array of state policy coordination methods, including the use of most of the tools and techniques discussed in this report.

Thus, various techniques are available for use in coordinating employment and training programs. Those techniques range from organizational arrangements to planning requirements to coordination incentives to the development of specific coordination requirements. A survey of state JTPA agencies in 1989 (Jennings, 1989) revealed a considerable array of such strategies and tools. In all, forty-one different approaches were identified. That survey asked state JTPA liaisons to describe coordination approaches used in their states and provide documents such as the governor's special services and coordination plan.

State job training and employment coordination can follow a variety of approaches. The 1989 study (Jennings, 1989) revealed five general categories of approaches followed by the states:

1. organizational
2. communication and decision making
3. mechanisms for operational coordination
4. planning
5. tools for use by the service delivery areas

Each of these approaches encompasses a variety of mechanisms and techniques of coordination. While mechanisms from more than one category may be used in combination with each other, the categories provide a useful framework for discussing approaches to coordination.

Organizational Approaches

The states vary in their organization of employment and training activities. Such variations reflect the broader diversity of arrangements by which states organize themselves to pursue public policy objectives. States vary, in particular, in terms of their major organizational units and the assignment of functional responsibilities to those units. Such differences are a product of historical patterns of development, the unique political patterns of each state, and beliefs in each state about governmental purposes and priorities and how governmental functions are interrelated.

Some states have tightly structured organizations for employment and training, while others scatter these functions across two or more major departments. Typically, vocational education and elementary and secondary education are found in a state education department. The Family Support Act and other social services are found in a state department of human services, department of social services, or department of public welfare. Employment and training programs under the Wagner-Peyser Act and the Job Training Partnership Act can be concentrated in one agency or divided among multiple agencies.

Of the thirty-five states providing information about the organization of employment and training activities, twenty-three placed administrative responsibility for the two laws in the same department. Of those, nine organize JTPA and the employment service in the same division of the department. In twelve of the thirty-five states, the employment service and JTPA are administered by different departments of state government with major responsibilities for economic development, commerce, community affairs, or community development. Several organize JTPA as a separate state function.

Communication And Decision-Making Approaches

If states are to coordinate employment and training activities, agencies with diverse missions must interact effectively to bring together the elements of the job training and employment system. To do this requires that they find ways to communicate effectively and develop shared goals. At a minimum, they must find how their goals interrelate.

Communication and decision-making approaches to coordination include a variety of structures, procedures, and policies for ensuring that effective communication develops and shared goals are identified and pursued. Planning activities, discussed in the next section of this report, are central components of the effort to develop shared goals and effective communication. They also provide the opportunity to develop operational coordination procedures.

States report a variety of communication and decision-making approaches to coordination. Agency-head policy groups, interagency task forces, and interagency committees address specific coordination issues and concerns. The focus of these groups is probably more specific and project oriented than the cabinet councils used by some states, which provide an opportunity to address general policy issues. These cabinet councils and clusters bring together the heads of major agencies with interrelated missions to address policy issues and concerns and provide general coordination of activities.

The use of the state job training coordinating council as the single policy body for all employment and training programs allows either joint or consolidated planning to take place and centralizes authority for policy recommendations for separate programs. Joint meetings of advisory councils do not go as far to coordinate decision making, but they bring together groups such as the state job training coordinating council, the Wagner-Peyser advisory council, and the state council on vocational education.

The use of interdepartmental liaisons and outstationing JTPA personnel in other agencies facilitates coordination of JTPA funds with other employment and training activities by fostering information exchange and understanding.

Appointment of the heads of agencies engaged in employment and training or related programs (or their representatives) to the state job training coordinating council involves them directly in JTPA planning, encouraging the expression of their concerns and the contribution of their knowledge. As with all participatory mechanisms, appointment of agency heads to the SJTCC can improve the base of information for decision making and build program commitment of the participants.

Information sharing can be an important means of fostering coordination. Regular meetings help. Working partnerships of agencies focusing on specific problems or programs help target communication and coordination at areas of shared interest. Common geographical boundaries facilitate coordination across agencies by making it easier to integrate planning and other activities.

Planning Approaches

Planning is a central component of communication and decision making in an interorganizational setting. Planning approaches to coordination involve the use of planning processes and techniques and plans themselves to foster coordination among agencies at the state level. At its simplest level, the use of planning for coordination purposes would involve having the state job training coordination council review the plans of programs in addition to JTPA that contribute to employment and training. Such a review is required under the Job Training Partnership Act and the legislation providing for a number of other programs, including Wagner-Peyser, Carl D. Perkins, and JOBS. Some states go further to include in the review process plans for purely state programs, which are not subject to federal review provisions.

Beyond plan review, states use a number of planning approaches to foster state-level interagency coordination. Specific guidelines for SJTCC use in reviewing plans of agencies involved in job development and training can focus attention on coordination concerns. The use of common definitions and quantifiable outcomes across human investment programs facilitates joint action and makes it possible to share credit and compare accomplishments. Specific goals for coordination among agencies provide targets for action and criteria by which to assess agency efforts. Joint planning of Wagner-Peyser and JTPA activities is common, but a number of states have moved to adopt consolidated plans for these two programs and, in some cases, other programs. Consolidated plans provide an opportunity for greater integration of resources. Uniform planning periods for programs make it easier to compare plans and coordinate their requirements.

Mechanisms for Operational Coordination

Agencies have to do more than plan and communicate if coordination is to take place. They must also develop mechanisms for operational coordination. Mechanisms for operational coordination typically formalize relationships among programs or organizational units or create particular operational patterns.

Operational coordination can involve a variety of activities, each providing some degree of integration of programmatic operations. Cooperative agreements, for example, take a variety of forms and can cover diverse activities, but their basic purpose is to identify how agencies will coordinate their activities and cooperate with each other in the delivery of employment and training services. They might specify the particular activities to be undertaken by each agency, the division of labor between or among agencies, activities to be coordinated, and ways in which activities will be coordinated.

Contracts involve not only agreements about shared responsibilities and a division of labor, but also provide for a transfer of resources between agencies. In other words, one agency pays another to do something. This, of course, provides considerable incentive to coordinate.

States identified joint funding, joint administration, and joint operation of programs as coordination tools, but did not provide detailed information about these techniques. Although there may not be sharp distinctions among them, some differences appear to be possible. Under joint funding, two agencies provide financial resources for the operation of a program that might actually be carried out by some third party. Joint administration of a program would involve joint decision making about and oversight of a program. Joint operation would bring the agencies together in the direct provision of services.

Joint marketing brings agencies together to publicize their programs. It is a way of developing a common message and concentrating resources. Sequential funding involves applying funds from different sources or funding categories in a way that maximizes the support for a set of objectives in pursuit of state goals. Funds from one source are used until they are exhausted or until an allowable limit is met; then funds from another source are used.

Tools for Use by Service Delivery Areas

State-level coordination is important because it provides a framework for coordination at the service delivery level and can provide vital support for activities at the local level. In the end, the important thing is what happens at the point of service delivery. Thus, states have attempted to develop a variety of tools to promote and facilitate coordination at the local level. These tools are crucial to some aspects of coordination, and service delivery areas are limited in what they can accomplish until states provide more support of this type.

Tools for local-level coordination typically involve the local JTPA program's relationship with various state agencies or cooperation and coordination among state agencies to support an activity at the local level. They sometimes involve an attempt to mirror at the local level things that are taking place at the state level.

Ten activities identified here support coordination at the service delivery level. One of these, support for one-stop shopping, can take the form of financial, policy, and technical assistance that allows and facilitates collocation, cross-training of personnel, and shared intake and assessment procedures that make it easier to bring together a variety of employment and training services provided by different agencies. Model memoranda of agreement or local coordination agreements make it easier to develop coordination at the local-level by clarifying what is possible in the relationship between the administrative entity and other organizations, including local offices of state agencies. They also identify the elements that need to be included in a cooperative agreement. The provision of specific coordination criteria for use with state agencies at the local level also provides guidance on what is expected and can be accomplished with respect to coordination. It can give structure to the negotiations between agencies.

Variance in eligibility criteria and information requirements of different programs often stands as a barrier to local area coordination. Universal eligibility and referral mechanisms and consolidated application forms help reduce these barriers. One state, in an experiment, has developed common intake and assessment procedures, requires the development of one local employability plan for each client, and provides each client of employment and training programs with an opportunity card that provides eligibility determination and access to an array of services. These foster local level coordination by reducing the work that service delivery areas have to do to develop common forms and procedures across agencies.

Structuring performance evaluation systems to allow the employment service and service delivery areas to share credit for placements creates an incentive for them to work together.

Allowing local private industry councils to manage Wagner-Peyser resources in addition to JTPA funds provides authority to enforce coordination mandates. Requiring a combined plan for JTPA and Wagner-Peyser activities at the local level also forces more active coordination than might otherwise take place. Interagency coordination is fostered by resource sharing when SDAs contract with the other agencies, like the employment service, for such things as intake, eligibility determination, and assessment.

STATE USE OF APPROACHES

Although states can follow many approaches, it is important to know the extent to which those approaches are being used and how helpful the states find the different approaches to be. The author conducted a survey of state agency directors in 1990 to answer these questions. The survey, endorsed by the National Governors' Association, included the agency directors for the state agencies responsible for JTPA, the Wagner-Peyser Act, the Carl D. Perkins Act, and the Family Support Act. Eighty-four percent of the agency directors responded to the survey, providing a rich, comprehensive base of information about state coordination activities.

The survey sought information about (1) the extent to which forty-one different coordination techniques are used in the states, (2) the degree to which each of those techniques contributes to successful coordination, (3) the degree to which each of twenty-three factors is important for successful state-level efforts to coordinate employment and training programs, (4) the extent to which various factors serve as barriers to coordination, (5) the effect of state-level coordination activities on performance at the local level, and (6) the quality of coordination between different agencies.

The following set of tables reports the extent to which the states use the different techniques and the extent to which the techniques contribute to successful coordination. Respondents to the survey were asked to rate each of the coordination techniques used by their state in terms of its contribution to successful coordination. The response categories were: contributes very much; contributes some; makes no difference; and hinders coordination. Few respondents indicated that any of the techniques hindered coordination.

The more specific analysis and interpretation can be prefaced by noting that the respondents generally saw some virtue in almost all techniques. Perhaps this is because only respondents from states using a particular approach indicated their assessments of the contribution of that approach. Presumably states are more likely to use approaches their agencies regard favorably. In addition, virtually all of the approaches have the potential to make at least some contribution to coordination, no matter how small that contribution. Because of this, the presentation will focus on responses indicating "contributes very much."

Table 6.1 reports data on state use of various communication and decision-making approaches and the percentage of respondents who judged each technique to contribute very much to coordination. As can be seen in the table, use of most of these approaches is fairly widespread. Information sharing and the use of interagency committees, used by nine out of ten states, lead the way. Other highly utilized approaches include the appointment of relevant agency heads to the SJTCC and workshops. More than 60 percent of the states also use interagency task forces, working partnerships, and regular meetings of staff.

The least-used communication and decision-making approaches include joint meetings of advisory councils and having one advisory council as sole policy body for all employment and training programs.

Two items stand out as receiving the highest percentage of respondents indicating that the techniques contribute very much: regular meetings of staff from different units, and working partnerships. Both of these items contain the potential for operational interaction, as well as communication or decision making. The approaches that generate the least support are joint meetings of advisory councils and the use of cabinet councils. Each of these, of course, brings together decision makers who are far removed from day-to-day operational concerns.

The data in Table 6.2 provide information about state use of various planning approaches. States almost uniformly view the review of plans as required by law as a coordination tool. In addition, almost three-fourths of the states include coordination criteria for all agencies in the Governor's Special Services and Coordination Plan. More than 60 percent report joint planning by agencies involved in employment and training programs. Among the least frequently used approaches are consolidated planning, the development of common definitions for use across programs, and the development of quantifiable outcomes for use in reviewing programs and making comparisons across programs.

Naturally, users view some approaches more favorably than others in terms of their contribution to coordination. Among the planning techniques, significantly higher proportions of respondents indicate that four techniques contribute very much: the use of uniform planning periods for all employment and training programs, joint planning by agencies involved in such programs, consolidated planning for employment and training programs, and development of quantifiable outcomes for use in reviewing programs and making programmatic comparisons.

Table 6.1

Percentage of States Using Communication and Decision-Making Approaches to Coordinate Employment and Training Programs and Percentage of Respondents Indicating Each Approach Contributes Very Much to Coordination

Techniques	Percent Using	Percent Indicating Contributes Very Much
Interagency committees	88	45
Information sharing	88	56
Appoint relevant agency heads to SJTCC	82	43
Workshops	81	39
Interagency task forces	71	51
Working partnerships	67	65
Regular meetings of staff from different units	63	63
Development of joint policy statements	56	48
Interdepartmental liaisons	56	54
Use of one advisory council (e.g., SJTCC) as sole policy body for JTPA and Wagner-Peyser	50	43
Use of cabinet councils	46	28
Agencies use common geographical boundaries	42	49
Joint meetings of advisory councils	25	18
Use of one advisory council as sole policy body for all employment and training programs	23	47

Techniques receiving the weakest support, including a significant number of respondents saying they make no difference, include SJTCC review of plans of other programs, including both those required under federal law and those not subject to federal review requirements; specific guidelines for the SJTCC to use in reviewing the plans of other agencies; the SJTCC including coordination criteria for all state agencies in the Gover-

Table 6.2
Percentage of States Using Planning Approaches to Coordinate Employment and Training Programs and Percentage of Respondents Indicating Each Approach Contributes Very Much to Coordination

Techniques	Percent Using	Percent Indicating Contributes Very Much
SJTCC reviews plans of other programs (e.g., Wagner-Peyser) as provided under federal law	96	18
SJTCC includes coordination criteria for all state agencies in Governor's Plan	71	29
Joint planning by agencies involved in employment and training programs	63	49
SJTCC sets specific goals for coordination among agencies	54	36
Use of uniform planning periods for all employment and training programs	38	50
SJTCC also reviews plans not subject to federal review requirements (e.g., purely state programs)	35	13
SJTCC has specific guidelines for use in reviewing plans of other agencies	35	31
Consolidated planning for employment and training programs (e.g., one plan for JTPA and Wagner-Peyser)	27	46
State has developed common definitions for use across programs	21	39
State has developed quantifiable outcomes for use in reviewing programs	13	48

nor's Special Services and Coordination Plan; and the SJTCC setting specific goals for coordination among agencies.

Thus, administrators view items involving formal review requirements and the development of guidelines for evaluating coordination with little favor. All of these items make specific reference to the state job training coordinating council, as is the case for communication and decision-making items that receive the least favorable responses. Those receiving the strongest support are those that bring agencies and programs together or deal with concrete aspects of planning and operations (uniform planning periods, quantifiable outcomes).

Table 6.3 indicates that cooperative agreements and joint funding of programs are the most common mechanisms of operational coordination. Joint marketing of activities and sequential funding of activities are used by less than half of the states. Among the mechanisms for operational coordination, users give none overwhelmingly favorable or negative ratings. They view joint funding of programs, joint administration of programs, and joint marketing of activities most favorably. They view cooperative agreements and sequential funding of activities less favorably.

Finally, we discover in Table 6.4 that only one tool for use by service delivery areas has been adopted by at least half of the states. That tool is support for one-stop shopping approaches to employment and training services. Beyond that, the most common forms of support for SDA coordination have been the development of common intake and assessment tools, the development of consolidated application forms, and the provision of specific coordination criteria for SDAs to use in working with state agencies at the local level. Only a small number of states allow PICs to control local employment service offices and plans. Just slightly more have worked to create universal eligibility and referral mechanisms.

It is interesting that only slightly more than half of the respondents (56%) report using federal coordination requirements as a means of pursuing

Table 6.3
Percentage of States Using Operational Mechanisms to Coordinate Employment and Training Programs and Percentage of Respondents Indicating Each Approach Contributes Very Much to Coordination

Techniques	Percent Using	Percent Indicating Contributes Very Much
Cooperative (non-financial) agreements	98	31
Joint funding of programs	77	51
Joint administration of programs	52	44
Joint marketing of activities	48	42
Sequential funding of activities	33	32

Table 6.4

Percentage of States Developing Tools for Use by Service Delivery Areas as a Way to Coordinate Employment and Training Programs and Percentage of Respondents Indicating Each Approach Contributes Very Much to Coordination

Techniques	Percent Using	Percent Indicating Contributes Very Much
Support for one-stop shopping approaches to employment and training activities	63	39
Development of common intake and assessment tools for use across agencies at the service delivery level	44	45
Development of consolidated application forms for use at the service delivery level	42	51
Provision of specific coordination criteria for SDAs to use in working with state agencies at the local level	40	35
Creating framework for there to be one local employability plan for each client	35	49
Requiring combined JTPA/Wagner-Peyser plan at the local level	29	41
Establishing electronic client service systems	29	70
Provision of model memoranda of agreement for use at the SDA level	23	31
Shared credit mechanisms	21	50
Creating universal eligibility and referral mechanisms	13	67
Allowing PICs to control local Employment Service offices and plans	10	24

coordination goals. Perhaps others find these requirements to be a formality without substance.

As can be seen in Table 6.4, users rate the development of two tools for use by service delivery areas more favorably than any others: establishing electronic client service systems and creating universal eligibility and referral mechanisms. Also, fairly high proportions of respondents indicate that the following activities contribute very much to coordination: development of consolidated application forms, shared credit mechanisms, creating the framework for one local employability plan for each client, and the development of common intake and assessment tools for use across agencies at the service delivery level.

Many respondents believe that some activities contribute modestly, at best, to coordination: allowing PICs to control local employment service offices and plans and the provision of model memoranda of agreement at the local level. Two other items found less than 40 percent of respondents indicating that they contribute very much: provision of specific coordination criteria for SDAs to use in working with state agencies at the local level and support for one-stop shopping approaches to employment and training activities.

The items receiving high levels of support deal with client eligibility and processing, both key issues at the service delivery level. Eligibility criteria are also a matter of some concern in national policy-making circles because interprogram differences in eligibility criteria can complicate program operations and coordination. Items viewed less favorably are generally somewhat removed from day-to-day operational concerns. Finally, it can be reported that only 9 percent indicate that the use of federal coordination requirements contributes very much.

Are there variations in the extent to which the states draw upon the different categories of coordination techniques? Yes. The items in the communication and decision-making category are used on the average by almost 60 percent of the states. Items in the planning category, on the other hand, are used by only 45 percent of the states, on the average. Almost 62 percent of the states use mechanisms for operational coordination, on the average, whereas only 32 percent use the development of tools for use by service delivery areas, on the average.

One interesting question is whether the approaches receiving the highest use are also the approaches that are perceived as contributing the most. Within each area—communication and decision making, planning, use of mechanisms for operational control, and development of tools for use by service delivery areas—correlations between the percentage of respondents indicating their state uses the approach and the percentage indicating that it contributes very much are quite interesting.

The correlation between the percentage of states using communication and decision-making approaches and the percentage indicating that it contributes very much is .41. This is the one arena in which there is a positive relationship, indicating that the tools used most extensively have the most favorable rating from users. In two other categories, this relationship is negative. The correlation between use of planning tools and the percent believing the tools contribute very much is –.44. The correlation between the development of tools for use by SDAs and the percent who believe those approaches contribute a great deal is –.32. In these two arenas, then, the tools that are used most extensively have the least favorable rating. There is no correlation between the use of mechanisms for operational control and the percent viewing those tools favorably.

These findings are somewhat discouraging. Although they should not be interpreted to demonstrate causal relationship (e.g., in planning, the use of techniques leads to their being viewed unfavorably), they do suggest that the use of techniques has not generally led to favorable impressions of those techniques, with a subsequent winnowing of approaches. They also suggest a great deal of wasted effort as state decision makers and administrators continue to pursue approaches that are perceived as having low payoff.

FACTORS IMPORTANT FOR STATE-LEVEL COORDINATION SUCCESS

Respondents were asked to identify the extent to which twenty-three different factors were important for the success of state-level efforts to coordinate employment and training programs. These items, derived from previous studies of employment and training coordination, reflect the kinds of concerns often raised in discussion of coordination activities. Table 6.5 reports the percentage of respondents indicating that each item is "very important."

These data indicate that the leadership role is crucial for successful coordination. The first three items, each of which receives significantly higher proportions of "very important" responses than do other items in the survey, deal with the role of leadership. Leadership itself is viewed as very important by 71 percent of the respondents. Seventy percent find communication by the leadership that coordination is important to be very important to success. Furthermore, 67 percent say that the governor's commitment to coordination is very important.

Coming a bit behind these in importance are a set of items that involve decision making and the distinctive roles of different contributors to the employment and training system. Extensive involvement by the appropriate decision makers and administrators is recognized by more than 57 percent as being very important. Almost as many say that it is very important to recognize that different programs have their own goals which have to be respected in the process of developing coordination. Fifty-two

Table 6.5
Percentage of Respondents Indicating Factors are Very Important to the Success of State and Local Efforts to Coordinate Employment and Training Programs

Factor	Percent Indicating It Is Very Important to Success
Leadership	71
Communication by the leadership that coordination is important	70
Commitment of the governor to coordination	67
Extensive involvement of the appropriate decision makers and administrators	58
Recognizing that different programs have their own goals that have to be respected in the process of developing coordination	57
Recognizing the unique contributions of different agencies to the system	52
Clear definition of the roles of various organizations	52
Organization of programs in a way that fosters coordination	49
Shared understandings among actors in the system	49
Skills at interpersonal relations	47
Negotiating skills	38
Use of planning processes and techniques	32
Establishing procedures to insure effective communications among programs/agencies	29
Shared knowledge	29

Table 6.5 (continued)

Factor	Percent Indicating It Is Very Important to Success
Personal relationships among agency heads	26
Shared Role definitions	26
Development of coordination tools for use at the local level	22
Development and use of appropriate incentives and sanctions to encourage coordination	21
Establishing procedures to insure that agencies and programs develop shared goals	18
Use of plans	17
Consolidation of employment and training programs in fewer agencies	13
Centralization of authority for employment and training programs	12
Careful attention to technical detail	11

percent assert that it is very important to recognize the unique contributions of different agencies to the system and have clear definitions of the roles of various organizations.

Another cluster occurs with just under 50 percent attributing great importance to the organization of programs in a way that fosters coordination, shared understandings among actors in the system, and skills at interpersonal relations.

Finally, a third or less of the respondents find a set of items to be very important to the success of state and local coordination efforts. Most striking among these are the centralization of authority for employment and training programs (12%) and consolidation of employment and training programs in fewer agencies (13%). Clearly, these administrators of employment and training-related programs give little credence to the notion that organizational approaches relying on centralized systems will make a difference.

Almost as striking is the finding that only 21 percent believe that the development and use of appropriate incentives and sanctions is very important. In this day and age, when so much attention is devoted to reward systems in public policy and management, this is an important finding. It is made more important by the frequent suggestions in policy deliberations that the way to improve coordination is to provide more incentives for it to occur. For example, proposed revisions to the JTPA that were considered by the 101st Congress included a provision that would have created a new Title II-C, funded by up to 5 percent of the appropriations for Titles II-A and II-B, which would provide grants for state coordination activities (Spar, 1991).

BARRIERS TO SUCCESSFUL COORDINATION

Discussions of employment and training coordination often turn to presumed barriers to successful coordination efforts, including such things as turf protection and the varying priorities of organizations. The survey included a set of seven items that have been discussed as barriers to coordination and asked respondents to rate these as barriers on a scale running from one for "not a barrier" to five for "very much a barrier."

As can be seen in Table 6.6, one thing stood out as a barrier in the responses of agency officials—technical issues. Forty-five percent scored it as a five on the scale and more than two-thirds scored it as a four or five. Thus, a considerable number of administrators believe that technical issues are a barrier to successful coordination. The second most important barrier according to the respondents is ineffective communication, rated as a five by 22 percent of the respondents and as a four or five by 57 percent. Close to this is different priorities of organizations, rated as a five by 21 percent and as a four or five by 55 percent.

In keeping with the finding in the previous section, very few respondents rated the lack of incentives or sanctions as a serious problem, with only 8 percent and 5 percent respectively assigning these a score of five. It should be noted, however, that just more than a third assigned a score of either four or five to the lack of incentives.

Only 7 percent assigned turf protection a score of five, although another 25 percent rated it as a four. Thus, almost a third of respondents see a barrier in turf protection. Although this does not approach the numbers one would expect given how much people talk about the problem of turf protection, it does seems to suggest the continued importance of this consideration in some areas.

Table 6.6
Percentage of Respondents Indicating that Various Factors are Barriers to Effective Coordination

Item	Percent scoring item as four or five on five point barrier scale
Technical issues	67.8%
Ineffective communication	56.9
Different priorities of organizations	54.8
Belief that coordination doesn't affect performance	36.1
Lack of incentives	34.9
"Turf" protection	32.5
Lack of sanctions	16.2

GUBERNATORIAL ENCOURAGEMENT AND THE EFFECT OF STATE-LEVEL COORDINATION

More than half of the respondents indicated that their governor has very actively encouraged coordination of employment and training programs. Only 7 percent indicate that their governor has not encouraged coordination at all. In addition, only 9 percent of these officials say that state-level coordination activities have had a very strong effect on performance at the local level; however, 42 percent indicate that this effect has been strong, and 39 percent report that it has been moderate. Only 10 percent assert that state-level coordination activities have had a weak or very weak effect on performance at the local level.

CONCLUSION

This wide-ranging survey yields a variety of insights about coordination processes at the state level. These insights involve the use of various techniques, the effectiveness of those techniques, the factors that affect success, and barriers to successful coordination. One thing stands out: *State managers believe that leadership is crucial to successful coordination.* This is consistent with findings from other studies of coordination. It suggests that organization, planning, incentives, and mandates will accomplish little without effective leadership to make things happen.

It also seems, from these data, that leaders must be sensitive to the diverse mandates of organizations involved in employment and training activities, recognizing and respecting their unique contributions. Success depends on the leadership's ability to define systems that allow multiple agencies to contribute within the frameworks of their own missions and capacities.

Such concerns as organizational centralization, concentration of authority, planning, and incentive systems receive short shrift from these state administrators. This may reflect a natural aversion to structures, procedures, and mechanisms that may undermine agency autonomy, but it also reflects the realities of a pluralistic system, where some degree of duplication and overlap is viewed as being healthy. It also reflects the fact that the employment and training system is populated by agencies responsible for a diverse, only partially overlapping, set of programs. While JOBS and JTPA both serve welfare clients, JTPA also serves a broader constituency. In addition, JOBS is only a small part of the responsibilities of social service agencies, which must also contend with a broad set of programs involving income maintenance, health care, and family counseling.

Planning is probably viewed with limited favor because it is so often a mandated activity that is carried out because of legal requirements, rather than because the various participants expect it to produce beneficial results. When planning is differently motivated and effectively managed, it quite clearly can produce positive outcomes, as the discussion in Chapter 7 makes clear.

It is probably for similar reasons that many of the activities associated with state job training coordinating councils receive lukewarm endorsements. The SJTCC performs a necessary function, but it is a product of federal mandate and is often viewed as meeting legal requirements, rather than making positive contributions to the system. This is particularly likely to be the case when it is seen as a setting for interagency strife and accommodation, rather than the focal point for substantive efforts to deal with the needs of state citizens. While a grant of greater authority, such as occurs when the SJTCC is designated as a human resource development council, may foster movement toward more effective coordination, it is probably the case that such a designation must be accompanied by effective leadership and a well-defined agenda if it is to make a real difference.

REFERENCES

Burbridge, Lynn C., and Demetra Smith Nightingale. 1989. *Local Coordination of Employment and Training Services to Welfare Recipients*. Washington, D.C.: Urban Institute.

Grubb, W. Norton et al. 1990. *Order Amidst Complexity: The Status of Coordination Among Vocational Education, Job Training Partnership Act, and Welfare-to-Work Programs*. Berkeley: National Center for Research in Vocational Education, University of California. August.

Jennings, Edward T., Jr. 1989. *Job Training Coordination: Issues and Approaches*. A report prepared for the Missouri Division of Job Development and Training. Columbia: Department of Public Administration, University of Missouri-Columbia. June.

National Commission for Employment Policy. 1991. "Background Paper on Federal Public Assistance Programs: Coordination and Eligibility Issues." Washington, D.C. February 20.

Spar, Karen. 1991. "Job Training Partnership Act: Pending Legislation and Budget Issues." Washington, D.C.: Congressional Research Service, Library of Congress. January 1.

Trutko, John, Larry Bailis, Burt Barnow, and Stephen French. 1989. *An Assessment of the JTPA Role in State and Local Coordination Activities*, vol. 1. Submitted to the Employment and Training Administration, U.S. Department of Labor. Washington, D.C. December.

Chapter 7

Planning and Organizing to Coordinate Human Service Delivery in the States

Edward T. Jennings, Jr., William Tracy, and Kathleen Wimer

State public assistance efforts take place in the context of a complex legal and political environment, a broad array of human resource development problems, and a diverse mixture of human resource programs. Central issues of human resource policy have to be addressed if states are to act effectively in this context. Planning provides the means for addressing the issues and developing policies in a way that will target resources on high priority objectives and coordinate the many agencies and programs that contribute to human resource development.

States normally engage in a variety of planning activities to develop effective, coordinated human resource investment efforts. This can include such actions as requiring that the state job training coordinating council (SJTCC) review all human resource development plans and activities in the state, in addition to those it is required to review under federal law; joint planning by agencies engaged in human resource development; the establishment of uniform planning periods; development of specific guidelines for SJTCC use in reviewing plans of other agencies; and development of consolidated plans.

Strategic planning processes provide a framework for developing consolidated human resource development plans. A study of strategic planning in the states (Van Horn, Ryan, and Tracy, 1990) reports that this process allows for (1) an environmental scan to identify conditions that affect policies and programs; (2) analysis of the competitive advantages and disadvantages of various approaches to human resource development; (3) an analysis across programs and functional integration of program and service delivery; and (4) adjustments in long-range strategy to meet contemporary needs.

Although strategic planning has been applied in the public sector in recent years, it is not easy for a variety of reasons, including the fragmentation of authority and responsibility in public policy systems (Bryson and Roering, 1988; Bryson, 1988; Wechsler and Backoff, 1986). Thus, while strategic planning may provide the means to integrate services and activities in a coherent strategy, it also requires organizational and procedural mechanisms to allow it to occur. A consolidated planning body may be what is required for such efforts.

In recent years, there have been proposals that Congress require states to establish human resource investment councils that would be responsible for policy development, planning, and oversight for the vast array of human resource programs (Job Training Partnership Act Advisory Committee, 1989; King, 1988). Such bodies would have more extensive responsibility and authority than that possessed by the current job training councils. At a minimum, they would consolidate planning for JTPA and Wagner-Peyser. Under more ambitious formulations, they would consolidate planning for those programs, the Job Opportunities and Basic Skills program of the Family Support Act (JOBS), vocational education, adult education, and all other programs that contribute directly to the employment and training system. Some states have already initiated efforts to provide this centralization of planning, as the two case studies in this chapter suggest.

While planning can point the way to human resource development effectiveness, organizational arrangements can inhibit efforts to make sense of service delivery and facilitate program activities. The states have very diverse organizational arrangements for the delivery of human services. Those arrangements are a product of the history of policy and organizational development in each state and reflect political compromises, the accretion of programs over time to respond to specific needs, and constitutional mandates. Although there is no one best way to organize for the delivery of human services, it is clear that the fragmentation of human service delivery among multiple competing agencies often stands as a barrier to the effectiveness and efficiency of programs. This, of course, is why public officials so often speak of turf problems. Planning activities may suggest better ways to organize for human services delivery at the state level.

New Jersey and Connecticut have created human resource investment councils and undertaken extensive planning efforts to reshape their work forces. Those planning efforts have led to substantial organizational changes in New Jersey and a significant plan for action in Connecticut. Their experiences provide insights into the stumbling blocks to strategically planned change and the results that can be obtained with persistent, successful efforts. They highlight the role that a human resource investment council can play in planning for change and action.

NEW JERSEY'S WORKFORCE READINESS SYSTEM

New Jersey took several steps over the past few years to prepare for its first statewide comprehensive planning model. In the mid-1980s, when Workforce 2000 and related issues were getting widespread attention, then-Governor Tom Kean established an Employment Policy Task Force to look at the issue of employment policy and how state government was structured and how it acted to deliver employment and training services. The task force (comprised of six cabinet officers, the chair of the state job training coordinating council, and the governor's director of policy) deliberated for about a year. It developed a set of recommendations to better connect the employment and training system in New Jersey. One of these recommendations was to establish a state employment and training commission.

In January 1990, the state legislature passed legislation creating the New Jersey Employment and Training Commission (NJETC). This bipartisan commission was signed into law during the early days of the Jim Florio administration as a conscious, symbolic effort on the part of two governors who believed that work-force development policy was broader than a partisan agenda and needed longer than a four- or eight-year cycle to be addressed effectively. Substantive institutional change had to go beyond the electoral cycle. They believed that a council or commission could provide continuity, community, and energy to sustain long-term change and development of policy and organization.

The commission faced serious questions as it began operations. People wanted to know what the new entity was. Some said it was either a Trojan horse for the state's Labor Department or a power play by Job Training Partnership Act (JTPA) officials to take over the world. Many of these questions originated, of course, because the commission is the linear descendant of the Comprehensive Employment and Training Act (CETA) and the SJTCC.

The commission differs significantly from its predecessors, including the SJTCC. The old council was located in the Department of Labor, was solely a creature of federal legislation, and focused only on JTPA and other areas connected by federal rules. The new commission extends its focus across all departments and programs. It is not bound to a particular department and reports directly to the governor. Its staff is appointed by and is responsible to the director of the commission. The commission has thirty-four members in proportions consistent with JTPA requirements, but no more than one-half can be from the same political party. The governor appoints the members, who are confirmed by the state senate and serve staggered three-year terms.

These differences are important. They contribute to the commission's ability to act independent of the forces of bureaucratic protection. The commission can exercise much greater influence because it has statutory authority for oversight, policy development, and evaluation of work-force development activities that it defines as falling within its reach.

The commission began its activities in July 1990. One of the first issues it faced was how to approach the problem of constructing a work-force readiness system that was accessible, simple, and effective. As the commission grappled with problems of service delivery and the needs of multiple clientele groups, such as youth and dislocated workers, it struggled with the question of how to define the structure of the work-force readiness system. Particularly important to the commission was the need to define the work-force readiness system in a way that would meet the needs of all the residents of the state.

The commission used a framework that suggested that it had to define a set of functions which provided some services for all people, rather than try to connect, in a linear fashion, a variety of client-driven responses or client-driven priorities as an all-encompassing system. It recognized that residents need holistic services; a systems approach would allow different systems to interact to provide this holistic set of services. The commission defined work-force readiness as that set of functions or services that affect labor market efficiency, supplement supply through enhancement of individual skills, or induce demand in terms of economic development catalysts on the basis of a highly skilled work force available for high wage work. The commission believed that the work-force readiness system, however it was defined, had to be an economically driven system. It had to have value in the market, both to its employer-customers and to its client-customers.

An intervention strategy approach was then used to take a look at the structure of state government as a precondition for articulating and mobilizing a human investment or work-force readiness plan. That strategy used a producer-consumer model, taken from Stanley Davis's *Future Perfect*, to classify entities of state government. Departments, agencies, and programs were assessed on the basis of whether they produced services or were advocates for the customers of the system, New Jersey employers, or residents.

Using that analysis, staff developed a "wheel of fortune" depicting sixty-four work-force related programs, a number determined in part by the technical limits of a typeface readable with the naked eye. These programs, operated by six departments of state government, have spent about $1.5 billion annually from state and federal sources.

Applying the producer-consumer model, the commission decided that three departments of government would remain as producers of work-force readiness service: the Education Department, Higher Education Department, and Labor Department. The three other departments would become consumer departments and would no longer produce services. As part of the trade-off for giving up the territory and control for operating these programs, the three latter departments were given the power and authority to drive the planning process.

Sticking with that principle, the consumer departments would determine what services are needed and how well the system is functioning. The Department of Human Services, for example, is involved in developing the work-force readiness plan that determines how services will be produced and plays a key role in determining how well the producers hit the targets.

The six departments remain as a planning structure, both within the executive branch of government and as part of the commission, but the departments that remain as producer departments have gone through wide-scale consolidations. It was decided that sixty-four separate employment and training programs could be consolidated into fifteen distinct program areas in the three producer departments. These programs are being reorganized and reassigned to the appropriate unit. For example, the state Labor Department is now in the process of reorganizing all of its U.S. Department of Labor funded programs—JTPA, unemployment insurance, employment service, and, in a more gingerly fashion, vocational rehabilitation—into one delivery system, with one field operation, one program office, and one customer support unit, rather than a Division of Unemployment Insurance, a Division of Employment Services, and the like.

Several shifts of programs back and forth between departments have been made, again using the producer-consumer logic. For example, apprenticeship training moved from the Education Department to the Labor Department. Oversight and monitoring of private proprietary schools, which had been dispersed among twelve different agencies, was consolidated into one unit under the Department of Education.

These changes allowed the state to develop the commission's capacity to perform third party, neutral, intermediation functions to resolve issues. None of these structural changes came without widespread debate.

To facilitate the structural changes, an ad hoc committee of commission members was formed to gather facts, hold public hearings, and engage in other activities to resolve issues whenever there was disagreement in the executive branch. This process worked better than was expected. For example, it opened new doors for recommendations and for understanding how programs interrelate. A small senior citizens employment program—with two missions—operated by Community Affairs provides a case in point.

One mission is the transition of employment for all workers. The second is a social service support mechanism for senior citizens that includes work experience. On the surface, members of the commission walking into the fact-finding session were pretty well sold on a particular viewpoint: "Well, this is really an employment program; we will move it to the Labor Department; this will be a fifteen-minute meeting." Three hearings later, however, the commission concluded that the Labor Department needed a better articulated older-worker strategy before it was given responsibility for additional older-worker programs. A conclusion was also reached that the agencies needed to look at the young-old and the old-old in different ways and seek to differentiate and articulate plans on how to deal with older workers in New Jersey.

This has put New Jersey on its way to evolving plans to spend special JTPA funds for the training of older workers (the so-called 3% money) more effectively and connect it with some other resources. It provides an example of the changes that have been made possible under the planning structure.

To facilitate the commission's work, there is an executive branch work group composed of a subcabinet appointee of each of the six cabinet members on the commission: Labor, Education, Higher Education, Commerce, Community Affairs, and Human Services. This group serves as the commission's extension into the executive branch of government and provides operational connections for the planning process of the commission.

Occupational education was the first substantive area to be reviewed. The goal was to rethink occupational education, because occupational education is currently defined as where you are in terms of years in school or location in the state or county. The overriding impact of the subsequent report and recommendations was to say that occupational education is a means to an end. The higher education community has to discuss it at the level of the associate's degree.

Getting the chancellor of higher education to agree to the goal was a major step. All the community colleges and the entire vocational education structure entered into a conversation on articulation that transcended the traditional "I will accept yours if you will accept mine." Instead, those involved looked at the issue from the customer's perspective. How do we define occupational education? How do we articulate between high school and postsecondary experiences? How do we assure that there is value added along the way?

Focusing on the customer's perspective is an effective way to discuss how the work-force readiness system connects with other components of the system. If we talk about connecting clients from different systems, we should talk about points along a value-added continuum where someone from any system, whatever his or her background or barriers are, can move into a work-force readiness system. With assessment and an individual plan, participants can plug into the continuum at the adult basic education level, at the GED level, at the tech prep level, or at a technical apprenticeship level—however the continuum of value added to lifelong learning is defined. This is really the first step in that trip.

An interesting process is underway. Decision making and governance stand side by side. The commission (NJETC) is an external representation of community, political, employer, and labor interests. It interacts with the executive branch of government on a daily basis in terms of planning and helping to develop the structural changes. This allows New Jersey to construct a state-level structure that is capable of changing its delivery system.

Thus, New Jersey's experience demonstrates that creation of a human resource development council and the use of strategic planning approaches can foster both a reorganization of work-force development activities and new approaches to issues. The dual processes of commission planning and executive branch work-group activity have facilitated the reorganization of agencies and services.

Leadership has been crucial to the success of the effort. The governor has been absolutely essential to the planning and reorganization processes. He appointed both the commission and the cabinet with the understanding that the most important thing to do was to develop a strategic response to the needs of the state. His commitment reinforced their work throughout the process of developing the work-force readiness system.

Connecticut's Plan for Action

As Thomas Corbett points out in Chapter 11 of this volume, compelling issues often provide the impetus for change. In Connecticut, a set of compelling issues gave rise to the Connecticut Employment and Training Commission as a successor to the state job training coordinating council.

Connecticut's SJTCC had a troubled history. It was supported initially by the Department of Labor (DOL), the agency the governor designated as the state JTPA liaison. DOL had been accustomed to the Comprehensive Employment and Training Act (CETA), a program with considerable federal guidance. In the rush to get JTPA started, DOL failed to recognize the increased state role that JTPA created. As a result, DOL got off on the wrong foot with the SJTCC, which was poised to influence the program.

Consequently, the SJTCC chair went to the governor and asked permission to exercise the option under the law that allows some of the 5 percent money to be used to staff the council. The governor approved this request and the council acquired an independent staff about six months into the program. The SJTCC's office was initially located in the Department of Education. By executive order, it was transferred to the Department of Economic Development on the theory that JTPA is not a social service program; rather, it is an economic development program to help employers fill unfilled jobs, both for their own benefit and that of unemployed people.

At the time, both houses of the Connecticut state legislature were controlled by a party different from the governor's. The legislators looked at the array of job training programs in the state and decided it needed a coordinating council. As they pursued state legislation to create one, some members of the SJTCC pointed out that the state already had a state job training coordinating council. The legislature responded by making the council a separate state agency. Thus, it went from Labor to Education to Economic Development to being an independent state agency.

Within the council itself, a couple of committees were chaired by commissioners of executive branch agencies. They reported out recommendations to the full council that commissioners from other state agencies found objectionable. This led to public disputes among the commissioners. To avoid splitting ranks in public, commissioners of the various agencies stopped attending meetings. Without participation from executive branch agency heads, representatives of major Connecticut-based corporations serving on the council became increasingly disillusioned about their ability to influence policy. This was one impetus for change.

Another compelling issue that provided impetus for change emerged from New England's economic strength in the mid-1980s. Connecticut had unemployment levels of about 3 percent. Young people were making $7 to $9 an hour in fast-food jobs. The legislature eased child labor laws to permit fifteen year olds to work in certain retail occupations because the labor shortage was severe.

The Connecticut Business and Industry Association (CBIA) formed an alliance with the black and Hispanic legislative caucus. Neither thought its needs were being met by employment and training programs. Minority groups felt that fragmentation and disarray among job training programs resulted in limited access and ineffective services, while business and industry confronted a dearth of qualified job applicants. In addition, an active community-based organization with a broad political following, located in the state capital of Hartford, made direct pleas to the governor for assistance in dealing with employment problems in a depressed city neighborhood.

On top of this, the Office of Policy and Management, a Connecticut agency similar to the federal Office of Management and Budget (OMB), analyzed employment and training programs in the state. That analysis demonstrated that there were sixty-five employment and training programs administered in fifteen separate agencies, with a total annual budget of about $280 million. With such a large commitment of resources, the legislature and the business community raised further questions about why large segments of Connecticut's work force were inadequately prepared to contribute to the state's economic health.

In an environment characterized by a dysfunctional SJTCC, widespread dissatisfaction with state job training efforts, and growing recognition of the fragmentation of employment and training programs, the governor appointed a new commissioner of Labor. Her first agenda item was to give the SJTCC some direction. She introduced legislation to create a Connecticut Employment and Training Commission and bring it into the Department of Labor, which was recognized as the appropriate locus for coordinating employment and training programs.

At this same time (1988), federal legislation required reconstitution of SJTCCs. The result was state legislation renaming the council as the Connecticut Employment and Training Commission (CETC). Its membership is consistent with that required under federal law, and it has responsibility for continuing to serve as the state job training council under JTPA.

The commission has a broader state statutory mandate than JTPA. It is responsible for an inventory of all employment and training programs. It must produce an annual plan to coordinate the programs administered by fifteen different agencies and is responsible, in the name of the commissioner of Labor, to monitor implementation of the plan. Furthermore, it is responsible for evaluating the effectiveness of the state's employment and training services in meeting the needs of business, individuals, and the economy.

The governor appointed the first commission members in June 1989 and gave them four goals, each with a set of objectives. The goals became the cornerstone for the annual plan the CETC was to produce to coordinate all of the state's employment and training services. It is important to note that these goals and objectives were not simply proclaimed by the governor. The deputy commissioner of the Department of Labor consulted with a cabinet-level group of commissioners from the other state agencies and developed consensus around the goals and objectives prior to the governor's pronouncement. By the time the governor delivered them to the commission as a whole, the state agencies were on board and in support of the goals and objectives: (1) match work-force skills with those required in the workplace; (2) ease the school-to-work transition for young people; (3) create opportunities for the disadvantaged to develop a permanent attachment to the work force; and (4) coordinate the system.

Committees are created around each of the four goals and are charged with making recommendations to address each of the goals and objectives. The committees decide if they need additional expertise for decision making and, if so, add to their membership subject-matter experts. The committees then enumerate the kinds of things they need to read and the kinds of people with whom they need to speak to be in a position to make responsible recommendations about how to achieve the goals and objectives. Each committee undertakes significant, arduous, involved, and thorough fact-finding around the major issues identified by the goals and objectives.

While the committees do their work, agency staff meet with cabinet members to keep them apprised of developments within each committee. There are no recommendations from the CETC that the commissioners of the various state agencies have not participated in formulating as members of the committees or through negotiations with the cabinet. Connecticut's decision makers believe that the involvement of agency commissioners throughout the process and the practice of keeping them apprised of developments within the committees is an essential element in the successful development of Connecticut's strategic plan for human resource development. The process and behavior contrast dramatically with the public conflict among commissioners that occurred within the precursor SJTCC.

It is worth elaborating on how the process of engaging state agency commissioners works. The governor established a Human Services Cabinet of state agency commissioners. In addition, there is a process called Interagency Initiative Day, which is scheduled for the first Friday of each month. Whenever one of the commissioners on the Human Services Cabinet has an issue that needs to be discussed with commissioners from the other agencies, he or she can ask for time on the Interagency Initiative Day agenda and name the other commissioners needed at the meeting for the discussion. An agenda is sent to those commissioners, and they meet and work through the interagency concerns involved in addressing the issue. The deputy commissioner uses the Interagency Initiative Days frequently throughout the commission's planning process.

In addition to the fact that agency commissioners participate actively as members of the CETC's committees and separately through the Human Service Cabinet in developing recommendations, another aspect of the planning process, the "do it yourself" approach, is extremely important to its success.

Planning committees that advise departments of government often begin with a staff person from the department providing members a copy of a staff-produced draft plan. In the case of the commission's strategic plan for human resource development, staff do not draft a plan. Instead, at their first meeting, committee members review the goal they have been organized to address and the objectives associated with it. They are charged with developing recommendations for attaining the goal and objectives themselves and told that they should have the recommendations ready in six months. They are told that staff will help them get the people they need in order to be informed enough to make major recommendations.

During development of the commission's first annual plan, even after the six months of substantial fact-finding that committees undertook, members still anticipated staff would put a piece of paper in front of them with a draft plan on it. The staff did not do it. As one observer notes, "Commission members sort of blanched when they realized they were going to have to materialize the recommendations to the governor themselves." Members had to come to a consensus about their own recommendations.

In the end, of course, this "do it yourself" approach is critical. It means there is buy-in from disparate organizations and interest groups, all of which claim the plan as theirs. They know it is theirs. They see it materialize through their discussions and negotiations.

This is not to minimize the importance of sufficient staff support. While staff do not develop the CETC's plan, they do provide members every resource needed, whether it is a document, a report from another agency, or statistical information descriptive of the current environment or predictive of future trends. Staff are the couriers, librarians, and scribes to the process. They also play a central role in facilitating the interagency process among agency commissioners within the Human Services Cabinet, so that they and their staffs are informed of what is happening. This allows the various commissioners to anticipate whether or not developments are consistent with their own agency's objectives and interests, and enables them to participate fully. This staff attention to the needs and concerns of other agency heads assures that no one feels blind-sided or embarrassed by recommendations she or he cannot support.

Difficult problems that could have destroyed the effort the first time around were encountered during this process. First, four-fifths of the way through the six-month planning period the governor announced that he would not run for reelection. About that time, the full extent of the state's deficit became known and a hiring freeze was placed on state government. In that environment, the commission staff went to the Interagency Initiative Day intent on extracting commitments from agency directors to designate staff to form interagency planning groups to translate the commission's recommendations—recently approved by the governor—into specific, strategic plans for implementation. The commissioners refused. They did not have the capacity to devote their staff's time to the interagency teams that commission staff proposed.

To compensate, commission staff located some federal money to hire consultants who negotiated back and forth between the agencies whose cooperation and participation were required and worked with them to develop the required written documents. This worked because the commissioners were willing to cooperate and participate; they just did not have staff available to sit down, work out action plans, and commit them to paper.

The committees developed fourteen action plans calling for specific activities. The committees brought these action plans to the full CETC for adoption. The entire set was then forwarded to the governor in fulfillment of the mandate to develop an annual plan for the coordination of all employment and training programs.

The overall process involved agencies in the development of a strategic, action-oriented plan. Each of the agencies had to come back and say what it was going to do, who would be the lead agency with responsibility for getting it done, which would be the cooperating agencies with the resources and expertise that were needed to get this activity underway and accomplished, which resources each of those agencies would bring to the table, and the specific outcome that would be achieved.

Although implementation of the Connecticut Human Resource Development Plan is well underway, much remains to be done, particularly with regard to the commission's responsibility under state statute to evaluate the effectiveness of state employment and training programs in serving individuals, businesses, and the economy. The fourteen action plans were all devised to incorporate specific outcomes that would result from their implementation. It turns out, however, that in many instances the stated outcomes actually represent input or output measures rather than results. For example, the first goal had to do with matching work-force skills to those required in the workplace. For this, the first objective focused on the needs of dislocated workers. The plan specifies that an outcome resulting from implementation of the associated action plan will be an increase of 65 percent in the number of dislocated workers served over the previous year. To provide services to more people than before is an output, but it is not really an outcome.

The Connecticut planning process has several key characteristics:

- Early collaboration on the part of all affected state agency heads in devising goals and objectives as a basis for devising strategies
- Simultaneous and continuing participation by agency heads in the public-private sector committees made up of appointed commission members supplemented by subject-matter experts *and* in executive-level cabinet meetings
- "Do it yourself" policy development undertaken by volunteer gubernatorial appointees based upon their thorough investigation of concerns at hand, not review of staff-generated proposals
- Adequate staff support

CONCLUSION

Several things stand out in these accounts of human resource development planning in Connecticut and New Jersey. In both states, it was an employment and training commission with a broader mandate than the standard state job training coordinating council that led the way in developing more comprehensive, change-oriented approaches to work-force development. Leadership by the governor was central to the effort to create such broad-based commissions and provide them with both formal authority and informal capacity to act.

Careful attention to the stakes of different agencies and efforts to help them find different ways to identify their interests were crucial to the development of collaborative planning processes. Allowing the agencies to develop a sense of ownership in the plan facilitated their cooperation in it. In New Jersey, it has led to a willingness to transfer functions among agencies as interests are redefined. The broader authority of these employment and training commissions has enabled them to do more than the standard state job training coordinating council.

At the same time, the experience of these two states illustrates that there may not be a "best" home for a human resource investment council. The New Jersey Employment and Training Commission has operated successfully as an independent entity. The Connecticut Employment and Training Commission is succeeding while linked to the Department of Labor. Different circumstances can call for different organizational arrangements.

In addition, these case studies suggest that creation of human resource investment councils does not by itself solve policy and organizational problems. There must be careful attention to the linkage between such a body and operating agencies. In addition, group and organizational processes must be followed that allow attention to the interests of different stakeholders, if the cooperation of those stakeholders is to be obtained. Issues must be thoroughly examined in light of their implications for existing programs and organizational arrangements.

REFERENCES

Bryson, John. 1988. *Strategic Planning for Public and Nonprofit Organizations*. San Francisco, Calif.: Jossey-Bass.

Bryson, John, and William D. Roering. 1988. "Initiation of Strategic Planning by Governments." *Public Administration Review* 48 (November/December): 995–1004.

Job Training Partnership Act Advisory Committee. 1989. *Working Capital: Coordinated Human Investment Directions for the 90s*. Washington, D.C.: U.S. Department of Labor. October.

King, Christopher T. 1988. *Cross-Cutting Performance Issues in Human Resource Programs*. National Commission for Employment Policy Research, Report 88–12. Washington, D.C.: National Commission for Employment Policy. August.

Van Horn, Carl E., Ken Ryan, and William Tracy. 1990. *Workforce Futures: Strategic Planning in the States*. Research Report No. 89–06. Washington, D.C.: National Commission for Employment Policy

Wechsler, Barton, and Robert W. Backoff. 1986. "Policy Making and Administration in State Agencies: Strategic Management Approaches," *Public Administration Review* 46 (July/August): 321–27.

Chapter 8

The Eight Percent Set-Aside as a Coordination Incentive

Robert G. Ainsworth and Barbara B. Oakley

The Job Training Partnership Act (JTPA) states that 8 percent of a state's grant be set-aside to promote coordination between the state's education and training programs. Recent policy debate has raised questions about whether the set-aside has been used in some states in a manner not fully supportive of JTPA goals.

This chapter analyzes the effectiveness of the 8 percent set-aside in promoting coordination activities. Following a description of the program and an overview of the questions that have been raised about its possible misuse, the next part of the chapter describes the states' uses of the 8 percent set-aside for education and training coordination grants. Data were obtained from several sources: state JTPA and education officials in fifty states and the District of Columbia, officials of the U.S. Department of Labor (DOL), state plans, and other literature on the subject. The chapter's final section presents conclusions and recommendations.

THE JTPA SET-ASIDES

JTPA provides funds nationwide to the states to distribute to more than 600 service delivery areas through formula grants administered by the governors. Title II-A provides training services for disadvantaged adults and youth. Title II, part B, provides summer programs to serve disadvantaged youth. The act sets aside 22 percent of the funds from the Title II-A allocation for each state to spend on certain activities for specific target groups through four separate set-aside programs (National Commission for Employment Policy, 1987). This includes the set-aside for education coordination.

Section 123 of the act authorizes the governor to provide 8 percent of the state's total allocation of JTPA Title II-A funds to any state education agency responsible for education and training. These funds are further divided into two parts. At least 80 percent of the set-aside (6.4% of the Title II-A total allocation) must be used to provide education and training services to eligible participants through cooperative agreements between the state education agency(ies), local service delivery areas, and local education agencies (if any). Not more than 20 percent of the set-aside (1.6% of the Title II-A total allocation) may be used for coordination of education and training services. Such funds may be spent on technical assistance, professional development, job placement, counseling, curriculum development, and other indirect activities aimed at coordinating education and training (National Commission for Employment Policy, 1985).

The set-aside may be used by the governor at the state and local levels to (1) facilitate coordination of education and training services for eligible participants; (2) provide literacy training to eligible youth and adults, dropout prevention and reenrollment services to youth, a statewide school-to-work transition program, or any combination of these activities; and (3) provide education and training (including vocational education services) and related services to eligible participants. Such services may include services for offenders, veterans, and other individuals who the governor determines require special assistance (Labor and Human Resources, 1986).

In providing these services to individuals, not less than 75 percent of the 80 percent funds are to be expended for services to economically disadvantaged individuals. Not more than 25 percent of the 80 percent funds may be spent for services to noneconomically disadvantaged individuals, including dislocated workers. (The flexibility given the states to serve this group is frequently referred to in the employment and training community as the "25 percent window.")

The uses of the education-coordination set-aside funds differ in several ways from the rest of the Title II-A funds. For example, federal performance standards do not apply to programs funded by the set-aside. States have flexibility in whether or not, and how, they establish goals and guidelines for their programs. Also, as previously mentioned, 25 percent of the state's set-aside funds can be used to serve noneconomically disadvantaged individuals. In Title II-A programs, 10 percent of the participants do not have to meet the eligibility criteria.

The normal Title II-A spending caps—70 percent minimum on training, 30 percent maximum on administration and support services of which not more than 15 percent can be spent on administration—apply differently. There is no administrative cap on the 20 percent that can be spent for coordination. There are no caps on the training or support services costs for the 80 percent portion.

The final difference is that the education-coordination set-aside has a matching requirement for the 80 percent portion, although the other Title II programs have no such requirement. The state education agency or agencies or the local education agency receiving "80 percent" funds must match these funds dollar for dollar (100%). The match can include use of other federal funds (excluding JTPA funds) if permissible by the statutes governing the funds. Matching funds may include

> direct costs of employment and training services provided by state or local programs, for example, vocational or adult education programs, cash, equipment, facilities, services and supplies funded from other sources, such as attendance-based formula aid, college full-time equivalency and high school equivalency aid and other state categorical grants, as well as in-kind contributions. (National Alliance of Business, 1984: 12)

If no cooperative agreement is reached between JTPA and education, the set-aside funds become available to the governor for use in coordinating activities that have been described in the state plan (as mandated under Section 121).

QUESTIONS ABOUT THE EDUCATION-COORDINATION SET-ASIDE

In recent public policy debates, several questions have been raised about possible misuses of the education-coordination set-aside. In general, the issue is that the set-aside is not being used in some states in a manner fully supportive of JTPA goals. Listed below are three examples of this criticism:

- The funds are sometimes used as a substitute for state and local education and training funds rather than as a complement to them
- In some states, the funds are simply turned over to state education agencies, which then do little to coordinate their use with JTPA administrators. Moreover, once the funds have been turned over to

a state's department of education, JTPA officials often have little control over their use

- The 20 percent allotment that is to be used for coordination activities between JTPA and the education agencies has been spent primarily for administrative costs by the department of education in some states

Reports raising these issues indicate that part of the problem may be that the act does not fully define "coordination" as it applies to this set-aside. As a result, confusion may exist in some states as to the legitimate uses of the money. Furthermore, little guidance has been given to the states on how the Congress and the U.S. Department of Labor intended the funds to be used and meshed with other federal, state, and local employment and training related programs (National Commission for Employment Policy, 1987, 1990).

A similar concern was raised in a report issued by the National Center for Research in Vocational Education. This report indicated that "the underlying problem with the eight percent funds is that federal legislation does not specify intended uses for the eight percent funds" (Grubb et al., 1990: 63).

The authors offered suggestions to remedy the problem. For example, if the Congress intended that these funds be used to foster stronger institutional relationships between vocational education and JTPA—or between JTPA and any other agency, including welfare-to-work and the employment service—then it would be appropriate for Congress to specify this intent and include legislative provisions to further it. In addition, federal regulations should be developed so that the programs are jointly operated by service delivery areas, educational institutions, and states. Finally, the U.S. Department of Labor should be required to collect information about successful models funded by this set-aside and share this information with other programs (Grubb et al., 1990).

Although there are concerns regarding this set-aside, there is also evidence that the funds have been used in ways that promote JTPA goals. Evidence from hearings on Hispanics in JTPA held by the National Commission for Employment Policy in 1989 indicated that some states are using the set-aside in innovative and important ways, such as English as a second language (ESL) programs, dropout prevention, and basic skills remediation. In addition, witnesses at the hearings indicated that states used the funds to serve individuals who were less likely to be served with regular II-A monies because they require lengthy training and are not easily placed. The absence of federal performance standards was said to be the major reason why programs funded under this set-aside serve a harder-to-serve clientele (National Commission for Employment Policy, 1990).

Participants in a series of seminars sponsored by the National Commission for Employment Policy on federal, state, and local issues in coordination of government-sponsored public assistance programs indicated that the set-aside program gave the governors flexibility in determining their states' needs for services and for improving coordination between employment and training programs.

USES OF THE EDUCATION-COORDINATION SET-ASIDE: REPORTS FROM THE STATES

States vary on their uses of the set-aside to facilitate coordination and provide services to eligible individuals. This section describes states' goals, uses of the education-coordination set-aside funds, services provided, trends in uses of the funds, how JTPA coordinates with the education system in the use of funds, and the states' views on the need for changes in the program.

State Goals

One of the first steps in using the education-coordination set-aside funds is to set goals that reflect the state's understanding of the flexibility available concerning services that can be offered to target groups. Our canvass of the states revealed a variety of goals in providing activities and services under the 8 percent set-aside. Among the most frequently mentioned state goals were the following:

- Enhance coordination and promote linkages among local education agencies (LEAs), service delivery areas (SDAs), and private industry councils (PICs)
- Provide literacy and basic skills to participants as participants have more success in other training activities when this component is provided first
- Prevent dropouts and help adults obtain a general equivalency degree (GED)
- Ensure that education has the fullest opportunity to be part of the planning process in local areas to leverage resources that education contributes to employment and training for youth and adults

- Seek creative and innovative partnerships with education
- Assist the hardest-to-serve populations

Uses of Eight Percent Funds and Services Provided

Designated Agency(ies) and Allocation of Funds. Governors of thirty-nine states have designated one or more educational agency(ies) to provide services with the 8 percent set-aside funds. Forty-four states allocate their funds by Title II-A formula, by request for proposal (RFP), or by a combination of the two. The majority of these funds flows locally to K through 12 school systems, postsecondary schools and colleges, and SDAs.

Programs Provided and Persons Served with 80 Percent Funds. The most common programs provided with education-coordination funds are literacy (basic skills), dropout prevention, occupational training, and school-to-work activities. Literacy programs are offered in nearly all states and dropout prevention programs are offered in more than 60 percent of the states.

According to state officials, the absence of federal performance standards for the education-coordination set-aside program enables services to be provided to economically disadvantaged at-risk youth and adults who are the hardest to serve and would not likely be served under other Title II-A programs. In most states, these individuals include high school dropouts or potential dropouts, welfare recipients, and offenders. For example, thirty-five states specifically mentioned serving high school dropouts or potential dropouts; fifteen states specifically mentioned providing services to welfare recipients; and ten states mentioned serving offenders. Generally, it appears that more youth than adults are being served under the 8-percent program.

How 80 Percent Funds are Matched. As noted earlier, the education set-aside program requires 100 percent matching grants by the state or local education agency or agencies for the 80 percent portion used to provide services to individuals. In approximately half of the states, the required match is made from a combination of in-kind contributions (e.g., equipment, space, and personnel) and local, state, and federal cash contributions. Among the sources of federal cash contributions were the Carl D. Perkins Vocational and Applied Technology Act, Adult Education Act, vocational rehabilitation grant, and Pell grants.

About 30 percent of the states appeared to receive only an in-kind match, while approximately 14 percent appeared to receive cash only. Three states, or 6 percent of the states, did not receive matching funds because of the absence of an agreement on uses of the education set-aside funds.

As a result, the 8-percent funds became available to the governor in these states for coordination activities described in the Governor's Coordination and Special Services Plan.

Use of the 25 Percent Window. As noted earlier, 25 percent of the 80 percent funds may be used to serve noneconomically disadvantaged individuals. However, many states do not use the 25 percent window because there are so many economically disadvantaged individuals that they focus entirely on that group. Those states that do use the 25 percent window noted that the individuals served do not "technically" meet the JTPA Title II eligibility criteria; however, they do have serious barriers to overcome before they are employable. Examples provided by the states include offenders, drug abusers, and dislocated workers who are in need of occupational training and remedial services.

Utilization of the 20 Percent Funds. All states use a portion of the 20 percent funds for the administration of the 8-percent program. Forty-eight states specifically mentioned using a portion of the 20 percent funds for coordination activities. Each of these states has an 8-percent coordinator who is responsible for assuring that JTPA and education officials work together in implementing the program.

States use the 20 percent funds in a variety of ways. For example, thirty-eight states indicated that a portion of these funds were used for evaluating and monitoring the education-coordination program; thirty-four states for staff training and development; and twenty-eight states for the development of the curriculum for the education-coordination program. Four states specifically mentioned using these funds with the 80 percent portion for other activities such as dropout prevention programs, establishing learning centers, literacy programs, and alternative school projects.

Trends in Uses of the Education-Coordination Funds

Over the past few years, the two most noticeable changes in the use of the 80 percent funds have been (1) a shift in emphasis from providing occupational skills training to providing assessment and literacy, and basic skills for at-risk youth and adults and (2) a shift in emphasis toward serving more youth than adults.

There have been no major changes regarding the use of the 20 percent coordination funds. However, six states indicated one or more of the following changes: improved state agency oversight and technical assistance to PICs and SDAs; increased emphasis on assessment, testing, literacy and basic skills; and a more focused coordination in high school dropout prevention programs.

How JTPA Coordinates with Education in the Use of Funds

Private industry councils in thirty-three states are involved in planning, approving, and monitoring education set-aside programs in their local areas. In eleven of these thirty-three states, the PICs set priorities for both the populations to be served and the services provided to participants with the 8 percent funds.

There is a range in the types of coordination activities involving education and JTPA at both the state and local levels. Coordination activities include written formal agreements and contracts at the state and local level; 8 percent advisory councils at the state level; planning groups at the local level; and JTPA staff located within the education agency.

Education's general administrative and policy-making role (both state and local) is significant in a majority of the states because services are provided by educational entities. Educators are represented on the state job training coordinating council, on similar statewide groups, or on private industry councils that determine policy for the use of JTPA funds in each service delivery area.

States' Views on the Need for Changes in the Set-Aside Program

Forty-two states recommended retaining the education-coordination set-aside program. Among the reasons given for retaining the program were the following:

- The absence of federal performance standards has enabled states to assist the hardest-to-serve individuals, including some persons who would not receive services under other Title II-A programs
- States have more flexibility in the types of programs they can offer and are therefore able to provide long-term training to clients with multiple barriers to employment
- The program has helped forge coordination links between JTPA and education and provides a way for leveraging resources

Among the reasons given by the nine states that suggested eliminating the program was that it may not be meeting congressional intent. State use of the funds would be more flexible if the program were replaced with a coordination grants program that included other agencies, as well as education.

If the education-coordination set-aside program were eliminated, the nine states that recommended elimination reported that the following changes would occur: JTPA funds would flow directly to the SDAs; the education system would become more involved in JTPA Title II-A programs in order to receive funding; and other state agencies would continue to provide services currently funded out of the 8 percent program with other JTPA Title II funds and other funding sources.

Although most states were generally pleased with the education-coordination set-aside program, fourteen states cited the small amounts of money available and ten states alluded to the matching requirement as obstacles to providing services with the 80 percent portion of the education-coordination funds.

About half of the states reported that no changes were needed in the set-aside program. The change most often mentioned by the other states was the elimination of the matching requirement. Officials that recommended eliminating the matching requirement were concerned about the difficulties in generating a match and the burdensome paperwork required once a match is made. Most states that received all or mostly cash contributions were in favor of the matching requirement. Of particular concern to the states were in-kind matches that generated little, if anything, toward total resources.

States recommending changes also suggested (1) clarifying the act's language and regulations to more clearly define coordination, (2) enacting more stringent requirements so that education agencies can make a real connection between 8 percent funds and other funding sources administered by education agencies, (3) improving accountability and specificity in the use of education-coordination funds, and (4) expanding the emphasis on coordination beyond education to include other state and local agencies such as welfare, the employment service, corrections, and vocational rehabilitation.

Sixteen states specifically cited the need for more leadership, direction, and proactive technical assistance from the U.S. Department of Labor in contracting and procurement, interpreting the regulations, clarifying proper uses of funds, and monitoring and overseeing activities.

The views of state officials regarding the need for change in the education-coordination set-aside program can be broken down according to whether the respondent is a JTPA official or an education official and whether the program is administered by the state's JTPA agency or its education agency. The survey covered 50 states and the District of Columbia (included as a state here). The state-designated contacts included forty-one JTPA officials and ten education officials.

Thirty-two of the forty-one JTPA officials recommended retaining the set-aside program. In the thirty-two states, the set-aside was administered by JTPA in eleven states and by an education agency in twenty-one states. In the other nine states where JTPA officials recommended that the program be eliminated, the program was administered by JTPA in two states and by an education agency in seven states. Nothing in the data suggested that the response of JTPA officials was affected by whether their agency or the education agency administers the set-aside.

A comparison was made of the responses from the twenty-one JTPA officials who wanted to retain the program with the responses from the seven state JTPA officials who wanted to eliminate the program in states where the program is administered by the education agency.

The analysis of these responses from the two groups was inconclusive. There appeared to be little or no difference between the two groups as to how the 80 percent funds were allocated and how they flowed locally, the types of services provided and who received services, and uses of the 25 percent window. Furthermore, there appeared to be no discernable differences between the two groups as to the effects of the absence of federal performance standards on who was being served and the types of services provided, the uses of the 20 percent funds for coordination activities, the extent of involvement by the PICs with the program, or education's administration and policy-making role in operations of all JTPA titles.

The analysis did, however, reveal differences in three areas. First, of those twenty-one states where the program is administered by education and state JTPA officials want to retain the program, 86 percent (or nineteen states) had made changes in the way the 80 percent funds have been used in the past several years. In contrast, only 55 percent (or five of nine) of those states that recommended eliminating the set-aside made changes in the use of the 80 percent funds.

Second, those same twenty-one state officials were less likely to identify any further changes needed in the use of the 80 percent funds than were those officials who recommended eliminating the program.

Finally, state officials who recommended that the program be eliminated were somewhat more likely to have some concerns about the matching requirement than those state officials who wanted to retain the program. Of the seven state officials who recommended the elimination of the program, officials in five states (or 71%) specifically referred to the burdensome paperwork exercise involved with the match, particularly with in-kind matches. Only three of the twenty-one state officials (or 14%) who wanted to retain the program had such concerns about the matching requirement.

ACTION RECOMMENDATIONS

As this chapter has indicated, the current education-coordination set-aside program could be viewed as having explicit and implicit goals. The explicit goal is to foster closer coordination between the JTPA and education systems through cooperative agreements. The implicit goal of the program in the absence of federal performance standards, is to provide services to the hardest-to-serve individuals. The fact that one goal is explicit and the other is implicit may be one of the sources of confusion as to the program's purpose.

This study has four major conclusions. First, isolated cases of misuse of education-coordination funds that may occur in some states do not outweigh the positive and innovative programs that have resulted from the flexibility that states have under Section 123 of JTPA to coordinate education and training programs.

Second, the absence of federal performance standards allows states to use the 80 percent portion of the set-aside to serve economically disadvantaged individuals who are the hardest to serve and who may be out of the reach of other Title II programs because of the performance standards attached to them. However, many states have established their own benchmarks or goals for measuring outcomes among these harder-to-serve individuals.

Third, the 25 percent window for serving the noneconomically disadvantaged has been of great benefit to persons not technically eligible who, nevertheless, have serious barriers to employability, although this window has not been used extensively by the states.

Fourth, some states need clarification of how the U.S. Department of Labor interprets "coordination" and how Section 123 funds can be used to further improve coordination among JTPA, education, and other relevant programs.

Three recommendations are warranted based on the findings contained in this chapter. First, the current education-coordination program should be retained as authorized under Section 123 of the Job Training Partnership Act. Second, the secretary of labor should clarify the Department of Labor's interpretation of "coordination" through a technical assistance guidance memorandum and explain how the Section 123 funds can be used to further improve coordination among JTPA, education, and other relevant agencies. This explanation should include specific examples of options for allowable activities in the areas of contracting, procurement, technical assistance, and programs. The secretary of labor should provide full information about the standards and requirements that will be used in the Department of Labor's monitoring and oversight activities. Finally, a percentage of funds should be retained for states that have a need for serving those individuals with serious barriers to employment even though such individuals do not technically meet JTPA eligibility criteria. However, the percentage available to serve the noneconomically disadvantaged should be reduced from 25 percent to 10 percent since most states do not fully utilize the 25-percent window.

REFERENCES

Grubb, W. Norton, et al. 1990. *Order Amidst Complexity: The Status of Coordination Among Vocational Education, Job Training Partnership Act, and Welfare-to-Work Programs*. Berkeley: National Center for Research in Vocational Education, University of California. August.

Labor and Human Resources. 1986. *A Compilation of Job Training and Related Laws*. Washington, D.C.: Committee on Labor and Human Resources, U.S. House of Representatives. December.

National Alliance of Business. 1984. *Business Currents: Technical Report*, Technical Report No. 2, February 3.

National Commission for Employment Policy. 1985. *Getting 100 Percent Results from the Eight Percent Education Set-Aside under the Job Training Partnership Act*. Research Report 85–06. Washington, D.C. April.

———. 1986. *Facts and Findings* 4, no. 4 (Spring). Washington, D.C.

———. 1987. *The Job Training Partnership Act*. Washington, D.C. September.

———. 1990. *Training Hispanics: Implications for the JTPA System*. Report No. 27. Washington, D.C. January.

Chapter 9

State Government Coordination of the JOBS Program

Edward T. Jennings, Jr. and Dale Krane

An already crowded arena of employment and training programs became even more crowded with the entrance of the Job Opportunities and Basic Skills (JOBS) program into the field following the adoption of the Family Support Act (FSA) of 1988 (Congressional Quarterly, 1988; Rovner, 1991). JOBS is the latest federal effort to address the employment and training needs of the disadvantaged, particularly welfare recipients. It joins an array of programs sponsored under the Job Training Partnership Act (JTPA), the Wagner-Peyser Act, the Carl D. Perkins Act, the Adult Education Act, and other federal, state, and local statutes, raising new questions about the coordination of employment and training programs. This chapter reports the results of a study of the implementation of JOBS that focuses on its coordination with other programs.

ASSESSING COORDINATION BETWEEN JOBS AND PREEXISTING PROGRAMS

Much of the experience of JOBS would probably parallel that of earlier programs like JTPA. JOBS could be expected to encounter numerous opportunities for and barriers to coordination because it has been implemented in the context of multiple employment and training programs, and adds to rather than replaces any of them (Bailis, 1989; Burbridge and Nightingale, 1989; Jennings and White, 1987; Jennings, 1989; Trutko, Bailis, Barnow, and French, 1989; Grubb et al., 1989, 1990). Because of the experience states acquired with other employment and training programs and welfare-to-work experiments, JOBS should have been easier to implement and coordinate, although that possibility was mitigated by the failure of Congress to consolidate JOBS with preexisting programs.

To determine the extent and type of coordination of JOBS with the preexisting programs, we conducted telephone interviews with officials in eight states selected to provide diversity of socioeconomic conditions and programmatic arrangements. In each state, we interviewed individuals in positions of responsibility with respect to JOBS, JTPA, the employment service, vocational education, and the governor's office. We sought information about the implementation of JOBS from the perspective of the different agencies. We asked about planning for jobs, administrative responsibility for the various activities associated with JOBS, barriers to and facilitators of coordination, and aspects of federal policy that could be changed to improve coordination.

The states included in the study are California, Florida, Illinois, Kentucky, Massachusetts, Nebraska, Oregon, and Texas. These states differ considerably in terms of size, region, degree of urbanization, and administrative structure. The patterns they exhibit are probably shared by other states. More important, they provide illustrative examples of the coordination issues raised by the JOBS program.

In succeeding sections of the chapter, we describe the major provisions of FSA and JOBS, indicate the relationship of JOBS to preexisting employment and training programs, and examine coordination issues that have arisen in the implementation of JOBS.

THE FAMILY SUPPORT ACT AND THE JOBS PROGRAM

The Family Support Act of 1988 (PL 100–485) is a major reform of the beleaguered Aid to Families with Dependent Children (AFDC) program. Its wide-ranging provisions include (1) increased child support enforcement efforts; (2) extension to all states of the AFDC-Unemployed Parent (UP) program, which provides benefits to eligible two-parent families; (3) work and participation requirements for AFDC-UP recipients; (4) an increase in the income that is not considered in determining AFDC benefit eligibility and prohibition on counting earned income tax credits in determining AFDC benefit eligibility; (5) permission for states to deny AFDC benefits to minor parents unless they meet certain living arrangement requirements or other conditions; (6) transitional child care and Medicaid benefits for families that become ineligible because of employment and earnings; and (7) the JOBS program.

The purpose of the JOBS program is to "assure that needy families with children obtain the education, training and employment that will help them avoid long-term welfare dependence." States were required to implement a JOBS program by October 1, 1990, and must establish the program in every political subdivision by October 1, 1992, unless the state demonstrates to the satisfaction of the secretary of Health and Human Services (HHS) that it is unfeasible or unnecessary to do so.

The JOBS program is required to include a number of components:

1. Basic educational activities, including high school or equivalent education (combined with training as needed)
2. Basic and remedial education to achieve a basic literacy level
3. Education for individuals with limited English proficiency
4. Job skills training
5. Job-readiness activities
6. Job development and job placement
7. Supportive services, including child care and transportation

Programs also have to offer two of the following four work activities: group and individual job search; on-the-job training; work supplementation programs; and community work experience programs.

States must require JOBS participation by all nonexempt AFDC recipients, as long as necessary child care is provided. Although there are a variety of exemptions, targeted groups include (1) families in which the custodial parent is under age twenty-four and (a) has not completed high school or is not enrolled in high school or its equivalent, or (b) had little or no work experience in the preceding year; (2) families in which the youngest child is within two years of being ineligible for assistance because of age; and (3) families that received assistance during more than thirty-six of the preceding sixty months.

Coordination Provisions of JOBS

Various provisions require coordination of JOBS with other employment and training programs. Each state must develop and periodically update a plan that describes, among other things, how the state will meet coordination requirements with the private sector and other programs. The program is to be administered at the state level primarily by the welfare agency, which is to assure coordination of JOBS, child support, and cash assistance services. Governors must ensure that JOBS activities are coordinated with activities under JTPA and other relevant education, training, and employment programs provided by the state. The state job training coordinating council (SJTCC) has the opportunity to review and comment on state plans. The welfare agency must consult with the state education agency and the agency responsible for employment and training programs. In addition, it has to use the services of each private industry council (PIC) to identify and provide advice on the types of jobs available or likely to become available in each JTPA service delivery area.

At the federal level, the Family Support Act created a new assistant secretary whose job it is to oversee and coordinate the JOBS, child support enforcement, and cash assistance programs. The HHS secretary must consult with the secretaries of Education and Labor during the implementation of JOBS and on a continuing basis to ensure maximum coordination of services. The secretaries of Labor and HHS are required to issue joint regulations with respect to provisions relating to working conditions, wage rates for the community work experience program, workers' compensation, and displacement of existing employees. Thus, substantial coordinating activity is required, even more than has been required for some of the other programs.

JOBS AND THE EXISTING EMPLOYMENT AND TRAINING NETWORK

JOBS came into existence in the midst of an array of previously created employment and training programs that encompass all of the activities envisioned under JOBS, including basic education, basic and remedial education to achieve a basic literacy level, job skills training, job-readiness activities, job development, job placement, and supportive services. The existing programs also offer group and individual job search, on-the-job training, work supplementation, and community work programs. In addition, JTPA, with its focus on the disadvantaged, serves much the same population as JOBS, although it is not limited exclusively to welfare recipients. Thus, JOBS was not created because of a perception that particular types of services were not available in the employment and training system. Rather, it came into being specifically to require states to institute mandatory welfare-to-work activities for AFDC recipients.

The question of where to locate JOBS administratively was interesting. Welfare agencies and JTPA administrative entities were logical candidates. Welfare agencies suffer from the perception that they promote dependency. There is also a perception that JTPA has been serving the easiest to serve of the disadvantaged, and that JOBS is targeted toward the most difficult to serve. This perception about JTPA is linked directly to its performance standards, which many feel cause it to emphasize the use of short-term, low-cost services for those most likely to take advantage of the services (Congressional Quarterly, 1989; Grubb et al., 1990; Job Training Partnership Act Advisory Committee, 1989; King, 1988; Levitan and Gallo, 1988). In addition, there may have been a feeling that integrated case management from the welfare side was required to ensure that essential support services are maintained and that the linkage between JOBS and welfare is not lost. Furthermore, the welfare agency would have to decide, at a minimum, who is required to participate in JOBS and keep track of that participation.

The fact that JOBS was created as part of a welfare reform effort explains why it was placed in the welfare agencies instead of being adopted as an extension of JTPA. As an amendment to the Social Security Act, FSA came under the purview of the Senate Finance and House Ways and Means committees. Placing the JOBS portion of FSA under the JTPA system would have required those committees to surrender authority over JOBS to the Senate Labor and Human Resources Committee and the House Education and Labor Committee. That they were unwilling to do; consequently, the tax committees won a struggle over this issue. Despite these considerations an entire new employment and training program for some of the disadvantaged was created just six years after the initiation of JTPA and was not directly tied to that legislation.

The program has multiple opportunities to draw upon existing service delivery arrangements and the capacities that agencies in the employment and training system have developed. For example, it can utilize the placement capability of the employment service, the educational skills of the vocational education system, and the brokering capacity of JTPA. In addition, if successfully coordinated, it can draw upon the resource base of those programs to supplement the limited funding made available under FSA.

IMPLEMENTATION, ADMINISTRATION, AND COORDINATION

The eight states in the study vary considerably in the extent to which they have implemented the JOBS program, the distribution of responsibility for program components, participation in the development of the state JOBS plan, provisions in the JOBS plan for coordination among agencies, the extent to which the JOBS program grew out of an existing welfare-to-work program, types of interagency coordination, moves toward various methods of operational coordination, and perceptions of coordination effectiveness. We discuss each of these topics next.

Administrative Responsibility

In each of the states, the agency that manages the Aid to Families with Dependent Children (AFDC) program is also responsible for the JOBS program. The names of the departments in which these programs are located vary, including Departments of Social Services, Human Services, Public Aid, Human Resources, Public Welfare, Health and Rehabilitative Services, and Social Insurance. Some of these are broad human service departments, encompassing an array of programs, while others have narrowly defined missions.

Extent of JOBS Implementation

Each of the eight states implemented the program by the October 1990 deadline. In some of the states—Massachusetts, California, Oregon, Illinois, and Florida—it has been implemented statewide. In the remaining states it has been implemented in only some areas, although it covers almost 90 percent of the eligible population in Texas. The extent of implementation here refers only to the extent of coverage of political jurisdictions and not the extent to which the target population has been reached or all program components are offered.

Administrative Responsibility for Program Components

The JOBS program has eight components in the processing of clients, in addition to support services and any actual education, training, or work experience activities: initial assessment of the client's needs; developing the employability plan; case management; job-readiness activities; group and individual job search; placement in training or education; and job development and placement. The states have developed a variety of organizational patterns for handling these components.

Most of the states report that the public welfare agency has sole responsibility for initial assessment of client needs, developing the employability plan, and case management. Five states report some work by others on these three functions, but even there the initial work is generally done by the public welfare agency.

The pattern of the remaining responsibilities is quite mixed. JTPA and the employment service frequently participate in job readiness, job search, job development, and placement activities. A variety of services are contracted out to public and private providers. In some states, JOBS has attempted to take advantage of resources available through JTPA, the employment service, and the vocational education system. In some instances, the welfare agency maintains direct control of most activities, using its own personnel to deliver services.

Thus, there is a mixed pattern of organization for the delivery of the JOBS program. As might be expected, the welfare agency generally handles initial assessment, the development of employability plans, and case management. There are diverse arrangements for other activities, with extensive reliance on contracts in some states, reliance on other agencies in other states, and an unapparent unwillingness to involve others in a couple of states.

From the perspective of our interest in coordination, two dimensions of agency responses to questions about the distribution of responsibility for various functional activities under JOBS are of interest: the extent to which the respondents in each state agreed with each other about the distribution of responsibility and the extent to which the JOBS agency relies upon the other agencies for various components of JOBS activity.

For most of the states, answers of respondents from different agencies indicated shared knowledge about the distribution of functional responsibilities. Some responses indicated some degree of confusion and the failure of a few respondents to be fully plugged in to what is going on in their state. On the whole, however, the sharing of knowledge about the distribution of functional responsibilities was fairly strong.

JOBS agencies rely on the other agencies to a moderate degree in the delivery of services. In some states there is considerable use of the capacity of the employment service and JTPA; in others, such use is more limited. The extent of such use was unclear in a couple of states because decision making is so extensively decentralized to the county level. Even less clear is the extent to which there is effective use of the capacity of the vocational education system. Full use is not being made of the capacity of the employment service and JTPA in some states.

Planning for JOBS

All eight states submitted JOBS plans prior to the October 1, 1990, deadline and had their programs approved. In several cases, plans were submitted and programs were in operation long before the deadline. Six states indicated that their programs began operation well before the deadline, some as early as 1989. The plans were all prepared by the agency with principal administrative responsibility for JOBS.

Most of the state welfare agencies reported extensive involvement of a variety of agencies in the planning for JOBS, including the range of agencies that one would expect, such as the employment service, JTPA, vocational education, and others. Some states had a fairly elaborate consultation process, with interagency committees operating at several levels statewide and at the local level; in other states, the arrangements were simpler. In one state, for example, there were six interagency committees, including representatives from seventy agencies, including the private sector. In another, committees operated at three levels in the executive branch, as well as at the SDA level. The JOBS agency reported very little in the way of interagency collaboration on the JOBS plan in two states, one noting that the only involvement of the other agencies was to review and comment on a plan that the welfare agency developed and circulated. Responses of the other agencies in those states indicated that they indeed had not been involved. In addition, JTPA, the employment service, and vocational education in a third state felt that they had minimal or no involvement in the development of the JOBS plan, although the JOBS agency said they had been involved. Thus, there is evidence of minimal involvement of non-JOBS agencies in planning in three of the eight states.

The legislation requires that each plan contain requirements for coordination with other agencies. A significant number of respondents from the other agencies knew little or nothing about coordination requirements that were built into the plans.

The JOBS plan was submitted to the state job training coordination council (SJTCC) for review in all states, as required by law. In all but two of the eight states, the SJTCC requested no changes in the plan. In two cases, state officials indicated that the SJTCC was involved in developing the plan and this might account for SJTCC concurrence. In one of the states where the SJTCC asked for changes in the state plan, it wanted on-the-job training programs to operate in all counties, but the state plan left that decision to the local areas. In another state, the SJTCC wanted the JOBS program turned over to the JTPA agency because JTPA already operated similar programs for the same population. The SJTCC was unable to convince the governor; consequently, the program stayed in the public welfare agency.

The overall evidence suggests a failure in a significant number of states to successfully incorporate all major employment and training agencies in the planning process. This is reflected in the interview comments on extent of involvement and the limited knowledge respondents have about coordination requirements contained in the plans.

Many of these states were operating welfare-to-work programs before JOBS came into being. In fact, several of their programs, such as Employment and Training (ET) in Massachusetts and Greater Avenues to Independence (GAIN) in California, provided part of the impetus for JOBS. Despite the widespread existence of these programs, they varied considerably in the extent to which they provided the basis for the JOBS program in each state. Respondents indicated little as to how these preexisting programs shaped the development of coordination for JOBS, but the states with extensive preexisting programs were no more likely than other states to exclude other agencies in the planning for JOBS.

Coordination with the State Education Agency

The JOBS agencies of the surveyed states report a variety of means for coordinating with education agencies, including contracts, consultation, board service, discussions, and interagency agreements. When asked about coordination activities, many of the administrators responded in terms of specific coordination agreements, instead of talking about coordination processes. Answers seemed to suggest that if another agency is doing something for the program, it constitutes coordination. There was one mention of funding being combined and several mentions of other agencies providing services with state funds to support JOBS activities or clients. This suggests attention to means of coordination that enhance resources to pursue program goals. In general, few things showed up systematically as being used in coordination with education across the states.

The vocational education respondents themselves gave similar responses, although in two states JOBS and vocational education gave somewhat contradictory responses. In addition, the employment service and JTPA respondents had quite limited knowledge of how JOBS is coordinated with vocational education in a number of states.

Coordination with the Employment Service

The reports by JOBS agencies on interagency coordination with the employment service suggest a relationship in all states, but it varies. In some states, administrators made little mention of state-level coordination, but indicated employment service involvement at the local level. Five states report direct arrangements with the employment service to provide various placement and readiness services. In at least one state, that activity goes to JTPA instead of the employment service. JOBS respondents simply did not report much in the way of coordination activities except specific programmatic arrangements. They seem interested in results rather than processes.

Employment service respondents talked about similar kinds of things. They and the JOBS people had shared views of how coordination between the two agencies is achieved in each state. In addition, the JTPA respondents generally had a working knowledge of how JOBS is coordinated with employment service activities. Vocational education respondents, on the other hand, had little or no knowledge about what goes on in this area.

Coordination with JTPA

The states report a variety of coordination activities with JTPA, including meetings, interagency committees, cooperative arrangements, liaisons, and specific contractual arrangements and operational relationships. The extent of coordination varies considerably among the states, ranging from one state where there is extensive cooperation and coordination at all levels to another where there has been little state-level coordination because of a program philosophy that emphasizes local planning and management. There is considerable antagonism toward JTPA by JOBS staff in at least one state. The degree of coordination is not as high as one might expect in a number of states, given the very similar purposes and clientele of JTPA and JOBS.

The JOBS and JTPA respondents reported similar information about how JOBS coordinates with JTPA. Employment service respondents seemed to have good knowledge of those coordination mechanisms. Many of the vocational education respondents, however, had little knowledge of how JOBS is coordinated with JTPA.

Summary on Interagency Coordination

The evidence with respect to coordination of JOBS with JTPA, the employment service, and vocational education suggests (1) moderately strong agency-to-agency coordination, but limited multiagency coordination; (2) stronger coordination than might be inferred from the data on involvement in planning; and (3) some degree of remoteness of vocational education from the rest of the system.

Governor's Actions to Ensure Coordination

States that were leaders in welfare reform, such as Massachusetts and California, report considerable gubernatorial support and pressure for coordination in the development of those programs. Although the governor or his staff actively encouraged coordination in some states, that gubernatorial involvement was absent in some states and fell off after initial actions in other states. Many respondents could not identify anyone from the governor's office who keeps track of the programs to help the governor fulfill the responsibility to ensure coordination between JOBS and other employment and training programs. Thus, despite impressive initiatives in some instances, the overall level of gubernatorial involvement is limited. In some states, it has been nonexistent.

PICs and Job Availability Information

The Family Support Act requires the welfare agency to use the services of each private industry council (PIC) to identify and provide advice on the types of jobs available or likely to become available in each JTPA service delivery area. Information from the state JOBS programs suggests that this requirement of the law is not being fulfilled. A couple of states assigned this responsibility to other agencies, and several other states report little activity of this type with the PICs. Only two states provided information suggesting that their PICs might be furnishing the job availability information.

Meeting the Deadline for a Statewide Program

Four states report having statewide programs in operation already. One said that it is so involved in getting the current activities operational that it had not given much thought to 1992. Little was reported about coordinating this activity, except for one state that was planning a meeting to coordinate further development. Several expressed concern about their ability to meet participation requirements and financial commitments for a program in all local jurisdictions.

Coordination Mechanisms

States might develop a variety of coordination mechanisms, such as a single state-based poverty measure, a framework for resolving eligibility and other problems, a clearinghouse on employment and training programs, single-purpose application forms, one-stop eligibility determination shops, collocation of programs, two-stop systems, and integrated case management. Evidently, little progress is being made on these fronts, although some individual states report efforts to develop frameworks for resolving eligibility problems, attempts to collocate programs, and discussion of single-purpose application forms.

Effectiveness of Coordination

Respondents were asked how effective the coordination of JOBS with other programs has been in their state. State JOBS administrators report varying degrees of effectiveness for coordination efforts, but most seem happy with developments to date. Some indicate that coordination has been very effective with some agencies but not with others. The responses from the other agencies are mixed. On the whole, the statements from a variety of participants suggest that coordination is working, but is far from perfect. More important, there is disagreement among agencies about how effective it has been. In very few states do the different agencies use similar language to discuss the quality of coordination.

The phrases officials used to describe coordination are real progress, tremendously effective, ineffective, working fairly well in about half of the areas, very effective, mixed, slow improvement, most critical part of program, seven on a scale of ten, better than anticipated, not like it should be, minimally effective, very good, largely superficial. Thus, while coordination is taking place and contributing to the programs, there is room for improvement. This conclusion is consistent with earlier observations about the coordination relationships between and among agencies.

KEYS AND BARRIERS

Respondents were asked to identify the keys or barriers to success or failure in the coordination of JOBS with other employment and training programs, as well as with public assistance programs. When asked to consider these keys or barriers, the twenty-nine officials, representing thirty-two different agencies in eight different states exhibited remarkably different perspectives about particular factors that account for success or failure.[1] Nineteen different items were mentioned by the respondents, of which fourteen were associated with barriers and fifteen were related to success. The respondents not only identified a wide variety of factors, but the factors were given very different rankings for success versus failure.

The most frequently mentioned obstacles to coordination are policy design (27% of changes suggested by managers), state agency behavior (16%), organization-structure (7%), and resources (7%). Among the flaws in national government policy design identified by the state officials were the need to impose or require coordination on all programs, lack of administrative flexibility, the absence of sanctions for duplications or inefficiencies, overemphasis on program rather than product or client service, wrong skills or training required, and faulty policy theory.

State agency behavior poses a second barrier to coordination. Respondents, themselves state officials, deplored agency actions such as turf battles, the welfare department's merely rolling over the previous welfare-to-work program into JOBS, the welfare department's failure to share JOBS funds with other agencies, and ignoring other agencies. Structural problems, such as fragmentation or the termination of a coordination commission, while not frequent problems, were nevertheless seen as quite serious. Financial retrenchment and insufficient facilities were mentioned as making coordination difficult to achieve. Most of the items mentioned have shown up in other studies of barriers to coordination in the employment and training area (Bailis, 1989; Burbridge and Nightingale, 1989; Grubb et al., 1989, 1990; Jennings and White, 1987; Jennings, 1989; Trutko, Bailis, Barnow, and French, 1989).

Respondents made few mentions of other frequently alleged barriers to coordination, such as communication problems, goal conflicts, human relations factors, incentives, operations, processes, and political conflicts. Perhaps the most surprising and interesting finding is that one-sixth of the state agency officials made no mention of barriers to coordination. Quite the contrary, these state officials expressed considerable satisfaction with the high level of coordination already achieved among agencies in their state.

Trutko and his colleagues (1989) also found aspects of policy development, such as eligibility restrictions, restrictions on the use of funds, and others, to be important barriers to the coordination of employment and training programs. Burbridge and Nightingale (1989) included conflicting regulations and reporting requirements among the barriers to coordination they identified. They also identified turf and resource protection as barriers, factors that show up in our interviews.

State officials also identified many different factors that accounted for success in coordination. They most frequently identified interpersonal relationships (17%) and leadership (16%) as keys to success. The respondents noted:

. . . focus on individuals, not on turf or on an administrator's glory. Personalities who can work together, arrive at a common goal.

. . . where we've had success, we've agreed philosophically on how to provide services to public assistance clients.

. . . built-in informal personal relationships where people feel free to telephone.

. . . good plans won't work unless you have people willing to work.

. . . where it has worked, local administrators have seen the merit of making it work.

Leadership as a key to success complements interpersonal relations:

. . . I have personally gone out with (head of human service department) and (head of department of labor) and spoke with local-level people.

. . . desire for success at state government. We have good leadership in the governor's office.

. . . the new governor is a 500-pound gorilla pushing (the human service department) to coordinate.

. . . must have CEOs committed (to coordination), not necessarily the governor, but at least department heads.

The administrators also suggested that coordination could be fostered by certain structural (14%) and operational (9%) changes. Suggestions for structural changes that would lead to successful coordination included consolidated agencies, an active state job training coordinating council, and agreements among local-level players. Operational changes that would encourage coordination included data exchanges among the different agencies, a delivery system run on a performance basis, and the use of interagency contracts. Other factors often cited in other studies as contributing to coordination (e.g., communication, finances, incentives, participation) gained little support from the respondents.

These results were not totally unexpected. After all, the devolution of welfare programs, as well as employment and training programs in the United States, places the burden for coordination on the shoulders of state government officials. In the administrative network of state capitals, it is the human dimension of management (that is, interpersonal relations and leadership) that makes things happen. Conflicts of interest, different constituencies, finances, operational procedures, and structural arrangements are all hurdles to be cleared by agency managers who want to implement their programs. So it should come as no surprise that these public servants see coordination emerging out of efforts to make programs work. It appears that the human relations dimension constitutes a first phase (building trust and exercising leadership) and then necessary operational and structural changes follow.

Other studies have produced similar results, at least with respect to some factors. Jennings and White (1987) found leadership and interpersonal relationships to be central to coordination at the SDA level. Trutko and his colleagues (1989) found leadership and cooperative attitudes to be crucial to the success of coordination, consistent with the emphasis here on leadership and human relations. Burbridge and Nightingale (1989) found leadership to be important, and data reported by Jennings in Chapter 6 of this volume suggest that state administrators consider leadership to be among the most important determinants of coordination success.

NATIONAL CHANGES TO ENHANCE COORDINATION AND EFFECTIVENESS

When asked what the national government could do to enhance coordination and effectiveness of the JOBS program at the state level, the state government managers asked in large numbers for changes in federal legislation or regulations (47% of the requested changes). Among specifically requested changes in policy design were (1) the need to include incentives or rewards for coordination, (2) reduce emphasis on process and allow state administrators more flexibility, (3) make JOBS more consistent with Food Stamps, (4) devise the same eligibility standards for the various programs, (5) put all the programs on a performance basis, (6) assess clients over a longer period of time, and (7) more clearly define the role of various agencies and programs, then restructure the employment and training system so that operations follow role assignment.

Structural changes (16% of changes suggested by managers) also accounted for several remedies the national government should pursue, including the establishment of an OMB-like entity to coordinate and standardize the language among the various programs, the encouragement of state coordinating commissions for human service and employment and training programs, and the centralization of certain procedures, such as initial assessment of clients. Eleven percent of the suggestions offered by state administrators were operational changes that the national government could initiate, especially in regard to the reporting requirements of different programs which affect the forms used by the different agencies and their ability or inability to devise a common electronic data processing system.

One recurring question about organization posed by the respondents was, "If the feds require us (state administrators) to coordinate, why can't the feds coordinate at their level?" Eliminating the lack of coordination at the national level was perceived as one of the most important changes that would foster state-level coordination of JOBS.

According to their answers to our questions, state administrators responsible for coordination of the JOBS program with other public assistance and employment and training programs would encourage the national government to decrease procedural controls, increase the incentives for coordination, and clarify the responsibilities of each agency and its programs to provide service to the individual client. These changes, the state administrators believe, will permit them to develop client-oriented systems that meet the goal of JOBS—to assist public aid recipients to find and hold jobs.

SUMMARY

The major findings from this study can be briefly summarized. States have developed diverse arrangements for delivery of program components. There is some evidence of tension and a failure to use preexisting services, but other evidence of careful intermingling of activities of various programs and providers. In general, JOBS agencies rely upon other agencies to a moderate degree for service delivery, but this varies considerably across the states.

There has been extensive involvement of other agencies in the planning of JOBS, although in three of the eight states that involvement has been largely pro forma or nonexistent. Diverse coordination tools are being used, but variety exists among the states with respect to the extent of coordination. There is some suggestion that the focus is on operational coordination, rather than planning processes.

All state JOBS programs use the employment service to some extent. Coordination with JTPA varies a great deal and some states do not make much use of JTPA. The degree of coordination is not as high as one might expect, given the similar purposes and clientele of the programs.

State JOBS directors perceive coordination to be fairly effective, but the perception in other agencies is quite mixed. Although coordination seems to be working, generally, there clearly is room for improvement. Perhaps most important for the operation of the system, there is disagreement among the agencies about the effectiveness of coordination.

There is considerable diversity in perspectives about what accounts for success or failure. Within this diversity, policy design and state agency behavior are cited most frequently as obstacles to coordination. State officials emphasize interpersonal relations and leadership as keys to coordination success.

If the national government wants to act to enhance state and local coordination, it will have to take different steps to satisfy different state and local officials, since there was little tendency for officials to suggest the same national policy changes. It would help, however, if federal agencies demonstrated greater capacity to coordinate at the national level.

CONCLUSION

Preexisting programs provided a framework for the implementation of JOBS in these states. Those preexisting programs included welfare-to-work experiments and the array of employment and training programs operating under federal legislation. In a number of cases, JTPA had laid a groundwork of communications and interpersonal relations that provided a setting for the development of JOBS activities.

Despite this, more could be done to coordinate JOBS with other employment and training services. Although many states have taken advantage of the diverse resources provided by these programs, some are missing those opportunities. In some states, the JOBS program has started anew in developing coordination processes, failing to draw upon established networks. This is most evident in states where the JOBS plan was developed exclusively by the welfare agency, without active participation by other agencies. It is also evident in the failure to fully exploit the resource base of JTPA and the service delivery areas.

Beyond this, these states are taking halting steps, at best, to develop operational coordination through such tools as single state-based poverty measures, frameworks to resolve eligibility issues, clearinghouses, single-purpose application forms, one-stop shops, and the like. While responses to our interview questions suggested an emphasis on operational coordination rather than processes of coordination, that emphasis has not extended to these measures.

On this score, however, it is likely that the states await leadership by the national government. Common definitions of terms and common eligibility rules are, in many cases, dependent on national rules and regulations. Some operational problems of coordination could be reduced through appropriate changes in national policy. Our interviews suggest that officials in these states perceive federal policy as the major source of barriers to effective coordination. In addition, they can see that coordination is weak at the federal level. If policymakers and administrators in Washington do not coordinate well, how can they expect people in the field at the state and local level to coordinate well? The people in Washington need to set the stage for coordination—both actually and symbolically. Further coordination mandates to state and local officials will do little to create a more effective employment and training system in the absence of changes in national policy and practice.

NOTE

1. In two states the same person administers the employment service and the JTPA program. In one state, the director of vocational education also served as interim director of the JTPA program.

REFERENCES

Bailis, Lawrence N. 1989. *An Assessment of the JTPA Role in State and Local Coordination Activities: Report on the Literature Review*. Washington, D.C.: Employment and Training Administration, U.S. Department of Labor. January.

Burbridge, Lynn C., and Demetra Smith Nightingale. 1989. *Local Coordination of Employment and Training Services to Welfare Recipients*. Washington, D.C.: Urban Institute.

Congressional Quarterly. 1988. "Congress Approves Overhaul of Welfare System," *Congressional Quarterly Weekly Report* (October 8): 2825–831.

———. 1989. "Job Training Act, Under Attack, to Shift Focus to Neediest," *Congressional Quarterly Weekly Report* (April 9): 747–50.

Grubb, W. Norton et al. 1989. *Innovation Versus Turf: Coordination Between Vocational Education and Job Training Partnership Act Programs*. Berkeley: National Center for Research in Vocational Education, University of California. April.

———. 1990. *Order Amidst Complexity: The Status of Coordination Among Vocational Education, Job Training Partnership Act, and Welfare-to-Work Programs*. Berkeley: National Center for Research in Vocational Education, University of California. August.

Jennings, Edward T., Jr. 1989. *Job Training Coordination: Issues and Approaches*. A report prepared for the Missouri Division of Job Development and Training. Columbia: Department of Public Administration, University of Missouri-Columbia. June.

Jennings, Edward T., Jr., and Jay D. White. 1987. *Coordinating Job Development and Training in Missouri*. An issues report from the Missouri Job Training Coordinating Council. Missouri Division of Job Development and Training. December.

Job Training Partnership Act Advisory Committee. 1989. *Working Capital: JTPA Investments for the 90s*. Washington, D.C.: U.S. Department of Labor. October.

King, Christopher T. 1988. *Cross-Cutting Performance Management Issues in Human Resource Programs*. Research Report No. 88–12. Washington, D.C.: National Commission for Employment Policy. August.

Levitan, Sar A., and Frank Gallo. 1988. *A Second Chance: Training for Jobs*. Kalamazoo: W. E. Upjohn Institute for Employment Research.

Rovner, Julie. 1991. "Raising the Curtain on Welfare Reform," *Governing* (January): 19–22.

Trutko, John, Larry Bailis, Burt Barnow, and Stephen French. 1989. *An Assessment of the JTPA Role in State and Local Coordination Activities*, vol. 1. Submitted to the Employment and Training Administration, U.S. Department of Labor. Washington, D.C. December.

Chapter 10

State Efforts to Influence Federal Policy

Dale Krane

> Local officials have to go to Washington, get on their knees, kiss the ring and tug their forelock to all these third-rate bureaucrats.
>
> U.S. Senator Thad Cochran (R-Miss.),
> *Jackson Clarion-Ledger* April 29, 1981: 1-B

> The key to American competitiveness is, as it always has been, a dynamic, innovative, market-driven private sector. The responsibility for achieving it belongs principally to the private sector itself. But the private sector will be successful only through partnership with government at all levels. Some states are well advanced in holding up their end of the bargain.
>
> R. Scott Fosler,
> *The New Economic Role of American States: Strategies in a Competitive World Economy* (1988: 3)

The global challenge to America's economic viability has been accompanied by two important changes in the formulation and implementation of public assistance programs. First, state governments have reinvigorated and expanded their traditional role of support for economic development. Not only are many states aggressively pursuing policies to assist the private sector (e.g., capital formation, promotion of new technologies, business incubators), some states are also actively pursuing work-force policies that have the twin purposes of building a highly skilled labor pool and, at the same time, reducing the number of poor who are outside the growth process. Second, the myth that state governments are mere administrative "branch banks" of the national government has been punctured as has the traditional distinction between public and private sector activities. Most domestic policy in the United States now incorporates a blend of national and state authority, finances, guidelines, and personnel. In addition, public programs increasingly rely on private sector and not-for-profit organizations to develop and deliver public goods and services.

These changes create important opportunities for state governments to influence national government policy as well as impose serious obligations on state governments to be more assertive in the formation of national policy. This chapter focuses on the channels through which state governments may communicate their perspectives on public assistance programs to the federal government. It is not exhaustive and inclusive, rather it is illustrative and suggestive.

STATE INFLUENCE ON NATIONAL POLICY MAKING

The reciprocal nature of American federalism and public-private connections opens many doors and windows through which state governments may exercise influence over national government policy making. Without taking an extended foray into the intellectual quagmire of the various definitions associated with the concept of influence, let it suffice to consider as *influence* any effort to shape the substantive content or the acceptability of a given policy proposal. Three types of state government officials are primarily involved in efforts to influence national policy making: governors and their immediate staff, state legislators, and state administrators, both appointed and civil service managers. In addition, state advisory boards and councils, state congressional delegations, and state "lobbying" organizations must also be considered as essential to state influence in Washington.

Attempts to influence policy making succeed or fail based on the strategic choices made and the commitment of resources to the effort. By selecting different courses of action, state officials can construct appropriate strategies by which to influence national policy making. Strategic choices for the exercise of influence can be classified along four simple dichotomies (see Figure 10.1). For example, state officials may act to influence either the formulation or the implementation of national policy, or both. Second, state officials can concentrate their influence efforts on the substantive content (e.g., goals, appropriations, regulations and standards, responsible agency, formulas, targets) of a policy or on a policy's acceptability, credibility, or legitimacy. Third, state officials can choose to act in their formal capacity within a given governmental institution (e.g., the state legislature), or they may act informally from their position within

Figure 10.1
Strategic Choices in the Exercise of Influence

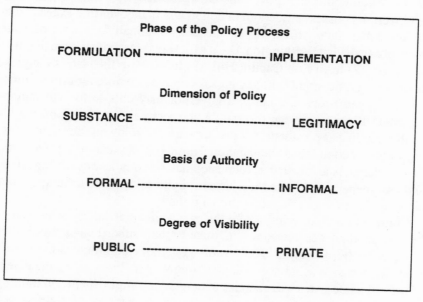

the political system (e.g., member of a particular coalition). Fourth, state officials may opt "to go public" with their efforts to influence, or they may work privately "behind closed doors."

The following subsections briefly discuss and illustrate these several strategic choices that confront state government officials in their attempts to influence the federal government.

Governors

The in-state official with the greatest potential to influence the national government is the state governor. Governors, as the prime source of state-level leadership, hold a pivotal place in the federal system. They can be the most effective voice in communicating their state's policy perspectives and preferences to all parts of the national government. Wright (1988), for example, identifies nine issue areas in which state governors can work to shape national policy. The list includes (1) designation of responsibility for federal programs, (2) approval of grant applications and state plans, (3) supporting or opposing federal legislation and regulations, (4) compliance issues and audits, (5) National Governors' Association (NGA) contacts, (6) contacts with the state's congressional delegation, (7) maintaining Washington offices, (8) organization and location of state-federal relations staff, and (9) contacts with regional groupings of other governors and other intergovernmental agencies.

Governors possess a freedom of action and maneuver that exceeds that of any other state officer. Even the constitutionally weakest of state governors can visit Washington, D.C., to (1) breakfast with the president— if invited, (2) testify on Capitol Hill, (3) lunch with the state's congressional delegation, and (4) hold a press conference before returning home, all on the same day. Similarly, a governor may choose to visit federal regional offices to present the state's perspective about program implementation. Just as presidents adopt a strategy of "going public" with ideas, proposals, or complaints about national policy, so also can state governors. Media channels as diverse as television news and talk shows, magazines and newspaper articles, and the lecture circuit allow state officials, especially governors, to influence national policy.

Contemporary prescriptions for the achievement of quality place a large burden on chief executives to articulate to their subordinates a vision of what is to be achieved. The vision governors communicate to state agencies and to Washington will go a long way in determining the extent of the influence states will exercise over national employment and training policy. By their choice to be active or not in support of state views, governors send important signals to the federal establishment about state priorities. Both individually and collectively, governors possess more authority, more legitimacy, and more respect than any other state official. Governors when reasonably united can be so influential as to stop a popular president's pet project, as demonstrated by the fatal blow the NGA dealt to President Reagan's 1982 New Federalism (swap and turn back) plan (Krane, 1990). Governors ought to concentrate their attention and "lobbying" efforts on the design flaws in federal statutes and regulations. Especially through the NGA, a consensus on the most serious design flaws can be developed and then communicated to the White House, the appropriate executive departments, and to Congress.

State Legislatures

State legislatures may also affect national policy. A legislature can choose to participate or not in federal grant programs by its vote to match funds. Similarly, state legislatures can exercise varying degrees of appropriations control over federal aid. Working with their counterparts in other states, state legislators can adopt uniform state codes (e.g., Uniform Commercial Code, Southern Building Code) and preempt the need for national government action. On the other hand, failure of state legislatures to act has been a major cause of national government action (e.g., clean air and water legislation, welfare programs). State legislatures can also establish in-state think tanks or provide the governor with a policy office, either of which could assist the state in its communications with Washington. State legislatures can enhance their state's capacity to influence national policy making by establishing and maintaining a state liaison office in Washington, D.C. Thirty-two states operate such an office. These Washington offices permit officials of a single state to express their state's particular policy preferences and to maintain close contact with the state's congressional delegation.

Another powerful mechanism for influence over national policy making comes from the state legislature's ability to lead by example. That is, state legislatures can establish innovative policy experiments that in turn attract national attention (e.g., California's Greater Avenues to Independence [GAIN], Florida's Project Independence, and Massachusetts' Employment and Training [ET] program). Equally important, state legislatures must not delay the establishment of necessary procedures and regulations (e.g., client support services) required for the coordination of Job Opportunities and Basic Skills (JOBS) with employment and training programs. Prolonged legislative battles over admittedly sensitive policy concerns can significantly slow progress toward meeting national policy goals. If state legislatures fail to maintain state capacity to serve the economically disadvantaged, the old argument that the states cannot administer national programs will be rekindled. Put another way, state legislatures need to ensure the development of well-functioning JOBS programs in order to keep the federal "wolf" from the door of state discretion.

Open meetings and open records laws have not put an end to politics behind closed doors. Efforts to influence national policy making also occur out of the vision of the general public. Such activities are neither illegal nor unethical; they are just not well-publicized. An unusual example illustrates a rare, covert approach states use to influence national policy. In 1991, reports filtering out of state capitals indicated that state legislators were using the decennial process of redrawing congressional districts as a means of extracting policy promises from their congressional delegations. Although unusual, this example should not surprise anyone familiar with the possibilities of state influence over national policy making.

State Administrative Officials

Programmatic and operational expertise form the foundations for the influence of state administrators in the policy-making process. Elected officials rely on appointed agency managers and career civil servants to develop policy options from which the elected officials may construct public programs (Kingdon, 1984). The single, most powerful method for influence in national policy making that state administrators possess derives from their creativity in problem-solving and their willingness to engage in action across agency boundaries. The history of policy innovation in America is replete with instances where new ways of program administration were invented first at the state level and then incorporated into national policy applied to all the states. The 1988 Job Opportunities and Basic Skills (JOBS) program, which has its roots in programs devised in California, Florida, and Massachusetts, is a recent example of how state action influences national policy.

Two crucial points in the federal policy-making process where state administrators may bring their expertise to bear are the drafting of legislation and the promulgation of rules. Although state administrators do not play a direct part in the drafting of national legislation, they can influence it indirectly. For example, state administrative officers may testify at congressional hearings or they may circulate to federal administrators and congressional staff position papers or research studies commissioned by the state agency. Second, state administrative officials may play an influential role in the writing of federal regulations and rules. The notice and comment process established under the Administrative Procedures Act guarantees access to the rule-making process. Problems with proposed rules and suggested modifications or remedies of proposed rules submitted by state administrators become part of the record on which federal rule writers must base their final drafts.

Functional links between national administrative agencies and state counterpart agencies create a vertical autocracy of program specialists, many of whom share professional training and values. This "picket-fence" federalism within a given policy area (e.g., mental health, child development) provides a channel for state administrators to use their specialized policy knowledge to communicate their state's position to their national colleagues. Telephone conversations and fax mail, for example, form the basis of a type of ex parte communication that can influence federal administrators. Similarly, state administrators can use their professional associations as forums to build a consensus on appropriate changes in national policy design and then lobby Washington for these changes.

State administrative officials also shape national policy through the discretion they exercise in the implementation of federally funded, but state-administered, programs. The devolution of public assistance, employment and training, education, and other national policies creates extensive opportunities for public managers at the state level to shape the impact of national policy. For example, discretion in the selection of program targets results in the now familiar "creaming" criticism of the JTPA program. "Creative accounting" is a well-known art form in administrative circles. Presenting federal program managers with a fait accompli—an action that the feds would be reluctant to overrule—is another commonly practiced skill. The "games" played by state officials in their efforts to shape the impact of national policies have become so well-known that textbooks now include them as a normal item of instruction (for example, see Wright, 1988). The specific gambit or tactic is less important than the existence of the game itself; the fact that national and state administrative officials engage in gamesmanship with each other confirms the reciprocal nature of influence in the intergovernmental policy process.

Also at the state level, administrative officials bear a responsibility to keep chief executives informed about program progress (or its absence). At a minimum, state administrators should ensure that the governor understands the requirements imposed on the chief executive by national legislation. Likewise, state managers can work to keep gubernatorial interest in JOBS alive, particularly as new governors come into office. Especially where obstacles are encountered, state administrators ought to use the governor to give weight to their communications with federal program officials. For example, a governor can visit the federal regional office with principal state managers for the purpose of negotiating items of difference between the state and the national government.

Other avenues of influence for state administrators also parallel those used by state elected officials. Administrators can form advisory groups composed of public and private persons who possess significant political clout. Public managers can engage in public relations and marketing strategies. They can even hold large conferences, invite federal officials, and then educate these federal policymakers about state views on policy. One of the most powerful tools (threats?) for influencing the course of national policy making that state administrators may choose to unleash is their program constituents. Whether from their agency office or through their professional associations or by way of advisory groups, state administrators can quickly signal their constituents about dangers to the benefits distributed through their particular program. Once the alarm goes out, the agency's clientele can send a message to Washington, often with great impact.

State-level program managers may engage in at least two different, relatively private methods of influence. First, state administrators can use insider knowledge in the same way their federal colleagues do by "leaking" information to the governor, to the state's congressional delegation, or to the press. A second, more pervasive influence on national policy making occurs over time when state administrators pursue state preferences, agency agendas, or personal objectives instead of national policy goals. The distortion or displacement of national goals by other goals can lead, as the history of CETA amply demonstrates, to a reaction that can dramatically alter national policy.

State Advisory Councils

One of the least visible (to the general public), but widely used, institutions for bridging the gap between public and private sectors is the advisory board, committee, commission, or council. Both national and state governments create advisory councils in large numbers and in surprisingly diverse policy areas. In 1982, more than 875 advisory boards functioned as part of the national government. State governments are no less timid in the creation of these liaison bodies. The expansion of federal grants and the emergence of the new politics demand for increased citizen participation in government led Congress to require the use of state advisory commissions as part of a state government's structure for the administration of grants. Among the policy areas where one finds state advisory boards are developmental disabilities planning, environmental protection, health care coordination, resource conservation and recovery, and vocational education.

State advisory councils play several important roles in policy formulation and implementation and serve the mutual interests and needs of government and the larger public. For example, "advisory committees are valuable [to the agency] not only because they provide access to information when and where it is needed but also they provide a means for channeling pressure from organized groups" (Schlozman and Tierney, 1986: 334). By bringing the interested parties within the policy-making framework, the policy gains added legitimacy and the administrative tasks become easier. On the other hand, the organized groups gain direct access to the executive branch and, thus, have an enhanced position for educating and influencing policymakers. Perhaps the most important function state advisory councils provide is "a mechanism whereby the solution of public problems can proceed through the voluntary cooperation between the government and those most affected by the policy decisions" (Schlozman and Tierney, 1986: 334).

The Job Training Partnership Act (JTPA) established state job training coordinating councils (SJTCCs) and assigned to the SJTCCs a lengthy list of coordination, planning, review and comment, and reporting functions (see Section 122 of the act). The SJTCCs are an extension of the "conviction that the training system will be most effective if business plays a substantial role in all aspects of local policy making, planning, administration, and program design and operations" (National Commission for Employment Policy, 1987: 41). Working with the governor and appropriate state agencies, the SJTCCs exemplify the public-private partnerships that have become common in the policy process. Consequently, SJTCC members, because they typically represent business, labor, education, community-based organizations, and the general public, have a unique vantage point from which to influence state workfare policy as well as national policy.

Given their access and knowledge, state advisory council members are in a powerful position to educate governors and legislators about changes in national policy that will enhance the coordination and effectiveness of employment and training programs. The experience and expertise of SJTCC members also gives them added credibility with which to educate and energize state congressional delegations about needed changes in workfare programs. Likewise, council members through their own lobbying organizations (e.g., National Alliance of Business or National Association of Private Industry Councils) can influence the president and the Congress.

State Congressional Delegations

State congressional delegations provide state governments with a powerful and continuous source of influence over the actions of the national government because the Constitution guarantees the representation of state interests in the U.S. Congress. No one doubts that individual members of Congress are, first and foremost, delegates from their home state or district. Members of Congress even if they differ by party affiliation or by ideological stance, frequently put these differences aside to work jointly for the achievement of their state's interest (e.g., the battle among the various states for the location of the superconducting Super Collider). Multistate coalitions also form to "bring home the bacon" to a given region of the country, as exemplified by the efforts of the Alabama, Mississippi, and Tennessee delegations to build the Tennessee-Tombigbee Waterway. Simply put, the original constitutional bargain ensures that the states can affect national policy through their direct participation in the legislative process. These representatives from around the country are not national government officials so much as they are ambassadors from the fifty states and the 435 congressional districts. One result is that much national policy is, in reality, state policy in disguise.

In addition to their vote, individual members of Congress may use their institutional prerogatives to foster their state's interests. Seniority confers many privileges. To protect the seniority power of a state's congressional delegation, state officials often work to support (or not openly oppose) congressional incumbents during reelection campaigns. Members of Congress constantly engage in constituency service (casework); for state government officials this service provides access to administrative officers in the national bureaucracy.

State Associations in Washington, D.C.

The increasingly competitive interdependence of national and state governments has spawned a significant growth in Washington-based associations that represent the interests of the states. Governors, other state elected officials, and state administrators transcend their institutional authority and extend their influence over national policy making through membership in these so-called public interest groups. The long list of associations lobbying for state government policy preferences makes it impossible to discuss all of them here, so a few prominent examples will illustrate their importance and utility.

Although formed in 1908, the National Governors' Association (NGA) for most of its history failed to wield much clout at any level. Since 1965, when the word "national" was added to the organization's name, the association has steadily increased its capacity for influence and its concomitant impact. Larry Sabato (1983) notes that "most important of all, the Governors' Association has institutionalized a national-level role for the state chief executives, enabling them to affect federal aid and regulations that directly influence their ability to perform their job well" (175).

Allied with the NGA are other official lobbying associations that represent other state elected officials (e.g., National Conference of State Legislatures, National Association of Attorneys General) and transmit a state-level viewpoint to the national government. The Council of State Governments (headquartered in Lexington, Kentucky) also works closely with the NGA in articulating state concerns to Washington, as well as to a larger audience. Since its establishment by Congress in 1959, the U.S. Advisory Commission on Intergovernmental Relations, as the only continuous organization designed to monitor and make recommendations for the improvement of America's federal system, has worked to promote cooperative intergovernmental management of public programs.

State administrators, like all public administrators, find themselves choosing or being forced to play politics. The belief that administration can be separate from politics died long ago. Just as elected officials form professional associations that represent the interests of their membership, so also do state administrators form these lobbying organizations. The roll call of associations is lengthy and includes examples such as the National Association of State Units on Aging, the National Association of Mental Health Program Directors, and the Conference of State Sanitary Engineers. These organizations provide forums within which professional norms and standards develop, innovations diffuse throughout the country, courses of action by the states or by the federal government are recommended, and even conflicts between members resolved.

ACTION IMPLICATIONS

What lessons can be drawn from this review of mechanisms by which states may influence national policy making, and how do these lessons apply to state government officials, especially governors, responsible for workfare and other welfare reform programs?

Gubernatorial Advantage

Governors must recognize that they occupy a unique and powerful vantage point from which to influence national and state policies for the coordination of public assistance programs. From their position as a linchpin between national and state governments, governors possess a fund of expertise and experience that gives their opinions substantial weight with national officials and opinion leaders. This advantage obliges them to go beyond the expression of complaints about the design and administration of current public assistance and employment and training programs. They bear a responsibility to contribute their positive ideas to the debates over the future course of welfare-to-work programs.

State Administrative Initiatives

Governors and their staffs can work with state administrators to devise innovative approaches to the coordination of public assistance with employment and training programs. Improving the coordination between JOBS, JTPA, and other employment and training programs can overcome many of the national concerns about the shortcomings of public assistance and work-force programs and serve as a foundation for an integrated work-force policy.

Coalition Building

Governors, state legislators, and senior state administrators must remember what Hedrick Smith (1988) pointed out in *The Power Game* about how politics works in Washington: "The coalition game—building coalitions and making coalitions work—is the heart of our system of government" (453). As Scott Fosler put it, state efforts to develop and implement strategies for economic competitiveness have been most successful when "both government and private sector leaders [work] to build consensus and integrate actions among groups in both the public and private sectors and at different levels of government" (Fosler, 1988: 323). At the National Commission for Employment Policy's seminar on "Improving Coordination In Government-Sponsored Public Assistance Programs" held in Washington, D.C., on March 27, 1991, Robert T. Jones, assistant secretary of Labor for employment and training, labeled this joint activity as "making policy together." Jones explained that this is what people really mean by coordination—not just funding, not just daily operations, but sitting down together at the beginning of the process and designing policy together. With no one in charge of coordination, unless interested parties act early in the policy process, only incremental changes can be made once the policy process is fairly far along. Unless the various groups make coordination their legislative priority, Jones noted, not much will change.

Building Acceptance

Governors, state legislators, and state administrators must also act to build a climate for the acceptance of coordinated work-force policies that integrate public assistance and employment and training programs. Coalition building, which often occurs behind closed doors, must be accompanied by a public education campaign that sells the work-force concept to the public, especially to small business. An official who was interviewed about the coordination of employment and training programs observed "happy JTPA bureaucrats have happy small businessmen . . . over a beer, they would say that serving the public assistance client alienates their small business constituents."

Change occurs in national policy in waves; that is, efforts to influence policy require the mobilization of public opinion in favor of change.

Another respondent of the survey who knew this elemental fact about the policy process concluded her remarks by stressing, "the business community doesn't understand the JOBS program, so there needs to be a whole lot better effort to educate the business community on JOBS, especially as a work-force strategy and as a reduction of welfare case loads." Unless private sector interests understand the importance of the JOBS program to state and national economic development, little progress will be made in altering national policies.

CONCLUSION

To conclude, the intergovernmental network through which national policies are formulated and implemented opens many windows of opportunity for the states to influence national policy making. Occasionally, as a nation, we have vacillated over the utility of joint action by public and private leaders. The recent history of domestic policy has been characterized by periods in which government has tried by itself to solve pressing economic or social problems. At other times, the shortcomings of those government-dominant approaches led us to rely solely on private-sector action.

Yet, a number of our nation's most pressing domestic problems fall beyond the scope of private action alone. David Osborne (1988), who studied initial state government responses to the challenges of the global economy for the Harvard Business School, identified two key strategies necessary for economic survival: (1) creating economic growth, especially through the development of a skilled, educated work force and (2) bringing the poor into the growth process because "the developed nations with the most competitive economies are also those with the least social inequality" (12). These new economic realities of our day challenge government officials and business leaders in each state to form partnerships in support of coordinated human investment programs and to build coalitions to carry that message to the national government.

REFERENCES

Fosler, R. Scott. 1988. *The New Economic Role of American States: Strategies in a Competitive World Economy.* New York: Oxford University Press.

Kingdon, John W. 1984. *Agendas, Alternatives, and Public Policies.* Boston, Mass.: Little, Brown and Co.

Krane, Dale. 1990. "Devolution As An Intergovernmental Reform Strategy." In *Strategies for Managing Intergovernmental Policies and Networks*, edited by Robert W. Gage and Myrna P. Mandell, chap. 5. New York: Praeger.

National Commission for Employment Policy. 1987. *The Job Training Partnership Act.* Washington, D.C. September.

Osborne, David. 1988. *Laboratories of Democracy.* Boston, Mass.: Harvard Business School Press.

Sabato, Larry. 1983. *Goodbye to Good-time Charlie: The American Governorship Transformed.* 2d ed. Washington, D.C.: Congressional Quarterly Press.

Schlozman, Kay Lehman, and John T. Tierney. 1986. *Organized Interests and American Democracy.* New York: Harper and Row.

Smith, Hedrick. 1988. *The Power Game: How Washington Works.* New York: Random House.

Wright, Deil S. 1988. *Understanding Intergovernmental Relations.* 3d ed. Pacific Grove, Calif.: Brooks/Cole.

THE LOCAL ROLE

More than the other parts of this book, Part IV draws upon specific examples of service delivery at the local level to formulate ideas about the kinds of coordination that are possible, the factors that hinder efforts at coordination, and the factors that facilitate coordination. Indeed, Part IV provides the necessary stimulation to develop proposals dealing with the following:

- The necessary ingredients for coordinating activities to serve multiple needs of those at risk
- Single-point-of-contact approaches to link various employment and training services
- Policies, procedures, incentives, and organizational arrangements and processes that make possible a system of integrated service delivery
- Organizational arrangements for policy development and delivery
- Processes for building linkages among disparate but related programs to facilitate client service
- The substance of public assistance policy as it bears on coordination issues

Coordination is difficult at the local level for much the same reasons that it is difficult at the national and state levels. The vast array of federally supported programs, with their competing definitions, rules, regulations, and organizational sponsors are augmented by separate state and local initiatives. Organizational diversity is usually even greater at the local level than it is at the national level.

Beyond problems of command and control, local administrators often report difficulties that originate in provisions of federal statutory and regulatory law. For example, as it prepared to implement the Job Opportunities and Basic Skills (JOBS) program, Maryland discovered that its plans to enhance coordination and program effectiveness would not be allowed because of the single-state agency provision written into the legislation. Needed flexibility was absent. As a further example, when twenty-nine state human service managers involved in implementing the JOBS program were interviewed about things the national government could do to enhance coordination and the effectiveness of the JOBS program, they generated ninety-three responses. Among these were forty-five recommendations for policy changes that they believed would make the job easier.

Local public assistance efforts take place in the context of a complex environment, a broad array of human resource development problems, and a diverse mixture of human resource programs. They are shaped by federal and state requirements, local needs, multiple actors, and fragmented authority. Clients and potential clients often find it difficult to identify needed services and to negotiate the system in ways that adequately address their needs. Because of these system shortcomings, numerous efforts have been made to bridge the gap and develop more systematic state and local service delivery efforts. Recent federal coordination requirements only scratch the surface and provide a modest framework, at best, for local efforts to integrate services for at-risk youth and provide one-stop shopping for a broad array of programs.

In Chapter 11, Thomas J. Corbett points out that street-level coordinating activities can occur and succeed only under particular conditions. He says that human resource systems for delivering employment and training services for the disadvantaged and welfare recipients have to address four sets of issues, including (1) a general framework of planning issues, (2) a vertical structure of organizational and management issues, (3) horizontal concerns about the way participants flow through the set of activities and obligations that constitute the new Job Training Partnership Act (JTPA) and Job Opportunities and Basic Skills (JOBS) systems, and (4) the use of data for client-specific decisions. Street-level coordination activities and service delivery depend on how the issues in each of these domains are resolved.

Corbett suggests a set of conditions that foster successful coordination, including (1) a compelling issue providing impetus for change, (2) agenda-driven efforts focused on client needs, (3) continuity of political leadership, (4) a willingness to experiment and evaluate, and (5) merit, as perceived at the local level.

The other chapters in Part IV deal with specific examples of efforts to coordinate and improve service delivery in a variety of settings with diverse clientele. They deal with employment and training, families at risk, youth at risk, and the JOBS program.

David Farley and Barbara King Misechok discuss Pittsburgh's Single Point of Contact program in Chapter 12, indicating how a state initiative provides the stimulus for local action. They discuss the operation of a program designed to make it easier for welfare clients to receive employment and training services by reducing the need for them to shuttle between various points of service. They then indicate some possibilities for such aggregation of services and some obstacles that need to be overcome to make it work.

In Chapter 13, Linda A. Harris discusses one of the most extensive one-stop shopping efforts in America, the Family Development Center of Lafayette Court, a high-rise public housing development in Baltimore. The center brings together in one facility a wide array of educational, health, employment, child care, and family intervention services. These multiple services are made available in an integrated manner by drawing upon the resources of eleven agencies that provide services, personnel, funding, or logistical support.

Several factors have contributed to the success of the Family Development Center. These include leadership, an articulated vision, accessible funding streams, an open and inclusive planning process, and a strong lead entity. The original planning was facilitated by an organizational structure in which the Housing Authority, the JTPA system, and Community Development Block Grants were all under the jurisdiction of one commissioner.

In Chapter 14, Kathy R. Thornburg points out that youth at risk face multiple threats to their well-being and development, including the prospect of personal and social failure, antisocial behavior, and long-term dependence. This can be avoided if action is taken to address their needs and reduce the risks they face while increasing their potential for personally, socially, and economically productive lives. The key to accomplishing this, according to Thornburg, is integrated community action to reduce risk factors and increase protective factors.

Thornburg discusses a Missouri experiment in community program development to improve the chances for at-risk youth. Demonstration communities work cooperatively with staff funded by a foundation grant, university personnel, and state agency personnel to create collaborative programs. Program development depends on community and youth boards with broad representation. Various coordination activities have been undertaken and a variety of new programs have been initiated. Even communities that were not selected to participate in the project have used their proposals to develop and implement programs.

In Chapter 15, Edward T. Jennings, Jr. and Dale Krane analyze the implementation and coordination of the JOBS program at the local level. Based upon documentary information and a series of site visits to interview program administrators and service delivery personnel, this original research describes and analyzes the arrangements used in the delivery of JOBS, with a special focus on coordination concerns, in an analysis of various aspects of program management. They identify and analyze specific coordination mechanisms and evaluate the effectiveness of coordination.

Chapter 11

Strategies for Coordination at the Local Level

Thomas J. Corbett

Program coordination, according to one apocryphal definition, is "an unconventional act between nonconsenting adults." In other words, it is easier said than done. This chapter is designed to get us to think about some of the issues and challenges related to securing coordination at the operational level. It examines actual state- and local-level coordination projects, using those experiences to identify salient issues and draw general lessons.

Coordination is a difficult concept to discuss, partly because it lacks definition. What is coordination? Why should we care about it? Would we recognize it if we saw it? It is one of those valued ends or sacred cows that remains frustratingly illusive. Despite this, achieving coordinated program structures and integrated functional systems is increasingly critical as more is demanded from a public-private partnership that increasingly must make do with less.

EXAMPLES OF COORDINATION

Tackling slippery policy problems might best be done by looking at some ongoing initiatives. Many examples of what appear to be exemplary coordination efforts are available, and those selected here are somewhat arbitrary. They range from state-level to neighborhood-specific undertakings.

State Examples: New Hampshire and Wisconsin

In 1987, at the governor's insistence, the state of New Hampshire undertook an employment training and welfare coordination project titled "Under One Roof" (New Hampshire, n.d.). The intent of the project was to achieve fiscal efficiencies and enhance program effectiveness by coordinating the functions of several state agencies: the welfare functions of the Department of Health and Human Services; the human capital enhancement functions subsumed under the Job Training Partnership Act (JTPA), as carried out by the state job training coordinating council; the labor-market linkage functions performed by the Job Service under the auspices of the Department of Economic Security; and (to a lesser extent) some functions located in the Department of Education.

The governor presumably anticipated the passage of the Job Opportunities and Basic Skills (JOBS) legislation under the 1988 Family Support Act (FSA) and sensed a fiscal window of opportunity given the good economic times in New England. He pushed a coordination agenda among these diverse agencies that resulted in the following systems changes: (1) the physical collocation of many key staff; (2) the development of common definitions and forms (where feasible); (3) a common interagency approach to orientation and assessment; (4) an interagency referral matrix (or grid) to clarify where a client should go within the system; (5) upgraded methods for keeping track of clients; (6) a system for developing common employment development plans (EDP) across programs; and (7) development of interagency implementation teams.

Wisconsin has a strong tradition of local control. For example, many welfare functions continue to be administered at the county level. New programs often are piloted on a volunteer basis and then allowed to "sell" themselves. In 1987, enabling legislation was passed to establish a limited number of Wisconsin Interagency Job Center Network Projects (Job Centers). Conceptualizing and implementing these centers required planning cooperation among the Department of Industry, Labor, and Human Relations (JTPA and Job Service), the Department of Health and Social Services (welfare and JOBS), the Department of Public Instruction (education), and the Board of Vocational, Technical, and Adult Education. The original four pilots have grown to about a dozen over the past several years. Among the coordination innovations to be implemented through these pilots are the physical collocation of staff from several agencies; a combined intake for the Job Service, JTPA, and some JOBS program activities; increased sharing of program information and client data; and movement toward common definitions, strategies, and marketing.

The most dramatic forms of physical, structural, and functional integration are likely to take place at the local level and are likely to originate with local individuals who sign on to the long and frustrating task of doing things differently. Kenosha County, Wisconsin, was a pilot site for a state work-welfare initiative called the Work Experience and Job Training (WEJT) program passed in 1986—a state-developed forerunner of the JOBS program. As originally developed, the Kenosha model appeared to bring all the major local actors (e.g., welfare office, the private industry council [PIC], the Job Service, the technical college, and so forth) together in an effort to improve the skill levels and labor-market participation of welfare recipients in the county.

What looked good on paper, however, was a disaster in practice. The organizations were linked in little more than name only. There were no agreed-upon goals, no shared perspective or language, and no methods for keeping track of what was happening to clients. Program operations suffered from massive confusion, excessive client loss to the system, and interagency scapegoating. In early 1987, the county welfare office, which had nominal responsibility for the program, shut down operations and slowly began to assemble a functionally integrated program. Four years later, it succeeded in assembling a model program that has attracted the attention of the federal Department of Health and Human Services, the Manpower Demonstration Research Corporation (MDRC), and private foundations.

The intent of the Kenosha model is to create a fully integrated and consolidated public welfare system that will forge the connection between receiving public assistance and preparing for work-based self-sufficiency in the client's mind. This means getting the clients involved in an employment and training regimen quickly and meaningfully, and keeping them involved in a substantive fashion that uses the skills and expertise available from various service providers. Partly, this is accomplished by collocating the income maintenance, JOBS case management, key Job Service functions, and several critical providers of service under a single roof to unify case management. Physical proximity is only one dimension of the innovation.

The system works as follows: Public assistance applicant data are entered into a computer system, and eligibility and benefits for all major assistance programs are calculated automatically. A JOBS case manager (who works with the economic support or welfare specialist) immediately does the JOBS intake, and the applicant undergoes an interagency-sponsored orientation by the end of the first week. The participant than begins a twenty-two- to twenty-three-week regimen, beginning with motivational classes, job-search skill training, vocational explorations, and in-depth assessments. Individualized employment development plans are prepared. Teams composed of an economic support specialist, two JOBS case managers, and a Job Service specialist work out of the same workstations. They share common telephone lines, are cross-trained to the extent possible, and do case management in an integrated manner. An automated case management system developed around an event history conceptual framework—a point-in-process (PIP) rather than a point-in-time (PIT) notion—facilitates ongoing client tracking. On-site child care, training rooms, and other services solidify the status of this innovation as a one-stop service center.

However, the model is incomplete. In time, child support personnel, additional basic education services, additional Job Service personnel, and selected PIC activities will be added. Although much remains to be done, it is already known that participation rates far exceed what is required under the JOBS program, and outcomes are encouraging. Welfare caseloads dropped by some 20 percent after peaking in 1986, despite the closing of the area's major employer (Chrysler Corporation). Moreover, more than 80 percent of new welfare entrants in Kenosha exit (at least temporarily) within the first thirty months (see Corbett and Wiseman, 1991).

Responding to complex social problems increasingly is seen both as a local responsibility and as a challenge to local ingenuity. Most agree that the era of "solutions from the center" is over. The mega-plans for federally initiated reforms of the 1970s, such as the Family Assistance Plan and the Program for Better Jobs and Income, are unlikely to be replicated. Equally apparent is that the locus of effective control over and responsibility for social programs is devolving from Washington to state and local governments. Moreover, the devolution of policy and program responsibility from the center has not been accompanied by a corresponding shift in resources. The proportion of state and local revenues from federal grants-in-aid dropped from 25.3 percent to 17.2 percent between 1978 and 1988 (U.S. Conference of Mayors, 1991). Finally, local governments confront their new responsibilities encumbered by the legacy of past policies and institutional arrangements. By some estimates, there were some 75 different programs (costing $176 billion in 1988) directed at the low-income population (National Commission for Employment Policy, 1991). Any local efforts to initiate a coordinated response must operate within this complex programmatic and organizational landscape.

This devolution of program and policy responsibility is not without some remaining controversy—namely, which levels of government should be responsible for what problems and how should responsibility be allocated between the public and private sectors. The virtual explosion of local innovation and experimentation in recent years affords some clues as to how such jurisdictional disputes might be sorted out. Production-type activities (e.g., the issuance of checks in entitlement programs) can be done at higher levels of government quite efficiently. Craft-type activities, such as getting involved in the "people changing" business for the severely disadvantaged (e.g., at-risk youth or chronic welfare dependents), demand levels of program coordination and institutional collaboration that are difficult to achieve at the federal, state, and even the county level of government. Typically, the technologies required are complex, intensive, and must be sustained over time—characteristics that are best realized when the geographical scope of the intervention is limited. Let us briefly look at two typical street-level coordination efforts.

Local Examples: Milwaukee and San Diego

The Milwaukee-based Neighborhood and Family Initiative (the "Initiative") is a community building project funded by the Urban Poverty Program of the Ford Foundation (Milwaukee Foundation, 1991). The project focuses on one central city neighborhood known as Harambee, which is a Swahili word meaning "pull together-come together." This neighborhood is plagued by a disproportionate number of unemployed, unhealthy, and poorly educated residents who live in deteriorated housing and have limited access to services and resources.

One guiding principle of the Initiative is that neighborhood residents actively participate in both the planning and implementation of the project. A second principle challenges the Initiative to harness the interrelationships among social, physical, and economic development strategies. To effectuate these principles, the project has established a nineteen-member collaborative (forum for planning and decision making) and, through a structured strategic planning process, identified three strategic directions: to facilitate educational, training, and career opportunities for Harambee residents to ensure meaningful employment; to assist residents to gain access to resources, including money, real estate, leadership development, and decision makers; and to assure access to facilities to provide for health needs, both mental and physical. Ultimately, the Harambee Initiative will provide several strategic points of intervention, or programs, that will be interdependent and interactive (i.e., job development, health care, revolving loan fund, housing collaborative, community network forum, and leadership development). Participants who enter the Initiative at one strategic point will have immediate access to other intervention programs.

The San Diego New Beginnings is a comprehensive project designed to change the way that social services are delivered to clients. Patterned after the New Futures initiative sponsored by the Annie E. Casey Foundation, the goals are to (1) integrate and coordinate services, (2) reduce duplication, and (3) ensure that families get the services they need. The program focuses on elementary school-aged children and their families living in the Hamilton elementary school area, a severely distressed neighborhood.

New Beginnings is an interagency collaborative project involving the city of San Diego, the County of San Diego, the San Diego Unified School District, the San Diego Community College, and the San Diego Housing Commission. Project staff provide a broad spectrum of social services, both directly and through referrals. Substantively, the services are in four categories: social service and counseling, health care, education, and community services and improvements. The ultimate benefits should extend beyond the clients and contribute to society's understanding of how to deliver intensive, integrated services to multiproblem families. Consequently, the larger purposes are as follows: to develop an integrated services approach based on a shared philosophy and a collaborative leadership structure; to develop a one-stop service center to provide multiple levels of support to troubled children and families; to develop a cross-agency training institute that can build commitment to the shared philosophy and enhance technical skills; and to develop an information management system that facilitates information sharing, referral and feedback, outcome monitoring, and evaluation.

All of the critical features of successful street-level coordination efforts are not fully understood. As the number and diversity of coordination initiatives increase, however, additional knowledge accumulates about which program features must receive careful consideration. Reviews of ongoing pilot initiatives indicate that those features where critical variation occurs include the composition of the target group, service scope, service intensity, delivery system features, service location, service-provider participation and sponsorship, level of commitment, and parental and community participation (Reisner et al., 1991).

In Chapter 6, Edward Jennings provides a convenient typology and summary of coordination tools. The tools are there and, as discussed elsewhere, examples of their successful application can be found, particularly at the local level.

ISSUES REQUIRING COORDINATION

The discussion above takes us into the "black box" of coordination efforts—what does it really take to make it work? No single set of guidelines or strategies will suffice. Some generic considerations do, however, merit discussion.

One way to look into the black box is to examine (by way of example) employment and training programs for the economically disadvantaged and welfare dependent as a system with certain common properties. These properties can be organized into four categories: general framework (planning) issues, vertical (structural/management) issues, the horizontal (process or systems flow) issues, and data management issues.

Framework Issues

Framework issues involve developing plans that determine who gets what, when, where, and how on an aggregate and not a client-specific basis. The development of collaborative planning teams composed of representatives of the relevant agencies is important here. These teams can be advisory only, temporary work groups, or standing work groups. They may exist under executive or legislative mandate or grow out of mutually agreed upon agendas and good working relationships. Whatever their structure, they generally must deal with some or all of the following: (1) common planning and funding cycles; (2) common service delivery areas; (3) common planning guidelines and procedures; (4) common program objectives, target group priorities, and other issues of systems mission; (5) common language and definitions (shared perspective); and (6) common standards for and ways of measuring success.

Vertical Issues

Vertical concerns involve key structural and management issues. They involve organizational concerns—ways to bring the different agencies together by administrative agreement or through physical proximity. Vertical issues deal mostly with what happens after the framework is established—ongoing management designed to ensure that the agreed upon coordination mechanisms are not undone in the implementation phase. This might include the formation of local coordination planning groups and the development of local coordination plans or capacities to monitor whether the intent to coordinate is being realized. It might include jointly planned training opportunities for state and local staffs on collaborative planning and program coordination. Ongoing structural arrangements and management processes that facilitate coordination occur on at least three levels: the strategic level, where basic framework issues continue to be resolved; the operations level, where day-to-day management problems and conflicts are identified and resolved; and the case level, where client-flow decisions are made and managed.

Horizontal Issues

Horizontal concerns deal with the way system participants might actually see the system—the way that participants flow through the sequence of activities and obligations that constitute new and emerging systems. A few key points are discussed below.

An initial gatekeeping problem concerns who gets in the system and how they enter. A variety of one-stop service strategies exist for looking at potential participants, identifying who needs or is eligible for help, and efficiently getting them into the system. Interagency intake teams, automated expert systems to aid intake, fully cross-trained or commingled staff, and jointly marketed programs deal with this concern. Single application forms and one-time collection of data are critical.

Assessment-allocation is a process of determining how the system can help the participant and getting the individual down the right path in multitrack systems. Choosing assessment and testing tools, deciding who uses them, and determining how to coordinate their use are key issues here. A shared vision about what programs are to accomplish, development of a common language, and compromise across varying institutional philosophies are essential.

Service delivery-case management is a process where all local network agencies deliver their respective technologies and share a plan for, track, and exchange data on the clients they have in common. A local system's interagency case-management methodology largely defines the extent to which the local system is coordinated.

Labor market linkage issues involve, among other things, coordinating job development efforts and sharing labor market information. Streamlining the number of staff from various agencies that make contact with employers to learn of job openings and offer employer incentives to hire participants requires a high level of trust among various agencies but has significant payback.

Data-Management Issues

The use of data and the making of client-specific decisions are at the core of all coordination efforts. Automated technologies offer the best hope of creating seamless interagency service networks. The common collection and storage of identical data elements (where feasible) are important. Access to manual or automated data files must exist across agencies. This may come down to where terminals are located and who has access. Automated systems must have advanced participant-tracking and case-management capabilities or software based on the point-in-process concept discussed earlier.

COORDINATION NEEDS AT THE OPERATIONAL LEVEL

State, county, and (perhaps more frequently) local initiatives are likely to constitute the driving force behind social policy change for the next decade. It is imperative that a systematic and inclusive investigation of state-county-local innovations in program coordination be done in order to derive valuable lessons. In Chapter 6 of this book, Jennings has made some initial steps in that direction. While there is still a long way to go, some aspects of what is involved in program coordination at the operational level are understood.

On a simple level, we can draw some rather transparent lessons from the examples reviewed earlier. The New Hampshire experience suggests that support from the top can be important. It is not clear that the changes would have taken place in the absence of a strong gubernatorial mandate. The Wisconsin experience credibly supports the usefulness of pilot efforts to work out initial problems and allow various models to sell themselves. Kenosha tells us at least a couple of things. First, coordination, when taken seriously, truly is a multidimensional process that involves structural, administrative, communication, technical, and other forms of change. Second, the process is never quite finished. The neighborhood-level collaborative efforts in Milwaukee and San Diego afford additional insights. One key lesson is that the probability of success for ambitious and comprehensive collaborative efforts may well depend on the selection of an appropriate scale on which to focus.

Looking more deeply, these and other coordination efforts offer further lessons.

- *Coordination is more plausible if there is serious high-level and external support.* Coordination is abetted if key actors (e.g., governor or legislative leadership) having some control over the relevant institutions make this issue part of their personal agenda.
- *Coordination is more likely if personal and institutional philosophies and agendas are made explicit and conscious compromise is achieved.* Typically, there are winners and losers in the coordina-

tion game, and it is easier to work out consensus when the stakes and stakeholders are known.

- *Substantive, as opposed to transparent, coordination takes commitment, tenacity, and energy.* The New Hampshire effort required weekly interagency meetings for more than two years before things fell into place. It took several meetings simply to arrive at a consensus on the term "placement." The Wisconsin projects have been under way four years and remain incomplete.

- *Personalities and interpersonal relationships are important.* Institutional networks have both formal and informal patterns of influence, emanating from position and from technical expertise, institutional memory, long-standing personal relationships, or personal charisma. People who trust one another because they have worked together and respect one another can do things that cannot be facilitated through administrative procedures or joint planning projects.

- *Substantive change is more likely to succeed if it starts small, if it uses pilots as real pilots* (i.e., opportunities to learn) *and if sufficient time is allowed to resolve problems.* The pilot concept assumes early mistakes and institutional resistance, including post-adoption sabotage during the implementation stage. It provides opportunity to work through these difficulties.

- *Substantive change is more likely if coordination models are built from the ground up with a lot of local input* (e.g., the Harambee neighborhood strategic planning group, the Kenosha effort, or the New Hampshire implementation teams) within the context of a supportive environment. Those institutional actors most affected by the changes have to sign on and make the changes their own.

- *Coordination efforts are more likely to be meaningful if an explicit effort is made to deal with all facets of the coordination challenge*: structural, process, technical, communications and training, management, philosophical, fiscal, and so forth.

CLOSING THE LOOP

This chapter has focused largely on coordination and collaborative efforts at the local level of government. It is axiomatic, however, that what happens at each level of government influences all other levels. Federal and state initiatives to enhance coordination at the county or subcounty levels effectively can be thwarted if local officials and program operatives do not sign on to the effort. Likewise, locally sponsored initiatives can be undermined by rigid program regulations and funding mechanisms handed down from above.

Clearly, the federal government is sensitive to the need for coordination. Virtually every major piece of recent legislation dealing with disadvantaged individuals contains substantive coordination requirements: The Carl D. Perkins Vocational and Applied Technology Act of 1990; Family Support Act (PL 100–485); Title II Job Opportunities and Basic Skills training program; Adult Education Act (PL 100–297); Job Training Partnership Act (PL 97–300).

A common mechanism used at the federal level to address the issue of coordination is to require that states applying for monies under grant programs, such as those administered under the Adult Education Act and the Vocational Education Act, describe in their state plans how relevant agencies will work together. Other commonly used mechanisms are administrative actions, such as the 1989 interagency agreement among several federal departments to provide joint technical assistance to states and localities to help them improve their JOBS program; reorganization at the legislative and executive levels to eliminate overlap and duplication; and coordination from the top, such as the creation in 1987 of the White House Low Income Opportunity Board to help facilitate and expedite the process by which states could secure waivers of federal regulations in order to experiment and innovate on the local level.

Nearly everyone agrees that coordination is a desirable goal. Agency representatives seldom refuse to collaborate in a public fashion. How the complex issues of coordination are defined and dealt with operationally determines success or failure. Lederer (1991) makes two critical points about coordination:

- All efforts to coordinate do not come free, but have costs that can be measured in additional planning and program development time, additional paperwork and other implementation costs.
- While there are a number of ways to conceptualize and measure the benefits of coordination, the perspective of the client should not be overlooked. Coordination efforts that primarily benefit program staff legitimately can be analyzed in terms of the time freed up to provide additional services to clients (or additional clients served) or increased efficiency in providing client services.

Higher levels of government can make the process easier by reducing incompatible regulations across categorical programs, rationalizing program oversight responsibilities, and generally granting more latitude to those who actually operate programs. They cannot, however, prescribe or mandate coordination. Collaborative planning committees, memoranda of understandings, and interagency agreements do not prove that coordination is taking place. It takes place when clients actually experience something different and, hopefully, more positive.

ACTION RECOMMENDATIONS

The best hope for substantive change appears to lie at the local level, but the process of change remains slow and uncertain. It remains hampered by restrictions, some defensible and some not, imposed by the federal government. And the long-term prospects for a rational outcome from the energy that has been unleashed are not certain. The "thousand points of light" are just as likely to blind us as to illuminate our way out of the darkness.

The impetus for change must emanate from a compelling issue. Coordination will not happen because it is rational, but rather because we cannot afford to do otherwise. Focusing on the plight of the next generation—our children—can rally disparate forces because it is both a compassionate thing to do and in our self-interest.

Change is more likely if it is agenda-driven. Tell people they should work together and you will get committees and memoranda of understandings, most of which will be insubstantial. Tell them you are no longer going to help poor kids through welfare-type programs and you are likely to spur serious efforts to develop new relations and methods of operation.

There has to be continuity of policy leadership. Substantive change takes a long time, certainly longer than the ordinary political frame of reference. A well-articulated vision or philosophy must be set out and mechanisms set in place to ensure that work toward that vision continues as individual actors change.

Change must be accorded the respect it deserves. Anything worth doing will take time. Managers and policymakers have to be willing to experiment and evaluate. They should not oversell or hide mistakes. They should not expect to get it right the first time. After all, it took decades to create the current mess.

Merit, not rhetoric, will ultimately sell change. Decision makers cannot prescribe rationality from above. People at the local level must sign on and invest in the endeavor. If it's worth doing, it will sell itself. In short, it is plausible that the best hope for substantive change is to try the "drop the bomb on a workable scale" strategy. Take a radical proposition and try it on a truly pilot basis. Give it time and share the credit. Keep an eye on where you want to be and develop structural mechanisms for getting there.

There is no single road to the goal of program coordination. Each situation presents its own circumstances, challenges, and personalities. Consequently, each coordinator must think through how he or she approaches the challenge of achieving greater program integration in each idiosyncratic situation.

REFERENCES

Anon. n.d. *Employment Training and Welfare Initiative: Under One Roof.* New Hampshire.

Corbett, Thomas, and Michael Wiseman. 1991. "Doing Jobs." A report prepared for the Kenosha County Department of Social Services. Wisconsin.

Lederer, John. 1991. *Measuring the Effectiveness of Coordination in Readjustment and Retraining Programs for Dislocated Workers.* Washington D.C.: National Governors' Association.

Milwaukee Foundation. 1991. "Neighborhood and Family Initiative: A Community Building Project for the Harambee Community." A proposal submitted to the Ford Foundation. March.

National Commission for Employment Policy. 1991. "Background Paper on Federal Public Assistance Programs: Coordination and Eligibility Issues." Washington, D.C. February 20.

Reisner, Elizabeth R. et al. 1991. *Service Integration for At-Risk Children.* Washington D.C.: Policy Studies Associates. February.

U.S. Conference of Mayors. 1991. *Human Resource Investment Policy: A Challenge to Mayors.* Washington, D.C.: Employment and Training Council. January.

Chapter 12

JOBS and JTPA: Single Point of Contact in Pennsylvania

David Farley and Barbara King Misechok

Increased federal emphasis on vocational interventions with targeted welfare populations spurred the passage of the Family Support Act of 1988. The Job Opportunities and Basic Skills (JOBS) portion of the Family Support Act requires states to offer educational and vocational skills training to certain eligible groups of welfare recipients. The welfare-to-work demonstration projects that preceded the Family Support Act generated considerable information about the difficulty of effectively delivering services to clients. Two central problems are to (1) tie together the many services a client might need, managing the transition among services, and (2) create service delivery systems that emphasize service outcomes rather than service processes.

Collocation of services and case management provides ways to address the problem of integrating services. Collocation brings together the personnel from two or more organizations that provide services required by public service clients. It attempts to make it easier for clients to access services by providing one-stop shopping for multiple services and facilitating coordination of services among providers. Case management involves assignment of a case manager to each client. That case manager is responsible for overseeing the delivery of multiple services to a client, even when those services are offered by several different providers. The case manager tracks the progress of the client, makes sure that the appropriate mix of services is provided, and addresses problems in the coordination of services. Thus, case management can be a powerful aid to the coordination of services in welfare-to-work programs.

Although it is important that services be delivered in an effective, efficient manner that takes into account the multiple needs of clients, it is also important that those services accomplish the goals and objectives of welfare reform. In particular, they should lead to enhanced functional capacity of clients and placement in jobs that permit independence and self-support.

This chapter addresses these two central problems by examining (1) the Single Point of Contact (SPOC) program in Pittsburgh, Pennsylvania, and (2) the role that service delivery areas (SDAs), developed under the Job Training Partnership Act (JTPA), can play in delivering services in a performance-based management system. After describing SPOC and its role as a method of coordinating service delivery in the welfare-to-work program, this chapter examines several issues related to service delivery and the role of JTPA service delivery areas.

PENNSYLVANIA'S JOINT JOBS INITIATIVE AND SINGLE POINT OF CONTACT

In late 1987, officials of the Pennsylvania Departments of Public Welfare and Labor and Industry merged portions of JTPA funds with state and federal welfare funds to create the Single Point of Contact demonstration project. With the active involvement of the Pennsylvania Service Delivery Area Association (PSDAA), SPOC projects started in eleven JTPA jurisdictions. The SPOC demonstrations targeted welfare clients who volunteered through County Assistance Offices (CAOs) to participate. An expanded menu of supportive services, case management, and extended medical benefits was an important feature of the demonstration project, along with basic skills and vocational training. Staff of the agencies represented on a Local Management Committee (SDA, CAO, Job Service) were stationed at the local welfare office, which became the "Single Point of Contact." Services and access to services were coordinated and available at the SPOC site to the extent practical. The SPOC demonstration succeeded well enough that Pennsylvania extended SPOC to all twenty-eight SDAs, covering all the counties.

Implementing the JOBS portion of the Family Support Act in Pennsylvania was made easier by the experience with SPOC, and the SDAs became the delivery system for a majority of JOBS activity. Complementary activity is still part of the function of the employment and training program workers in County Assistance Offices. Local Management Committees coordinate local policy and program activity so that duplication of effort can be minimized.

SPOC has evolved with the advent of the Family Support Act to standardize support services, tighten the targeting of subpopulations of welfare recipients, and introduce performance standards similar to those in JTPA. In accord with provisions of the JOBS legislation, the SDAs must target the following eligible clients to comprise 80 percent of all individuals served: (1) clients on Aid to Families with Dependent Children (AFDC) at least thirty-six of the preceding sixty months; (2) AFDC custodial parents under the age of twenty-four who are not enrolled in and have not completed high school; (3) AFDC custodial parents under the age of twenty-four with little or no work experience; and (4) AFDC parents whose youngest child is within two years of ineligibility for welfare coverage because of age.

An additional 20 percent of clients may be served from among welfare recipients who do not fall into one of the above categories. Because Pennsylvania chose to fund existing employment and training program activities with JOBS money without also imposing any targeting requirements on that program, it had to severely restrict the groups that SDAs could serve in their SPOC projects in order to ensure that the state would meet the federal targeting requirements for JOBS.

Other parts of Pennsylvania's Joint Jobs Initiative serve special groups or explore various approaches to training welfare populations for employment. Two major projects are Transitionally Needy and Job Link.

Transitionally Needy is a competitively awarded set of contracts to train individuals who are cash-assistance grantees under Act 75 in Pennsylvania, which imposes a calendar cutoff date for eligibility to receive general assistance. Although a few SDAs have such contracts, most do not, and these projects operate through community-based organizations and local educational agencies.

Job Link is a joint project with the Pennsylvania Department of Commerce to use state funds for training in specific occupations. SDAs are involved in the planning of Job Link activities and may refer trainees to various openings. Some JOBS money is used to pay local high technology councils to coordinate Job Link in up to nine economic development planning regions in the state, and the state funds (Customized Job Training) are restricted by law for use in local educational agencies.

PITTSBURGH SPOC

The Pittsburgh SPOC Local Management Committee (LMC) consists of the executive director of the Allegheny County Assistance Office, the Pittsburgh regional director of the Pennsylvania Job Service office, the manager of the Pittsburgh Partnership (the local SDA), the regional director of the Pennsylvania Office of Vocational Rehabilitation, and an education representative. The LMC uses consensual processes to cooperatively manage the program. If a consensus cannot be reached by the LMC, issues may be referred to the Commonwealth of Pennsylvania's Joint Jobs Initiative Task Force for assistance in resolving them. Comprised of representatives of the state Departments of Labor and Industry, Public Welfare, Education, and Commerce, the task force provides oversight and policy direction for the New Directions initiatives, including SPOC. The task force organization parallels a cabinet committee created by the governor to coordinate policy for economic development and human resources across a broad array of federal and state programs.

The LMC solicits input from the direct service teams to foster cooperation in solving technical and policy difficulties in SPOC operations. In turn, direct service teams refer questions to the designated representatives on the LMC.

The direct service team is located at the SPOC site. It consists of individuals who work directly with the client to develop the program of services. It includes the SDA intake specialist, the Allegheny County Assistance Office case coordinator, the general case manager, and the job service specialist. This team makes sure the individual is eligible, gets enrolled, and is tracked through the program.

The Allegheny County Assistance Office is responsible for recruitment and is assisted by the Pittsburgh Partnership. Special recruitment methods have been developed and implemented to reach the target population. Those methods include targeted print and electronic media advertising, neighborhood recruitment by SDA staff and SPOC subcontractors, and specialized referral networks with agencies serving the SPOC population.

Case Management and Assessment

At each phase of the participant's activities, one person is identified as having primary responsibility for the participant's case management during that activity. Participants are aware at all times of who the primary case managers are as they progress through the system. Client-to-case manager ratios do not exceed fifty to one.

Coordinating the participant's movement through the employability development plan (EDP) phases is the general case manager. The general case manager is a part of the direct service team and is involved in case management at each part of the process. The Pittsburgh Partnership subcontracts with a local agency to provide these general case managers. These SPOC case managers provide participant assistance and advocacy, beginning with the first client intake meeting and assessment and continuing through training, job search, placement, and the follow-up period. One hundred percent of their time is devoted to case management. These general case managers complement the primary case managers and help achieve continuity of services for participants so that the effects of training and job placement can be maximized.

The role of the general case manager is critical during the implementation of the EDP to ensure smooth transitions for the participant. As primary case managers change, the participant knows that additional support is available at all times from the general case manager. Thus, there is general case management to provide continuity and tie things together combined with primary case management for particular activities.

Allegheny County Assistance Office staff are responsible for case management during orientation, which describes the SPOC program. Applicants who are interested in enrolling in SPOC are then assessed by the SDA subcontractor, with Pittsburgh Partnership staff assuming primary case management responsibility during this phase.

Each applicant then works with a direct service team to develop an employability development plan. The EDP outlines the applicant's employment goal and the specific steps to be taken to achieve the goal. The client's educational background, work history, and test scores are noted on the EDP. The County Assistance Office has primary responsibility for case management during this time.

The EDP may contain a variety of activities, including the feeder program, basic education (at several different levels), skill training programs, and job search. These generally occur in sequence, although the number of sequences a client goes through depends on that person's background and goals. As the participant moves through the phases of the EDP, the primary case manager changes.

During the feeder, basic education, and training programs, the primary case managers are the staff of training subcontractors. At the start of a class, the case manager is identified for the participant. During the job search phase, primary case management is handled jointly by the subcontractor staff and the general case manager. Subcontractor staff continue to provide primary case management for up to ninety days during the job search following completion of training.

During the postplacement period, primary case management is shared by the county case workers and the general case managers. Case workers are primarily concerned with ensuring that special allowances are received by clients. General case managers deal with the array of issues that may arise and hinder the participants from retaining their jobs.

Several aspects of SPOC foster effective service coordination. First, the joint location of service delivery personnel at SPOC sites increases interactions among service providers. It facilitates service delivery and reduces the need for clients to move around among different offices seeking help. It makes possible the direct service teams that bring together the service delivery agents working with individual clients. The general case managers have proved to be highly effective coordinators of client services under the Joint Jobs Initiative, providing a source of continuity for clients and giving attention to linkages among program elements.

WHY USE THE JTPA SYSTEM?

The logic is strong for merging certain types of human resource funding, especially at the state and local levels. In the case of welfare reform programs, such as JOBS, it makes good sense to use existing vocational training delivery systems that have solid records of successful placement, such as the JTPA system. Although other local service delivery systems—educational institutions, employment and training program units in local welfare offices, and an array of training providers and agencies—have worked with welfare populations, they have been relatively unsuccessful in retaining students and helping them find and keep good jobs when measured against current federal criteria. For example, local education agencies with whom the city of Pittsburgh contracted during program year 1989 placed 33 percent of the participants enrolled under their contracts, while the city's overall placement rate under JTPA's Title II-A program was 74 percent.

Thus, the JTPA system succeeds against the federal criteria, and, especially in urban areas, it has long targeted the same populations that JOBS is intended to serve. According to recent U.S. Department of Labor information, 30 percent of the participants served with JTPA Title II-A funds were welfare recipients. Of the welfare recipients served, 62 percent were placed in unsubsidized employment and 65 percent of those placed in jobs were off welfare after six months.

Outcome vs. Process

The outcome focus of the JTPA system is quite different from the typical process orientation of the welfare system. The U.S. Department of Health and Human Services has devoted considerable effort to rule making to implement the Family Support Act. Much of the law deals with process. In the vocational training and basic skills areas, however, the focus on process at the federal and state levels threatens to distort the intent of JOBS because it emphasizes counting the number of hours per week a client was assigned to an activity rather than either the efficacy of the activity, its effect on the client, or the job the client gets.

Creaming and Milking

Critics of JTPA have charged that its focus on outcomes causes creaming. That charge is not borne out by the facts in Pennsylvania, although it fosters some of the concern that welfare systems show toward SDAs. In the city of Pittsburgh, for example, almost 75 percent of all JTPA participants were welfare recipients before there was a SPOC project, and 54 percent were already in the JOBS target groups. During program year 1990, twenty-one of twenty-eight SDAs in Pennsylvania served at least 100 percent more long-term AFDC recipients than was required on the basis of their prevalence in the economically disadvantaged population. Maintenance of effort provisions in JOBS ensures that JTPA service levels to welfare recipients do not decrease because of additional welfare funding.

The JTPA system views these types of criticism as defensive milking of funding sources by schools and agencies, some of whom have already failed to perform under JTPA contracts. Some of those organizations have refined their pejorative attitudes toward the poor into an argument that it is just too difficult to serve some groups of people for anyone to be held accountable for what happens after they intervene with those groups. The proof that the hard-to-serve can be served successfully is available throughout the JTPA system.

Performance, Favoritism, and Credibility

States have a clear interest in getting the best possible JOBS outcomes for their welfare clients. Multiple approaches and different delivery systems should be investigated. If states select the JTPA system based on its performance, then the same criteria should be applied for judging alternative delivery systems. Pennsylvania's experience may offer some insight into the effects that a state's decision can have on how its intent is judged.

The Transitionally Needy project was created as a separate activity from SPOC, despite the fact that the clients were served successfully in the original demonstration. Respondents to the request for proposals must now specify a narrow range of treatment (e.g., training with particular vendor for a particular occupation) for a hard-to-serve population that demands flexible and multiple treatments. Most SDAs have declined to even apply for these funds because of the rigidity of the project model. When pressed to explain why these funds are not merged with SPOC so that SDAs can serve more Transitionally Needy clients, the Department of Public Welfare said it wished to maintain a network of agencies that it could fund directly.

Inherent in state implementation of JOBS is the conflict that can ensue when historic commitments to certain funding arrangements interfere with getting the best, most effective, vocational services to clients. Yet, in most states JTPA would be judged more successful based on service to welfare recipients and credible outcomes for those who participate in training. The difficulty created by state decisions that favor certain contractor groups or reserve to state workers the luxury of not having to be concerned about whether or not clients fall into hard-to-serve target groups is that SDAs and private industry councils (PICs) will rightly infer that they are being held to a higher standard than others who are supposedly their peers in the JOBS partnership.

As long as JOBS funds remain plentiful relative to JTPA funds, such behavior by a state may be tolerated by SDAs. But the instability that can be caused by states that play favorites in these ways is harmful in the long run to the integrity of local employment and training activities. Since SDAs and PICs, also created under JTPA, have had to be responsible for many years for the quality of local projects that they fund, a great deal of effort has been devoted to ensuring that high quality training continues to be offered. When a state funds employment and training activities in a local jurisdiction without regard for any judgment or input from the SDA or PIC, it risks creating a second-class training system. Although the risks to the state may be manageable, the risk to the credibility of the local SDA or PIC can be enormous because of the lack of control over the quality of what gets funded and the limited extent of integration with other sources that can be achieved by the SDA with that contractor, who now looks to the state for protection and sponsorship. In some notorious instances, states have funded directly these local organizations that were abject failures in the local JTPA system, while exhorting the SDAs and PICs to continue to perform at high levels.

JOBS AND JTPA

Using the JTPA system of SDAs and PICs to provide training and employment services to JOBS clients can be very effective. In many states, the JTPA system has established efficient linkages with employers on behalf of economically disadvantaged trainees over almost ten years. Many SDAs, especially urban ones, have extensive experience with successfully training welfare recipients and helping them to obtain jobs. Because of the performance-driven management of JTPA, trainees are directed toward jobs that pay better than minimum wage and jobs where the likelihood of retention is higher than average. The policy decision to utilize existing JTPA delivery systems to implement JOBS brings with it a recognition of the importance of the SDA and PIC structures for program oversight as well as implied acceptance of the performance- and outcome-driven aspects of local JTPA employment and training systems.

Pennsylvania's SPOC project has been successful in providing services to welfare clients, nurturing a partnership among state departments and local agencies to coordinate and streamline services. Under this system, JTPA provides employment and training services, welfare provides supportive services (income maintenance, Food Stamps, housing, transportation, child care), and the Job Service provides placement assistance. Participants experience less shuffling from agency to agency to get services. The participants are ultimately the winners in a system that capitalizes on this shared expertise so that employment and training services are provided in concert with supportive and special needs services.

Chapter 13

Lafayette Court Family Development Center: Bringing Social Services and Housing Programs Together

Linda A. Harris

Lafayette Homes is a Baltimore public housing high-rise development with 805 units and almost 2,400 residents. There are 1,200 children living within these units, 546 under the age of six. Eighty-five percent of the residents are receiving public assistance. The Lafayette Court Family Development Center recognizes that many residents of the high-rise development are held captive by poverty. Many would contend that this entrapment begins early in life. By the age of five, many youngsters are already lost. Inadequate prenatal care, lack of early childhood stimulation, disruptive family situations, abuse, neglect, and poor nutrition have stunted their development—without intervention, they will never catch up.

By adolescence, many more are lost to drugs, alcoholism, pregnancy, and crime. These problems are compounded during the teenage years with high drop-out rates, illiteracy rates, pregnancy rates, and addiction rates. Surely, there are those who will survive and succeed; they will make it against all odds. The creators of the Family Development Center recognized that the odds are high, the barriers awesome; thus, the intervention had to be comprehensive and sustained.

The Family Development Center is an on-site center that provides sustained comprehensive services for families to assist them in becoming self-sufficient. The underlying premises of the center are the family unit and development. The family unit, defined by the center as anyone residing within the household who is considered by that unit to be a family member, is the key target. Essential to this concept is a comprehensive plan of service for the family unit. For example, the center addresses the employment needs of a mother, as well as the day-care needs of her preschool child, programming for her latchkey child, remediation for her teenage dropout, and counseling and support as necessary.

Development is the basic goal. This means (1) developing the consciousness that there is a way out and up, (2) beginning to work toward the future with a structured plan, (3) developing the skills of the individual, (4) developing the abilities of the family to deal with and overcome barriers, and (5) developing a plan for self-sufficiency and independence.

July 1991 marked the beginning of the fifth year of operation for the Family Development Center. The center is a unique collaboration among city agencies, local service providers, and multiple funding streams to address the needs of the Lafayette Court families.

With the topic of comprehensive, integrated service delivery to at-risk families being very much in the forefront of policy discussions, the Family Development Center has attracted hundreds of national and international visitors. Although a great deal of enthusiasm has been expressed for the program model, there has been just as much interest in the planning process, the management structure, and the early impact results. This paper addresses these areas.

PROGRAM MODEL

The Family Development Center is a large physical complex that has been specially renovated and designed to provide convenient access to comprehensive services. To create this complex, nine housing units were taken off the market, a portable facility was procured to provide additional meeting space, and three floors of the elementary school directly across the street were renovated for additional literacy and day-care activities. In total, the Family Development complex encompasses 27,950 square feet of space.

The Family Development Center offers all residents of the development the opportunity to access a broad array of educational, health, employment, child care, and family intervention services. The on-site services were put in place exclusively for the use of residents who sign up for membership in the center. Similarly, to maintain continuous access to the services of the center, each member must adhere to the plan of service set out for him or her by the case manager. Although the center does make available to the residents an impressive array of resources, it is expected that the head of household, as well as the subordinate members of the family unit, will remain productively engaged. A broad menu of services has been put in place to ensure that the center can respond to the various needs and support the level of activity needed to maintain the interest and involvement of members. The following is a description of the components and activities of the Family Development Center.

Case Management

The point of entry to all services is through the case management structure. Three case managers provide outreach to the development and recruit residents to sign up for membership. Once the first member (usually a head of household) signs up, then the case manager works with that individual to bring in all the other members of the family unit. An assessment is conducted on the service needs of the entire family and the case manager then works with that family to implement the service plan.

The case manager's role can best be described as a brokering function—assuring that the Family Development Center member gets priority access to the services needed, arranging for the enrollment of the member in the appropriate programs, and intervening and advocating to resolve problems along the way.

Adult Education Services

Basic skills remediation is a fundamental need for the majority of residents who sign up for membership. Reading levels range across a broad spectrum. To meet this need, the center has in place fully equipped and staffed computer-assisted learning labs with state-of-the-art software.

The educational component has four separate elements: (1) a video disc learning lab for those reading below a fifth-grade level; (2) pre-GED computer-assisted remediation for fifth- to eighth-grade readers; (3) preparation for the general equivalency diploma (GED); and (4) college matriculation through Morgan State University in a program that begins at community-based sites. Residents are encouraged to sequence through the programs as long as they are making continuous progress.

Development Child Care Services

The center encourages the participation of adults and teens in a full-time program of activity. In creating the center, careful attention was paid to the design of a full range of developmental child-care options. On-site, full-day child care for three- to five-year olds (100 slots) provides a program of discovery learning, developmental assessment, parent workshops, writing-to-read, computer activities, and escort services to and from school for five year olds. A school-age child care program (150 slots, youth, five to thirteen) provides a year-round program of academic and cultural enrichment from 7:00 A.M. to 6:00 P.M. This includes peer tutoring, homework assistance, music, art, dramatics, sports, field trips, and parent involvement activities. The Head Start program provides activities for parents of infants and toddlers up to thirty-six months old. The program includes age-specific parent-child activities in the areas of expression, motor development, self-awareness, emotion, and social play. It includes group activity and home visits.

Health Services

The Family Development Center has under its jurisdiction, at any point in time, approximately 200 children whose parents are engaged in training or education activities or employment. For this reason, there is an on-site health clinic with a nurse practitioner. This clinic provides health and dental screening, well-baby clinic services, nutrition counseling, family planning, health-related education, and priority referral for diagnosed health problems. The clinic also makes available physician services on a continuing basis. It provides an ongoing series of workshops for adolescents. The clinic staff assures that every preschool child adheres to the regular schedule of immunization and developmental checkups.

Employment and Training Activities

The Job Training Partnership Act (JTPA) and Job Opportunities and Basic Skills (JOBS) funds training in more than twenty occupational areas and many special programs for targeted populations. The Family Development Center serves as a point of intake for all the activities funded by the JTPA and JOBS system. Thus, Family Development Center members receive priority referral to occupational training, on-the-job training, job search assistance, and all other JTPA-funded activities.

Programs Targeting Teenagers

The Family Development Center has a teen drop-in center. It provides an informal setting and less structured series of activities designed primarily to build a bond between youth and center staff. Social activities, rap sessions, field trips, videos, and motivation sessions are provided. Interspersed with those activities are counseling sessions and relevant workshops. Eventually, youth are attached to a case manager who will assist them in enrolling in appropriate activities, which might include (1) an educational learning center for youth who have dropped out of school, providing instruction, work experience, counseling, and job placement; (2) an alternative Baltimore city public school high school, Harbor City Learning, which offers the opportunity to earn a high-school diploma in three trimesters, along with ongoing work experience and counseling; (3) Futures, a high intervention, school-based program for students who are in transition to high school but whose profile suggests they are at imminent risk of dropping out; and (4) Commonwealth Services, a series of program activities during a youth's high-school years, which includes community service activities, year-round work experience, college camps, leadership development, assistance with college enrollment, and school-to-work transition.

Family Support Activities

In addition to the ongoing workshops, speakers, and parenting sessions, the case managers provide individual assistance to families dealing with problems of family violence, substance abuse, eviction, and other such barriers. Case managers are able to quickly connect families to services through their relationship with both the Family Services unit of the Department of Social Services and, for mental health referrals, the city health department.

Similarly, the nurse practitioner, in conjunction with the case manager and the child-care worker, has been successful in assisting numerous families diagnose and address the needs of children with developmental impairments.

Complementary to its school-age child-care service, the Bureau of Recreation also provides year-round recreational and cultural activities to all residents. These services are also housed in the elementary school.

The center staff also works with the parents to design activities that reinforce family unity. The Family Development Center has become a focal point in the community for activity involving parents and children. The Center sponsors the summer Family Fun Day, the annual Christmas pageant showcasing the talents of all the children in the child-care programs, the Halloween Haunted House, Family Portrait campaign, quarterly report card activities, and other such events.

THE PLANNING PROCESS

It took less than nine months to open the center after initiation of the concept. This included renovating the facilities, hiring staff, and negotiating interdepartmental agreements. Five key ingredients were responsible for the energetic pace that accompanied the implementation of the center: leadership, articulated vision, accessible funding streams, open and inclusive planning process, and a strong lead entity. It is important to note the organizational structure at the time the Family Development Center was conceived. The Housing Authority, the JTPA system, and Community Development Block Grant (CDBG) programming were all under the jurisdiction of one commissioner with a separate deputy commissioner for each of the above-mentioned functions.

Figure 13.1 identifies the stages of the planning process that were catalyzed when the commissioner indicated at the start of the CDBG planning process a desire to be more than just a landlord for the public housing high-rise complexes and suggested a willingness to set aside resources necessary to begin assisting the residents toward self-sufficiency. The deputy commissioners were challenged to consider the most appropriate intervention.

The Family Development Center concept was created out of the deliberations. A three-page concept paper served as the document that garnered the support of all the collaborators. Care was taken to present the concept paper in a small group setting to each important constituency—the health commissioner, the social services director, the school system, the tenant representatives, and others. The concept was greeted universally with support and enthusiasm.

The leadership and vision of the commissioner, the deputy commissioners, and the other key department heads were important in creating a sense of excitement and energy on the part of each participating agency. The Family Development Center concept was innovative and clearly articulated. Thus, subordinate staff in the participating agencies signed on with zeal and were happy to be part of actualizing this vision. This enthusiasm extended down to the Housing Authority construction crews who went above and beyond the call of duty to assure the completion of the center with all the necessary amenities. Having an easily understandable written concept around which people could rally was important glue to this process.

The planning process was open and inclusive. Beyond the basic concepts outlined in the concept paper, it was made clear that the specific design of each of the individual components would fall to the agency or organization that had the most expertise and that it was not the intent of the center to duplicate existing services or replace existing deliverers with a new set. Thus, each partner had an equally important role to play in designing and assuring the implementation of the center services. The intention throughout the process was to allow the residents to access directly the best services through a single access point. With the exception of Head Start, none of the services was available in reasonable proximity to the development. However, the city was rich with expertise that was tapped in the planning process.

Eleven organizations participated in planning the Family Development Center. These included city agencies dealing with housing, health, employment development, social services, recreation, children and youth, and tenant services. The Baltimore Private Industry Council, the public school system, the tenant council, and Morgan State University also took part in the planning effort.

A high-level staff person of each agency participated on a planning committee that provided hands-on direction to the implementation process. Since several of the programs required licensing, the persons responsible for licensing were brought into the early planning phases. A good deal of attention was paid to the inclusion of residents in the process. The president of the Tenant Council and the representative of the Resident Advisory Council participated actively throughout the planning and implementation phases. They were instrumental in organizing residents to assist in a door-to-door survey of the residents to create support for the center and solicit input on residents' needs and interests. This door-to-door survey was also essential because it provided a better profile of the population, including the actual number of people residing in each unit, their educational levels, their current health providers, and their interests, than was available through existing data.

The existence of accessible funding streams to cover the costs of physical renovation and the ongoing operating infrastructure took some of the pressure off participating entities. More attention was paid to what works best and what is needed as opposed to what the agencies' budgets could afford. To complete the center four funding streams were required. CDBG provided a $1 million initial outlay and $600,000 in ongoing annual support. Under Title XX Day Care, sufficient funds were set aside to guarantee reimbursement for 250 day-care slots. However, because of the developmental nature of the child-care programs, the day-care reimbursement rates were insufficient to cover the total cost. This deficit was covered in the first year by CDBG, and in subsequent years by the Housing Authority. The job training system, in addition to making JTPA funds

Figure 13.1
Stages of the Planning Process

Stages	Time	Actors
STAGE 1		
INTERNAL PLANNING PROCESS		
Commissioner catalyzed planning process	About 4 weeks	Commissioner
Deputies developed conceptual framework		Deputy Commissioners
Internal refining of concept		Agency Executive Staff
Development of concept paper		
STAGE 2		
GARNERING EXTERNAL SUPPORT OF KEY PLAYERS	About 4 weeks	Board of Housing Commissioners
Briefing of key players		Health Commissioner
Selection of specific highrise development		Director, Social Services
Assuring availability of funds		Tenant Council/Resident Advisory Board
Identification of delegated agency representatives		Office of Children and Youth, Day Care Division, Tenant Services
STAGE 3		
FORMAL PLANNING PROCESS	About 3 months	Housing Deputy Commissioner
Planning workgroup formed, conducted monthly meetings		JTPA Deputy Commissioner
Door-to-door resident survey to profile needs and interests		Assistant Commissioner of Health
Identify specific program needs/slot levels		Tenant Council Representatives
		Office of Children and Youth
Design format, policies, and protocol		Asst. Superintendent of Schools
Layout space configuration		Child Care Division, Tenant Services

Figure 13.1 (continued)

Stages	Time	Actors
STAGE 4 **IMPLEMENTATION PHASE**		
Negotiate agreements	About 3 months	Same as Stage 3 plus
Facility renovation		Housing Authority Crews
Recruit staff		Tenant Council
Community outreach		
Equip facility		
Hire/train staff		
Open facility		
STAGE 5 **REFINING AND REDESIGN**		
Revisiting policy and program design issues	Ongoing	Family Development Center Advisory Board

available as needed, also had access to a state general fund program called Investment in Job Opportunities, which was designed specifically to target welfare recipients for inclusive job training services. Thus, the service delivery area felt it could guarantee enrollment to all eligible members. The initial cost of the clinic was underwritten by CDBG funds, and a mechanism was devised to charge the Medicaid card for reimbursement for services rendered to establish the funding pool for subsequent years. This ran into difficulty once a local health maintenance organization (HMO) enrolled a substantial portion of the residents.

The final key ingredient was a strong lead entity. The Office of Manpower Resources, which is the JTPA administrative structure, managed the implementation process and was ultimately accountable for assuring that deadlines were met and agreements were negotiated. This was the particular strength of the local JTPA system, which had a great deal of experience in program development and contract negotiation.

This part of the process had the most potential for bogging down. The Office of Manpower Resources did not control the funding streams for any of the services for which agreements were being negotiated. This was the real test of the buy-in and trust. A great deal of bonding that occurred during the planning phase facilitated the ultimate delivery of signed agreements. Not all agreements were in place at the opening of the center, but they followed shortly.

THE MANAGEMENT STRUCTURE

Figure 13.2 shows the organizational structure of the Family Development Center. The staff of the Family Development Center report to the Office of Employment Development (formerly the Office of Manpower Resources). Solid lines indicate a direct supervisory line of authority; dotted lines indicate that the relationship is governed by a written memorandum of understanding.

The design of the Family Development Center brings together several delivery agents in one site to provide exclusive services to the members of the Family Development Center. These services are universally accessed via the case management structure, and all services operate subject to negotiated agreements and protocols that are established by the Family Development Center Advisory Board. The director of the Family Development Center is responsible for assuring coordination and smooth delivery of service to members. The director also convenes the advisory board. Each service provider occupies a seat on the board that convenes monthly. This board is the forum for ongoing program refinement. Here discussions take place on new services needed or potential resources that can be attracted to the center. It is also the forum for addressing problems and concerns that may require changes in program design or protocol.

Since its inception, the Family Development Center has served as a magnet for new program services, since each of the partners advocates on behalf of the Family Development Center for new resources that become available to their respective agencies. This is an important reason for encouraging individual service providers to maintain their individual agency identification as opposed to subordinating them to the Family Development Center or the Office of Employment Development management structure.

EARLY IMPACT RESULTS

The real impact will not be known for several years. Ultimately, it is envisioned that the existence of the Lafayette Court Family Development Center will result in the following:

- Proportionally fewer families dependent on public assistance
- Increased proportion of family heads working
- Better development of cognitive and social skills of children, resulting in higher promotion rates
- Increased school graduation rates

Figure 13.2
Organizational Structure of the Family Development Center

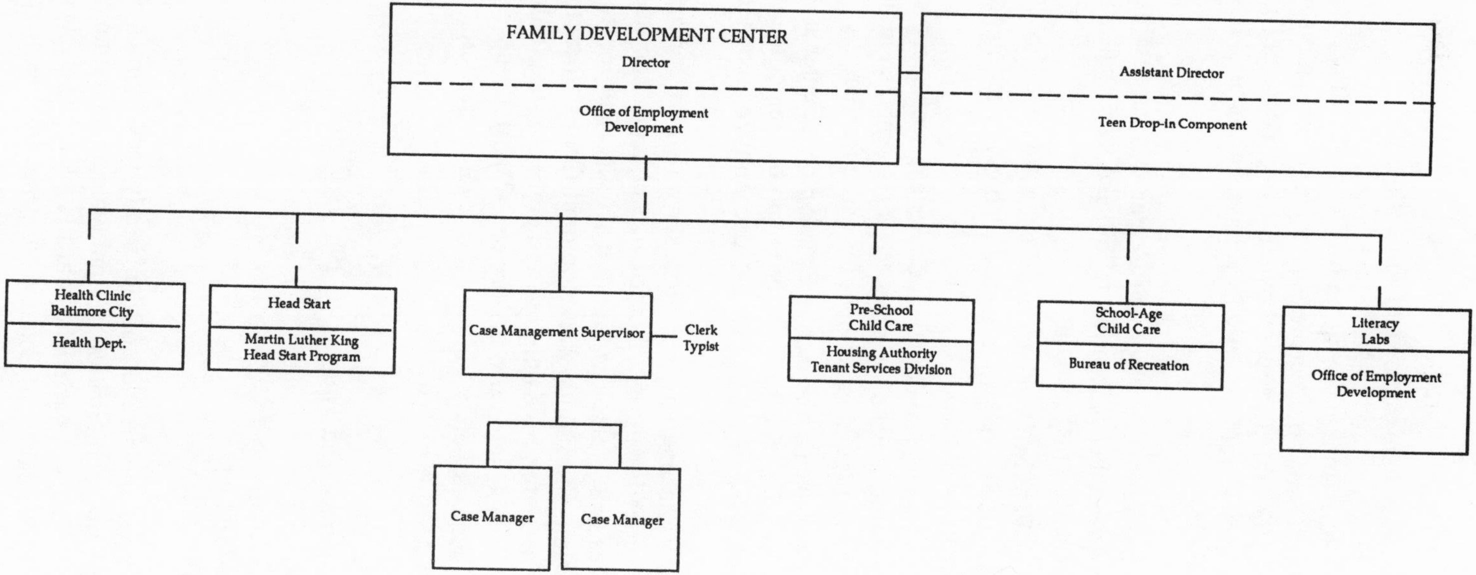

- Decreased pregnancy and addiction rates

The Johns Hopkins Institute for Policy Studies conducted an impact evaluation based on the center's first year of operation and issued a report in April 1991 titled, "Steps Toward Independence: The Early Effects of the Lafayette Court's Family Development Center." Its findings included the following:

- The Family Development Center was successful in attracting a large number of families to join and participate in Family Development Center programs
- The Family Development Center was able to show movement toward the long-term goal of achieving economic independence for its residents
- The Family Development Center has been successful in providing "comprehensive" services to its residents, an indicator of its success in providing services for entire families
- The impact of the Family Development Center as a coordinated set of services for families appears to be greater than if services were delivered in a conventional, decentralized manner

Other intermediate indicators show that the concept is working. One major question is whether such a concept can successfully engage families in sustained productive activity. During its first four years of operation, the Family Development Center attracted 689 families to join the center. Five hundred and eight of those families had all family members participating in services. That take-up rate is phenomenal. The statistics below indicate the level of participation by individuals in the various activities:

Education	259
Employment and Training	198
College	34
Youth Programs/Activities	182
Child Care	581
Job Placements	139

Prior to the creation of the Family Development Center, the level of community participation in employment and training activities was minimal, despite outreach. The Johns Hopkins' analysis of the impact of the Family Development Center documented that the participation of families in education and training activities far exceeded the levels for a similar high-rise development for the same time period.

The Family Development Center has successfully encouraged a public housing community to take part in charting its own destiny. Women are not just getting their general equivalency diplomas; they are going on to college. New life has been given to the elementary school that had been slated for closing. It now bustles with activity. Parents improve their basic education on one floor of the school, while their preschoolers attend the school-based child-care services and their older children receive before and after school care at the same facility. These parents now form the nucleus of the school's parent organization. The revitalization of the school is a definite by-product of the creation of the Family Development Center activity. The school reports that students coming into school after participating in the child-care programs are much more prepared for first grade. All evidence points to the fact that the center is working.

Chapter 14

Youth at Risk: Making a Difference at the Local Level

Kathy R. Thornburg

Ours is an aging society increasingly dependent on its youth. At the very time that we need educated and healthy children and youth, a disproportionate number of them are growing up poor and uneducated.

> To the extent that poverty of children is related to their poverty as adults, the quality of our future work force may be affected by the present poverty of our children. And the poverty of our children today may affect our long-term competitiveness with other wealthy countries that tolerate much less child poverty than does the United States. (Smeeding and Torrey, 1988: 877)

At-risk youth are the children and youth who spend all or a portion of their lives in low-income families. They are the children who are born to teen mothers, to high-school dropouts, and to illiterate parents. They may be minority children, or children of unwed mothers, or the victims of divorce or separation. They may be the children of parents who are homeless or one rent payment away from eviction.

A cause and effect relationship exists between the events young people experience and the way they approach problems they later face. Lisbeth Schorr (1988) identifies three themes that emerge from this relationship. The first theme notes that poor children and children who grow up in areas of concentrated poverty endure more frequent risk factors. As risk factors multiply in a young person's life, chances of overcoming the problems diminish. This, Schorr notes, requires a societal response to the risk factors (the second theme). The third theme, which eliminates excuses for lack of action, is that the knowledge to make a difference does exist: "there is a reasonably good match between known risk factors and the interventions to reduce them" (p. 20).

This chapter outlines some community-level structures and programs that are beginning to make a difference in the lives of children who are at risk for school failure, teen pregnancy, drug abuse, and other antisocial behavior. In addition, it suggests state and national policies to resolve the problems.

FEATURES OF LIVES AT RISK

Children face multiple problems as they mature, thus demanding a wide range of solutions. Spending more money on existing programs and services that we know work is necessary, but this alone will not solve the problems. Innovative community activities also need to be developed. A second point to keep in mind is the need to develop programs that will prevent, not remediate, problems. In addition to being aware of risk factors and how to eliminate them, we must begin to look at protective factors and the assets that youth can build upon.

Risk factors are elements that are present in the child's environment that make the child more vulnerable to negative influences. Such factors are low self-esteem, low socioeconomic level, family dysfunction, poor health, academic failure, and a negative peer group. Risk factors tend to increase in an exponential manner in a child's life. One risk factor may not pose a serious problem, but if a child has two risk factors present, that child's chances of developing serious problems are four times greater. When the number of risk factors increases to four, the chances of developing related problems increase twenty times (Bogenschneider et al., 1991).

Protective factors are positive elements of a child's environment. A positive relationship with a parent or mentor, a quality school, good self-esteem, good problem-solving skills, and a positive peer group are examples of protective factors. In the presence of high-risk factors, these protective factors begin functioning to help the child cope with or overcome the adverse situation (Bogenschneider et al., 1991).

Protective factors play a key role in combating the impact of risk factors and in preventing antisocial behavior (Webster-Stratton, 1990). Protective factors have a tremendous influence in the lives of resilient children. When faced with risk factors, children can draw upon the strength of the protective factors as a means of filling unmet needs or surviving challenging situations. Although some protective factors are innate (e.g., appearance, temperament, etc.), others are environmental and, therefore, can be found in a child's immediate surroundings: the family, peer group, school, and community. It is tempting to point to an impoverished family and note all the risk factors as being insurmountable. However, protective factors will also be operating for the majority of children, offering an opportunity and hope for successful intervention. It is at this level that communities need to intervene.

FRAGMENTATION OF SERVICES

One reason current government programs and services often fail in their efforts to intervene is the respective agencies' turf battles that prevent them from delivering a total range of services to clients with multiple needs. They exert so much energy fighting one another, that they have less time for needy clients. Meanwhile, these families require coordination of these services to solve their multiple problems. The present system, operating through myriad agencies, means fragmentation that results in an isolation of services, underservice, or a total lack of services to eligible children. In addition, the fragmentation often causes funding problems, an overburdened system, discontinuity of care, and conflict of goals and philosophies in helping children.

An example of the ineffectiveness of services resulting from inter-agency conflicts is the longstanding difference in the area of child care between the Department of Social Services and the Department of Education in California. "The former frames the fundamental purpose of child care services as custodial; the latter conceives of child care as a developmental problem. This elemental lack of agreement on general purpose has generated incapacitating suspicion and lack of cooperation between agencies at both state and local levels" (Kirst and Massell, 1990: 4). Unfortunately, it seems the dissension reported in California is common in a majority of the states. While children are in desperate need of both educational and social services, they are victims of this bureaucratic conflict.

To make a real difference, we need more cooperation among agencies at the national, state, and local levels. The recent consolidation of children's programs at the national level into the Administration for Children and Families has the potential to strengthen national policies for children and families. This could be a positive step in reducing problems in service delivery, conflicts in philosophy, coordination of funding, and the provision of comprehensive care. Although policies developed following this reorganization may be more "family friendly," we must not think that better policies alone can solve the problems our youth face.

WHAT'S HAPPENING IN MISSOURI?

Across the nation, communities are making efforts to address the youth-at-risk issue. We may be able to generalize from the experiences of these communities and suggest policy changes needed at state or national levels. Communities in Missouri provide examples of effective local efforts.

Missouri received a grant from the Kellogg Foundation for community programs designed to improve the chances for youth at risk. The three parts of the grant are a Youth Fellows Program, a Demonstration Community Program, and a Youth Data Base Project.

The Kellogg Youth Fellows and the Youth Data Base Project provide support to community-level youth activities, in addition to working to improve policies for youth at the state and local levels. A brief description of the Youth Fellows and Data Base Project should help in understanding their relationships to the communities.

Youth Fellows Program

Thirty interdisciplinary experts from five university campuses, university extension, and state human service agencies collaborate with one another and community groups to develop creative approaches to address the problems of Missouri youth.

Youth Data Base Project

Data analysts from state departments (Health, Mental Health, Elementary and Secondary Education, Social Services, and Public Safety) and the University of Missouri developed a new coordinated system for obtaining information about children and youth. The project analyzes youth and family data and makes them available to local and state policymakers, agency personnel, and concerned citizens.

Demonstration Community Program

Persons from six communities throughout the state work cooperatively with project staff, university personnel, Youth Fellows, and state agency personnel to create programs that are responsive to the needs of youth in each community. Only communities that could demonstrate collaboration of several agencies and organizations were eligible to apply for this grant. The six communities were chosen from 114 that applied for the grant monies to coordinate youth-at-risk programs.

These grants are less than two years old; therefore, the long-term impact on the lives of children and families cannot be assessed at this time. However, there have been positive outcomes from programs in youth leadership, substance abuse prevention, and delinquency prevention. There have also been encouraging results in school retention rates, personal responsibility, and reduced recidivism rates. For example, teachers in one school district provided the Taking Steps to Excellence (EXCEL) program to twenty-two of their most "at risk of dropping out" students. A majority of these students would normally have dropped out of school within the first few months of the school year. All twenty-two students in EXCEL not only completed the school year, but passed all of their courses.

SUCCESSFUL COMMUNITY PROGRAMS

The following sections describe some strategies that have been successful in all or most of the six communities.

Community Boards

Each of the six communities began with similar organizations and agencies represented on their policy boards. The board members were generally from state and private child welfare and mental health agencies, juvenile courts, public health agencies, and school systems. By the second year, the boards expanded to include representation from such groups as the local ministerial alliances, elected officials (including the mayor), police departments, sheriffs' departments, and county commissions. The community boards with the broadest representation have developed more programs, reorganized more services, and mobilized more outside funds than those with narrower participation.

Each of the six communities also has a youth board. Although each youth board has representation on the overall policy board, it also has its own separate structure. The youth board is widely representative of the community. Community leaders worked hard to avoid having a youth board made up solely of representatives of organizations such as the letterman's club, the honor society, and the class officers. A special effort was made to include at-risk youth on the boards. Some of the at-risk youth serving on the boards had appeared in juvenile court, attended alternative education programs, and been defined by the authorities as "problems." These communities have strived hard to make sure that both boards are representative of the community.

Coordination

The six communities have been able to coordinate some youth services. Activities relating to coordination include the following:

- Establishing community resource directories and youth "yellow pages" that make it easier to locate services
- Developing interagency staffing teams charged with developing resources and services for the children and families who are failing to receive adequate services
- Reducing transportation costs by combining previously separate bus service for the elderly, children with cerebral palsy, and children with other developmental disabilities
- Expanding the role of the school as a community agency with programs such as before-and-after school care, intergenerational nutrition sites, social services, medical screening, and parental education
- Developing a network of service agencies to work on prevention of child abuse and neglect

New Programs and Services

By working together for a little over a year, these communities have started some programs new to their areas. These programs include summer development camps that include techniques borrowed from the Outward Bound model to build self-esteem and leadership skills; a telephone hotline that provides families with information about parenting skills; mentoring programs in which youth at risk of dropping out of school are put into teams to work with preschool and elementary students; community resource networks with four-member teams trained in substance abuse prevention, parenting education, family life development, and child safety promotion; puppet shows developed by at-risk middle-school students to perform for elementary students; a homework hotline for middle-school children and their parents; summer literacy programs providing children who are at high risk of dropping out with a tutor for themselves and their families; and, a self-esteem-building three-day retreat for the tutors, students, and families held at the end of the summer.

Working Together for New Monies

The six communities, working in conjunction with the University of Missouri and other state agencies, have been successful in bringing additional monies into their communities. Their community coordinating boards have provided the impetus for federal and state grants from the U.S. Department of Agriculture, the Juvenile Justice and Delinquency Prevention Act, the private industry council, the Community Action for Substance Abuse Prevention Council, the Children's Bureau, and the U.S. Department of Labor. These grants have allowed some of the community programs to become a reality. Many of the grants were possible only because two or more community agencies worked together.

Beyond the Six Communities

Although the six Kellogg sites have the support of a half-time university extension employee and a modest budget, several communities that submitted proposals which were not selected also have active programs today. As a result of developing their proposals, which called for collaboration of community agencies and organizations, people from various agencies have continued to work together and implement those programs.

Examples of programs and activities in these communities include parenting education programs in the schools; before-and-after school programs; a four-part community plan, including programs to help youth develop a better self-image, development work with families to place more value on education, teacher workshops on methodology and communication, and consultants to work with administrators to encourage school reorganization; development of a coalition of eighteen community agencies that supported a Positive Youth Development program; and, development of a grant proposal on early identification of students who are at risk that was funded by USDA (50 percent matching dollars were provided by the Kellogg grant).

In all of these communities, it took people and money external to the community to make the programs work. Kellogg Youth Fellows, other university faculty, and state specialists worked with community councils. They went to the communities with no preconceived notions of the kinds of projects or activities that should be developed. They served solely to work with the advisory boards to help them develop the kinds of activities the communities wanted.

LOCAL, STATE, AND FEDERAL COORDINATION

Much has been learned from these and other community efforts. A kaleidoscope of useful ideas has emerged for local, state, and federal policymakers that might increase the effectiveness of community programs.

It appears that if cooperative programs are to be successful, coordination of services must occur simultaneously at a number of levels. A certain reciprocity among state departments' administrators and elected officials has served as an impetus for collaboration at other levels in Missouri. For example, the five major state agencies that have constitutional responsibility for children and the University of Missouri have a memorandum of agreement that mandates coordination and collaboration among the service delivery agencies at all levels. Appended to the agreement is a description of nine functions a coordinating council could perform. These range from the simplest level of information exchange to joint policy and program development requiring the pooling of resources. At the present time, fifty of Missouri's counties have Human Service Coordinating Councils that work on joint programs.

With the support and encouragement for joint projects, some concrete services have emerged. One of the most successful activities occurred in a community when the county extension agent, the superintendent of schools, and the director of the Division of Family Services became catalysts for building a community day-care center.

Redesigning Children's Services

Currently, Missouri is in the process of designing community-level prototypes of unified services for children and families. Some of the programs in the existing departments and divisions of family services, youth services, and mental health will be combined into new departments at the county level relating to children's services. Also, plans are being made for the possibility of delivering some of the services through local school districts.

This coordination of services within the schools as a means of reaching out to high-risk students uses existing protective factors found in each community: a school as a central gathering point for all children and youth, teachers committed to helping youth, and the facilities to make comprehensive services accessible to all youth. With appropriate services available to all children, there is the potential to reach youth and their families before serious and costly problems develop.

Perhaps we need to redefine the roles of our schools as community resources. After all, teachers do not just teach reading and writing; they teach children. Some children may be hungry, homeless, on drugs, or pregnant. Teachers should not be expected to "do it all," but schools can be a central point for service delivery. With the support of other professionals and social and health services readily available, teachers and other school personnel can be valuable links in the coordinated efforts to help children and their families.

Categorical Funding

While recognizing that an administrative agent is necessary for accountability, ownership or control by one agency can result in splintered and ineffective service delivery. Federal- and state-level categorical funding is often an impediment to effective integration of services. As mentioned earlier, Missouri is in the process of coordinating child-related departments at the community level. The Health Department, however, is attempting to hide behind the claim of a "federal mandate" to keep from cooperating. It claims to be the sole provider for certain programs because of categorical funding. In reality, however, it is a state problem. The federal government requires the governor to designate an agency for child and maternal health programs. The governor could change the designated agency to allow for coordination. This is an illustration of federal- and state-level policies intended to protect the clients that actually protect claims to power of a bureaucracy. The centralization of policy and program directives at state and federal levels can also become an excuse for local agencies or administrators who want to maintain their insularity.

Community-Level Planning

The goal of community-level planning for youth means the creation of new programs and resources. Before this collaboration can take place, however, people from various agencies must share information and develop common interests. Next, people must cooperate by extending one another's services and resources (Lofquist, 1989).

_LUSION

Policy changes are needed at all levels of government to improve community-level services to youth. Based on the author's experiences of professional work with children and families for twenty-five years, as an elected member of a public school board, and as the vice president of an organization of more than 80,000 professionals committed to the improvement of programs for children, the following recommendations come to mind:

- Communities need federal and state policies that encourage flexibility or mandate coordination of services
- Families need one-stop shopping for government services
- Proven programs that prevent later problems, such as Women, Infants, and Children (WIC) and Head Start, need to be fully funded
- Federal and state bureaucracies serving children need to coordinate services
- Efforts are needed to blend all types of service delivery and funding sources—government, private human service agencies, schools, churches, foundations
- Eligibility requirements and regulations for programs need to be more consistent
- Accurate data are needed to provide public awareness of the problems of youth
- Prevention, not remediation, needs to be the focus of new programs and services
- Programs must focus on assets of youth as well as needs
- Youth should be involved in community-level planning
- Programs need to stress empowerment strategies for youth and their families

A reexamination of current policies, funding levels, and knowledge of prevention programs can lead toward successful solutions. It is vital that action be taken now.

REFERENCES

Bogenschneider, K., D. Riley, and S. Small, 1991. *An Ecological, Risk-Focused Approach for Addressing Youth-at-Risk Issues.* Madison: University of Wisconsin-Madison.

Kirst, M. W., and D. Massell, 1990. *Rethinking Children's Policy: Implications for Educational Administration.* Bloomington, Ind.: Consortium on Educational Policy Studies.

Lofquist, W. A. 1989. *The Technology of Prevention Workbook.* Tucson, Ariz.: Associates for Youth Development.

Schorr, L. B. 1988. *Within Our Reach: Breaking the Cycle of Disadvantage.* New York: Anchor Press.

Smeeding, T. M. and B. B. Torrey. 1988. "Poor Children in Rich Countries." *Science* 242: 873–77.

Webster-Stratton, C. 1990. "Stress: A Potential Disruptor of Parent Perceptions and Family Interactions." *Journal of Clinical Child Psychology* 19: 302–12.

Chapter 15

Community-Level Coordination of the JOBS Program

Edward T. Jennings, Jr. and Dale Krane

Earlier chapters in this book, particularly Chapters 1 and 9, provide important background information about the Job Opportunities and Basic Skills (JOBS) program, including a description of major provisions of the Family Support Act (FSA) and an analysis of state-level implementation of JOBS. Implementing JOBS requires bringing together diverse agencies at the local level to provide multiple services to clients. How well the program administrators coordinate this activity will substantially determine the success of JOBS in promoting independence and self-sufficiency for welfare families.

In this chapter, we examine the implementation of JOBS in eight major metropolitan areas and provide an analysis of coordination processes and issues at the local level. That analysis includes the program's organization, decision structures and planning processes, client processing, and structures, processes, and tools of coordination at the community level. We discuss the extent to which local-level implementation and coordination are dependent on state-level decision making. We also discuss barriers to and facilitators of coordination. We conclude with a set of recommendations for improving coordination.

To help the reader follow the analysis, it is important to define what we mean by local- or community-level decision making and program activities as compared to the state level because state agencies are often important actors at the local level. We use the terms "local" or "community" to refer to decisions and actions of units that operate at the community level. Thus, field offices of state agencies are included in the definition of local. In some states, for example, the local-level agency responsible for social welfare programs is a county welfare department. In other states, it is a field office (typically, but not always, organized on the county level) of a state social service department. In both of these cases, we have both state decision making (made at the level of the state agency in the state capital) and local decision making (which may involve purely local agencies or a combination of local government organizations and local offices of state agencies).

The usual array of major actors at the community level includes the local welfare office (either the county office of the state welfare department or the county welfare department), the private industry council (PIC) and administrative entity of the Job Training Partnership Act (JTPA) service delivery area (SDA), the local school system and community colleges, and local offices of the state employment service. We use the terms "local level" and "community level" interchangeably. We use the term "local government" when we refer specifically to units of general purpose local government.

We selected major metropolitan areas for the analysis because they provide the most complex political and administrative environment for the program. The experience in such settings says much about the potential for successful coordination of JOBS with preexisting employment and training programs. For this purpose, we chose Boston; Jacksonville; Houston; San Diego; Portland, Oregon; Omaha; Chicago; and Louisville. Although these metropolitan areas do not represent a random sample, they are very diverse. Some have considerable experience with welfare-to-work programs; others have little experience. The areas come from every region and vary in patterns of development and economic conditions.

In site visits to each of these communities, we interviewed a variety of individuals involved in the administration and delivery of the JOBS program. In each community, we tried to talk with the director of the JOBS program, a case manager, the director of the local employment service office, an education administrator responsible for the delivery of basic education services to JOBS clients, the executive director of the PIC or the administrative entity for JTPA, and directors of community-based organizations involved with JOBS. Where the specific individual that we sought was not available, we generally interviewed a principal assistant. The identification of individuals to interview was modified where required by the organization of the JOBS program. We collected as many documents concerning the local JOBS program as possible, including, where available, the local JOBS plan. We were able to review a sample of case files in six communities.

THE ADMINISTRATION OF JOBS

In some ways, the administration of the JOBS program varies little among these eight communities. In all, the local welfare agency (the agency responsible for the Aid to Families with Dependent Children [AFDC] program) plays a central role, whether that unit is organized as a county welfare department or as a county office of the state agency. Invariably, that agency is at the heart of local decision making, to the extent that decisions are made at the local level. The welfare agency also does the initial assessment of client needs, develops the employability plan, and provides case management. In addition, in all of these communities there are a variety of agencies involved in delivering various component activities in the program.

In other ways, the administration of the JOBS program varies considerably among the eight metropolitan areas. Decision-making structures and planning processes differ in several ways, as does the organization of the program for service delivery. The differences are shaped partly by decisions made at the state level and partly by decisions made at the local level.

Centralization vs. Decentralization

In all of the communities, the program has been shaped in significant ways by decisions made at the state level, but how much this is the case varies. In some communities, decision making and administration of the program are so highly centralized at the state level that it is almost meaningless to speak of a significant local role. Indeed, in one of the states the administrators had difficulty distinguishing between the state and the local levels of decision and action. In the centralized states, decisions about what program components to offer, how to allocate resources, who to contract with for components, and what role to assign to other agencies are made in the state capital. There is virtually no local planning activity in these states.

At the other end are states where a substantial range of significant decisions has been made at the local level. In these states, local planning processes lead to decisions about the nature of the program, its goals and objectives, the division of responsibilities among various agencies, the allocation of funds among activities, and contractual relationships. In these decentralized settings, the state sets a basic framework and general policy, while allowing local administrators and decision makers to shape the program and its administration in significant ways.

In between are the states where a fair degree of centralization has been accompanied by some room for local discretion. In one state, for example, the state agency signs contracts with a state education agency and the state employment service to provide education, job readiness, job development, and job placement services. It leaves to local areas the question of how to involve the JTPA service delivery areas, what optional program components to offer from a list of options, and operational details of relationships with the basic education providers and employment service.

Planning

Planning processes vary considerably among these communities. Where decision making is highly centralized at the state level, there is limited or no local planning. In states with extensive local discretion, there generally is a well-developed local planning process. In most states, this planning is led by the local or county office of the human services agency, although there is one community where the state contracts with the regional planning agencies to provide overall management of the program at the local level, including convening an interagency planning committee. In another metropolitan area, planning is done on a regional basis that extends well into the hinterland of the central city, but the planning is led by a regional office of the welfare agency.

Planning actively involves numerous human service agencies (including the AFDC agency), the employment service, the private industry council, education agencies, child-care providers or brokers, and others in communities with local discretion and planning. In at least two of these communities, however, this is really a pro forma process. In reality, the human service agency and the SDA do the planning with the other agencies providing a supporting cast.

In a number of cases, the character of planning for JOBS depends on whether or not the state and locality had an extensive welfare-to-work program in place prior to adoption and implementation of the Family Support Act. Where this was the case, the planning structure that was used to develop the initial welfare-to-work effort was often used to develop and implement changes necessitated by federal requirements under the JOBS legislation. In at least one case, however, the county office for human services planned the changeover to JOBS without involving other agencies in the same way that they had been involved in planning the original program.

Organization of Service Delivery

JOBS programs typically include the following components: initial assessment of client needs, the development of the employability plan, case management, job-readiness activities, education, skill training, group and individual job search, job development, and job placement. These service delivery components can be condensed into three fundamental phases: (1) client diagnosis and supervision, (2) removal of employment barriers, and (3) work-force entry.

A particular agency or combination of agencies generally dominates each of these three phases. Client diagnosis and supervision normally rests in the hands of the local social service office. Various education, skills training, and job-readiness organizations provide barrier removal activities. The number and diversity of service providers is greatest during this phase. Clients usually receive work-force entry services through the job service or skill-training providers. Clients invariably remain under the supervision of social service caseworkers who provide case management through the multiple steps to employment. While follow-up of the client's work experience might provide a tenth component, it is not uniformly pursued.

There are several different patterns of organization for service delivery in the eight communities. At one extreme is a community where the welfare or social service agency directly provides all major components except education, training, and placement, and even shares placement responsibility with the employment service. Thus, in this community, initial assessment of client needs, development of the employability plan, case management, job-readiness activities, group and individual job search, and placement in training or education are provided directly by the local social service agency. Job development and placement are shared between the social service agency and the state employment service agency. At the other extreme is a community in which all but one of these activities are provided by contractors.

Client Diagnosis and Supervision. Important choices that can affect client treatment are made in local case processing procedures. Once eligibility is determined, JOBS participants may proceed through case processing individually or in groups and may report to one or more case workers (e.g., income maintenance or JOBS caseworkers). Assessment of client needs varies from the extreme of extensive, in-depth assessment of literacy and education, as well as interests, aptitudes, and values of the client, through a cursory, simple test of math and reading skills to the other extreme of no formal assessment.

The degree to which the client is "job ready" shapes the client's employability plan and largely determines whether the individual is placed in basic educational activities, skill training activities, or job placement activities. The employability plan is generally simple, seldom exhibiting extensive detail or elaborate scheduling.

In all of the communities, the social service agency has primary or sole responsibility for initial assessment of client needs. Case management is the responsibility of the social service agency alone in six communities. In two others, contractors have case management responsibilities. Thus, departments of social services dominate client assessment and supervision. This is true even in those localities where client assessment is contracted out or performed by other agencies or organizations. Caseworkers, while relying on tests of the client's basic skills, make an individualized judgment of the participant's degree of job readiness. Social service case workers typically have the ultimate say over the content of the participant's employability plan, even if parts of the plan are reviewed by the provider of the specific service.

Removal of Employment Barriers. Unlike previous welfare-to-work programs that concentrated on returning the client to the work force as quickly as possible, while doing little to remove barriers to employment, JOBS emphasizes the removal of barriers to self-sufficiency, particularly the obstacles associated with illiteracy or incomplete education and training. Although a full range of education is available through JOBS programs, most JOBS-supported education can be described as remedial. Case managers in the eight localities refer their clients to community colleges, public schools, and adult learning centers for adult basic education and general equivalency diploma (GED) preparation.

JOBS funds do not necessarily cover the costs of basic education. Boards of education may provide state money to adult education providers, whether they are local schools, independent school districts, community colleges, or adult learning centers.

Provision of education, one of the main components of JOBS, exhibits little duplication. In every case, the local JOBS agency referred clients to educational institutions and did not itself offer classes. There are, however, a diversity of service providers and settings, as well as coordination arrangements. Consequently, participants and case managers often have a variety of schools from which to select; if the client cannot attend one location, another is usually available.

Welfare recipients are at a disadvantage in the job market, not only because they lack education, but also because they lack job-readiness and more general life skills. As a result, all of the JOBS programs include job readiness activities that encompass such topics as goal setting, time management, stress management, communication, assertiveness, and networking. Local social service agencies rely heavily on a variety of outside partners (e.g., the local community college or employment service, a for-profit contractor, or a not-for-profit community-based entity) to teach these life-skills activities. While a modest amount of this training occurs at the JOBS office, clients usually go to contractor sites.

Job skills training is generally purchased from a local supplier, commonly the service delivery area (SDA), but JTPA funds often pay for this training. JOBS participants often undergo a reassessment when they enter the JTPA program to determine if their basic education has reached the level required by the JTPA program. Participants found to be job ready go directly to job skills training, on-the-job training (OJT), or work experience. Other participants are referred back for further educational activity.

Although SDAs gain performance payments for serving welfare clients, many JTPA managers prefer to work with job-ready or near job-ready individuals. The coordination arrangements between local social service offices and SDAs have not reduced the division of labor between the two—the SDAs still get the more skilled clients, while social services works with the less skilled. On the other hand, JOBS and JTPA managers point out the financial advantages of their partnership. JTPA participants who qualify for JOBS allow SDAs to pass the cost of support services to the JOBS budget; likewise, the local JOBS program can obtain job skills training paid for with JTPA funds. This allows both programs to spread their funds further, serving more clients than would be the case if each program paid for both training and support services from its own funds, particularly because JTPA has limited support service funds and JOBS programs have low levels of funding for skills training.

Work-Force Entry. Placement activities have been relatively low in most communities because most clients have been assigned to educational activities. Despite the relatively low level of activity, several different arrangements exist for assisting the JOBS client into the job market. This variety has importance for coordination and dictates the type of agency and milieu the client encounters.

Collocated social service and employment service personnel share responsibility for the JOBS participants entry into the job market in three communities. It is of interest that these three cities are in states that had demonstration programs prior to FSA and where the governor played a role in bringing agencies together to reform welfare. Clients benefit from the expertise of each specialist as they work with the collocated staff. The state job data bank is usually directly available in the JOBS office under this arrangement, relieving either the client or the job placement specialist from making visits to a separate job service office. A relatively minor role for the SDA is typical of this pattern. Some JOBS clients may go through

JTPA-funded training and receive job placement through the training provider or be placed in an on-the-job training position, but this path to a job is just for some participants, usually those who are job-ready and motivated to pursue work.

In two localities, a treaty-like agreement between the local job service office and the SDA forms the basis for moving JOBS participants into the marketplace. Large numbers of job-ready welfare recipients are assigned to JTPA for training and placement, while the support costs for these public aid clients is picked up by JOBS funds. In these cities, the employment service serves in a minor capacity as keeper of the state job data bank and provides no special services for welfare clients. The three remaining communities exhibit unique local patterns, in which one agency or organization (e.g., the employment service, the welfare office, or a contractor) acts as the main gatekeeper of work-force entry. The other employment and training agencies and organizations play a secondary role, usually as a vendor of services purchased by the gatekeeper.

Support Services. JOBS participants require support services, such as child care and transportation, if they are to successfully participate in education, training, and other program activities. In general, clients receive reimbursement for transportation from their case manager, who either authorizes payment from the social service agency to the client or directly dispenses cash, bus passes, or tokens. Occasionally, a contractor provides transportation and then files for reimbursement.

The eight communities exhibit several different patterns for organizing child-care delivery. Two localities rely on the social service office to arrange for child-care referral. One other JOBS agency covers most of its child-care needs (80%) through a flat $2 per hour reimbursement to the client who can arrange her child's care with any provider. The rest of the clients, mostly in training or work experience, receive child-care services via a voucher system managed by a state department different from the public welfare department. In the five other communities, the JOBS program uses a child care resource and referral (CCR&R) organization that identifies vendors, manages a data base system, handles referrals, and disburses payments.

Coordination of Activities

With such diverse arrangements for service delivery involving multiple organizations in service provision in most communities, the need for coordination is high, just to make sure that clients are served and the various parts of the program fit together. Beyond that, JOBS has been implemented in the midst of an array of preexisting employment and training activities. The legislative mandate called for coordination of JOBS with other programs and activities, presumably to enhance effectiveness and reduce unnecessary duplication and overlap.

Approaches to coordination of JOBS activities at the local level range from the highly formal to the very informal. In almost all communities, contracts provide a major means of coordination. Contracting is an important coordinating mechanism because it provides the opportunity to specify the division of labor, identify roles, assign financial responsibilities, and establish procedures for client processing and information sharing. Of course, whether a contract accomplishes all of this varies from community to community and across the relationships of different agencies.

Although contracts are used frequently between public agencies, they are central to the use of not-for-profit and for-profit service providers. Procedures for coordinating the activities of these service providers with other components of the program are often identified in contracts.

While contracts are used to obtain services from various public agencies, it is often the case that nonfinancial agreements provide the basis for formalizing relationships among JOBS, JTPA, the employment service, social service agencies, and educational systems. These nonfinancial agreements serve many of the same purposes as contracts without requiring a transfer of financial resources from one agency to another. They are particularly important where existing state and intergovernmental programs are being used to provide services to JOBS clientele.

Contracts and nonfinancial agreements are sometimes the product of bilateral negotiation between agencies at the local level, but they are often the end result of activities undertaken by interagency coordinating bodies, particularly planning efforts. This is especially true in those states where decision making is sufficiently decentralized for significant planning and choices to be made at the local level. In a number of communities, care is taken to make sure that all relevant agencies are represented on planning groups and coordinating councils as a way of encouraging coordination.

The provision of joint funding and joint staffing through contracts and agreements also fosters coordination. Joint funding is an important coordination device because it signals the commitment of both organizations and gives each a stake in the success of the program.

Numerous coordination activities take place at the operational level. Perhaps the most important of these is collocation of staff, which is done by three communities. This allows joint processing of clients, extensive information sharing, and careful sequencing of activities. It makes it easy to move clients between components without suffering slippage.

Establishing fixed procedures for referral and client tracking is another important operational mechanism of coordination. These procedures include paper flows in all communities and electronic information transfer in others as agencies track clients through the system. Joint training is used in some communities to ensure that staff from cooperating organizations have a common understanding of the procedures that are to be followed.

Regular communication is often cited as an important part of coordination and has been formalized in some communities where individuals are assigned by the Title IV-A agency (the agency responsible for administering Aid to Families with Dependent Children) to serve as liaisons and coordinators with other agencies. In two communities, for example, the social service agency has created the position of education coordinator. Education coordinators visit education providers regularly, address the problems of individual clients in education programs, keep track of client progress, and generally foster a close working relationship between the social service agency and the education provider. They link case managers with education providers.

Many communities rely on regular meetings among program managers to facilitate operational coordination and reduce procedural and policy obstacles. These meetings typically include a discussion of local policy issues, specific coordination issues, substantive program problems, and proposals for future action.

One community said that joint presentation of some activities, such as orientation sessions and job search training, promotes coordination. Another suggested that having several providers involved in the development of a client's employability plan is an important way to generate coordination.

Exchanging information about clients is an important way to coordinate service delivery and all communities have some sort of provision for this. Despite this, little progress has been made in developing shared, electronic information systems. In one community, the social service agency staff enter some information that is put in the employment service information system. In several communities where employment service staff are collocated with case managers, there is some ability to share information from the systems of the two agencies, but little integration of those systems. In another community, there is sharing of some information through an electronic system that links the social service agency and the employment service. Nowhere are the multiple agencies linked by an electronic client processing or management information system.

EFFECTIVENESS OF COORDINATION

At one level the effectiveness of coordination refers to the degree to which JOBS has been effectively coordinated with the range of preexisting employment and training programs, such as those operating under provisions of the Job Training Partnership Act, the Wagner-Peyser Act, and the Carl D. Perkins Vocational and Applied Technology Act. At a second level, it refers to coordination at the policy level of the various components of the JOBS program itself. At a third level, it refers to coordination at the operational level of JOBS components. Our analysis addresses all three levels of coordination, and we find considerable variation in the effectiveness of coordination among these communities.

At the first level, involving coordination among programs, there has been considerable effort to draw upon the capacity of preexisting employment and training programs in some communities. Thus, almost all communities make some use of the employment service and the capacity it has developed under Wagner-Peyser and related laws. The extent to which communities draw upon this capacity varies, with some communities making extensive use of it and others drawing on it to a minimal degree. In one community, the relationship between JOBS and the employment service is a weak formality with no special arrangements for employment service support of the JOBS effort. In another, the employment service plays a central role, drawing upon its accumulated expertise to deliver a range of services to JOBS clients.

The integration of JOBS with JTPA activities also varies considerably. While some social service agencies have established strong connections with the JTPA system, others seem to draw on it almost as an afterthought. All JOBS programs rely to some extent on the availability of training and on-the-job training positions through SDAs, but in some there is very little use of this resource. In a couple, formal arrangements for access to JTPA services for JOBS clients are weak to nonexistent. In other communities, however, there are strong formal connections with the JTPA administrative entity, well-established referral systems, and regular channels of communication.

Much the same could be said for the vocational education system that is funded in part with Perkins Grants. In some communities, extensive use is made of the public vocational education system, particularly community colleges and vocational-technical schools. In other communities, the link between JOBS and the vocational education system seems quite weak.

Thus, despite formal legislative requirements for coordination of JOBS with elements of the preexisting employment and training system, such coordination is not guaranteed. It ranges from strong to almost nonexistent. In some ways, assigning lead responsibility for JOBS to the Title IV-A agency has led to weaker interprogram relationships than might otherwise have existed. Had the responsibility for JOBS been shared between the welfare system and the JTPA system, there would have been considerably greater chance for strong program coordination. That, of course, would have had other consequences for the program, not all of which would necessarily be viewed as positive.

At the second level, or the JOBS policy level, there have been mixed results in terms of coordination of JOBS activities in local communities. Some communities have had strong planning efforts that led to thoughtfully structured programs that link components in an effective manner. In other communities, coordination at the policy level has been more tenuous, in part because of weak planning processes. This has happened in part because so much decision making was centralized at the state level in some states. Such centralization made it particularly difficult in some cases to plan for coordination with JTPA which, of course, is a highly decentralized system. In one case, the state human service agency has attempted to overcome this by demanding, in effect, that the service delivery areas act in a particular manner. In another case, the administrative entity makes JTPA training available to JOBS clients, but coordination at the policy level is weak.

Coordination at the third, or operational, level is very effective in some settings and only partially effective in other communities. We encountered few, if any, glaring failures of service delivery coordination, but there were communities where coordination of particular components seemed quite weak. This was particularly the case where formal arrangements, contracts, and strong interagency agreements had not been developed to spell out mutual responsibilities. This often happened when one agency was viewed as playing a minor role in the program, as in a couple of cases where the employment service was viewed almost as an accidental appendage or where it had not developed services tailored to JOBS participants.

Views of coordination varied substantially among actors in the different communities. As might expected, these differences show up in comparisons across communities. Even within individual communities, however, there were cases where actors had quite different perceptions of coordination. When this occurred, it was typically the case that social service agency managers had a more sanguine view of the effectiveness of coordination than did managers of other agencies. JTPA personnel were the most likely to think that coordination needs considerable improvement.

BARRIERS TO COORDINATION

Our interviewees actually identified only a small number of factors that they believed to be barriers to coordination, although the broader analysis of activities suggests several additional factors that hinder coordination efforts. Comments of the people we interviewed suggest that the biggest barrier to coordination at the state and local level may be instability: political instability, policy fluctuation, turnover of administrators and staff in the lead agency, and turnover of case managers. Time and again it turned out that managers found it difficult to coordinate when these forms of instability were present.

Political and policy instability undermine leadership and create great uncertainty about program directions and priorities. Under these conditions, it is difficult to plan a set of activities for clients, much less decide how to coordinate such activities. Such instability detracts attention from the problem at hand and leads to great speculation about what the future holds, dissipating energy that might better be devoted to program management and service delivery. Every policy change can mean that service delivery has to be changed; this, in turn, can lead to new requirements for coordination. Thus, more effort has to be put into planning coordination, instead of delivering services to clients.

Such instability is inherent in public policy processes. The struggle over the content and direction of public policy is ongoing, reflecting different conceptions of the role and purpose of government and how best to achieve its various objectives. Managers can do little about it, except to cope with it by adapting activities as necessary to meet changing political demands.

Policymakers themselves can be attentive to the problems created by instability. They can, for example, ask whether the marginal benefits to be brought about by some change in policy or administrative structure are worth the losses that will be experienced as a result of instability introduced by implementing the change. They can ask whether they leave their mark better by focusing their efforts on improving operations within current policy and structure or by trying to change structure and policy. The issue of staff stability is also crucial. Operational coordination depends not only on establishing formal coordination procedures, but also on the interactions and relationships that develop among those actually responsible for providing service and administering activities. Frequent changes in leadership and staff make it difficult to maintain the interpersonal relationships that foster and facilitate coordination.

Respondents also suggested that confusion over assigned roles and complex contractual arrangements can create barriers to effective coordination. If people are uncertain about who is doing what, it can lead to gaps in action and duplication of effort. If contractual arrangements are complicated, it can be difficult to initiate action and change. Complex contractual arrangements, for example, may result in a need for multiple approvals when some step is to be taken. In one instance, where the state welfare agency contracts directly with another state agency to obtain educational services for JOBS participants, the local managers find it difficult to get additional sites established for delivery of basic education services. Instead of dealing directly with the local education agency, they have to route a request through the state human service agency which then forwards it to the state education agency which then sends it on to the local education agency.

Perhaps most striking is the fact that few of the respondents we interviewed saw existing policy as a barrier to effective coordination. They simply did not raise broad issues of legislative policy or administrative regulation as significant problems. This may well reflect the fact that local actors have more immediate operational concerns that they do not see as being particularly tied to national, or even state, policy issues.

IMPROVING COORDINATION

As we talked with managers and service delivery specialists, we sought their ideas about things that could be done to improve coordination in JOBS. Many steps that individual respondents suggested have already been taken in some localities. Some would probably contribute significantly to program effectiveness if implemented in localities across the country. Others have more problematic consequences.

Respondents offered a number of ideas:

- One-stop shopping with collocation of JTPA service delivery area, employment service, and human service agency personnel
- Reduced workloads
- Placing greater reliance on employment service estimates of labor market demand in making decisions about training
- Federal and state officials providing a model for local coordination and reducing their turf wars that make it tough to coordinate at the local level
- Giving incentives and nonfinancial recognition for successful collaboration
- Developing on-line computer access to a shared information system

- Consolidating assessment in hands of the case manager
- Reducing client shuffling among agencies
- Reducing requirements for targeting and allowing more effort to be devoted to volunteer participants

Some of these ideas carry a compelling logic and have been demonstrated already to work in some of the communities. For example, it is eminently logical to create one-stop shopping arrangements that collocate service providers who are responsible for JOBS services. This automatically reduces the amount of running around the client has to do, allows close collaboration among service providers, and makes it easier to share information and provide effective case management. Collocation is in place to one degree or another in several of the communities we studied, and it is working reasonably well in those locations. Respondents from those communities generally perceived significant benefits from the arrangement.

Despite this endorsement, collocation by itself is limited in what it can accomplish. Without other efforts to collaborate on client processing and client services, it may simply mean that the client has to go to only one location in order to see different providers of distinct services. Several interviews suggested to us that it is interaction and collaboration that really make the difference.

A second idea with considerable merit is the notion of creating shared electronic information systems. Modest efforts have been made in this direction, but they are not enough. Most of the systems we encountered did not allow ready transfer of information among systems. None allowed the full mix of service providers that work with a client to have access to the information base. Most seemed to focus on management reporting requirements, rather than addressing service delivery needs. Information systems that overcome these barriers will reduce considerable duplication of effort, make it easier to track clients as they move through the system, and facilitate service delivery. Thus, they will enhance both management control and service delivery.

Several ideas would do little to improve coordination. Reducing the targeting of JOBS and allowing more emphasis on volunteer participants would unquestionably make the service provider's jobs easier, but it is hard to see how this will affect coordination efforts. It also runs counter to the JOBS philosophy of concentrating effort on the hard-to-serve. Reducing the shuffling of clients among agencies is more a goal of coordination than a way of improving coordination. The question is how one can coordinate in a way that reduces client shuffling.

Consolidating assessment in the hands of the case manager is an interesting idea. One of the classic signs of insufficient coordination has been the presence of multiple assessment processes that clients must undergo, as first one agency and then another attempts to identify their needs and develop service plans. Indeed, we found cases where JOBS clients were being tested more than once to identify their level of basic educational skills. Such repeated testing places unnecessary burdens on clients and depletes resources that could be put to other uses.

On the other hand, it may not be desirable or necessary to place all assessment activities in the hands of case managers. Others who deal with clients may have better capacity and skills for doing certain types of assessment. If nothing else, education and training providers are sure to assess learning that occurs in their programs. Some education providers may be better equipped than case managers to assess life skills. The key is to develop a sensible policy on assessment, one that clearly identifies assessment responsibilities and makes provision for sharing of assessment information among all providers who require that information to adequately and effectively deliver client services. In many instances, this probably will not place all assessment responsibilities in the hands of the case manager, but it will more effectively accomplish the same ends.

As for reducing workloads—it depends. Workloads should be structured to allow case managers adequate time to work on each client's case. They should be able to talk with service providers, as well as the client, to ensure appropriateness of services, coordinate activities, and monitor client participation and progress. If the workload is too heavy, they will not be able to do this and coordination will suffer. This may be a real threat in a time of severe budgetary difficulties at the state and local level. At least one community we visited had already reduced staffing to the point that it was threatening the viability of the program.

In terms of federal and state officials providing a model for local coordination by reducing their own coordination shortcomings, several observations are in order. First, exemplary behavior up high may foster better coordination at the service delivery level, but it is hardly any guarantee. In addition, there are numerous examples of excellent coordination despite continuing difficulties at the federal level. On the other hand, better coordination at the federal and state level would eliminate some difficulties that local programs face. Perhaps more than anything else, progress at the state and federal level would provide symbols of what can be accomplished and serve as a stimulus to improvements at the local level. With hierarchically-organized state agencies that have field offices at the local level, state-level coordination may be central to the success of efforts at the service delivery level.

Although local managers did not suggest it as a way to improve coordination, special steps need to be taken to involve the JTPA service delivery areas in the JOBS program when policy making is highly centralized at the state level. Under this condition it is too easy for the SDAs to be overlooked as significant contributors to the program because JTPA is such a decentralized program. Special efforts should be made to pull them into the circle, rather than having them standing around as passive observers who occasionally certify JOBS clients for JTPA training activities.

ACTION RECOMMENDATIONS

We limit our recommendations to three that are by far the most important things that can be done to improve coordination of JOBS at the service delivery level.

1. *If it has not already been accomplished, local communities should concentrate on efforts to create one-stop shopping with active collaboration and interaction in the shop.* This step, more than any other, has the potential to provide substantial coordination and improved program effectiveness.

2. *Cooperation is needed between state and local actors and among the various agencies to create information systems that allow shared use of a common base of client information.* Although this information is important for management reporting purposes, it is even more important to see that client needs are met and service delivery is coordinated. It is a crucial step, for example, in creating a system in which assessments are limited but the information is shared among all who need it. Creating such information systems is both a technical and a policy problem and must be approached at both levels.

3. *The administrators of the JOBS program at the local or service delivery level should make special efforts to establish effective working relationships with SDAs, involving them as full partners in the program.* JTPA and JOBS have overlapping objectives. The SDAs have considerable experience. It is possible to create great synergy by bringing welfare and employment and training organizations together in the administration of JOBS. This can only work to the benefit of both agencies and clients.

Part V

CONCLUSION

Chapter 16

Coordinating Public Assistance Programs in the United States

Neal S. Zank and Edward T. Jennings, Jr.

As demonstrated throughout this book, the public assistance system is overloaded with a multitude of agencies, programs, regulations, procedures, documentation requirements, and terminology that has the unintended effect of discouraging coordination and the efficient delivery of services. To many, the system is unworkable or at least seems to have broken down. Even the system's staunchest defenders find it too unmanageable. Yet, the many players and special interests underscore the difficulty of comprehensive reform.

Short of drastically eliminating or consolidating programs, improving program coordination is the only realistic solution. Yet, improving coordination is not a simple process. It is time consuming and requires continuous attention to operations; it may result in some loss of decision-making autonomy, while requiring increased interagency activity. Its benefits are in the future, and it requires action counter to much bureaucratic behavior, which tends to focus on the agency's specific responsibilities, legal mandates, and narrowly defined clientele.

We see clear-cut roles for all levels of government in coordinating public assistance programs. We believe that the federal government should have these objectives:

- Ensure that the economically disadvantaged have reasonable access to assistance programs

- Define overall goals and structure evaluations for federal public assistance programs
- Manage the existing disparate federal aid system in a way that promotes greater cooperation and coordination between implementing agencies and, when involved, the private sector
- Assist states to provide, expand, and modernize assistance programs in a flexible environment that allows for state experimentation, innovation, and design of their own programs

The state should have these objectives in promoting coordination in programs for the economically disadvantaged:

- Develop and maintain a service delivery system that ensures reasonable access to assistance programs
- Experiment with innovative service delivery systems that reflect the unique situation of that state, but may yet be replicable
- Coordinate the disparate federal assistance programs to the maximum extent possible

State and local efforts to promote coordination at the service delivery level should have these objectives:

- Develop innovative, responsive, and flexible service delivery systems that are tailored to client needs
- Integrate programs with different eligibility criteria, documentation, and funding streams into a unified, more manageable system
- Help public and private agencies participate and communicate within a framework of community planning, operation, and evaluation
- Utilize sophisticated referral and communications systems among agencies

There are many strategies for improving coordination, as well as streamlining and rationalizing the eligibility and related criteria of federal programs, to assist the economically disadvantaged. Implementation of these strategies should help make federal, state, and local programs more efficient and facilitate access for the poor to the programs. Over time, these strategies should lead to an administrative environment that allows for increased program participation and the allocation of savings from program administration to assistance activities.

Our proposed solutions to the coordination problem correspond to our identification of the elements of that problem. The proposed solutions all contribute, to one degree or another, to minimizing conflicting or overlapping provisions; identifying funding disparities; improving program management and administration; reducing administrative costs; and enabling states to deal with fewer contact points in Washington.

ELEMENT 1: PRESIDENTIAL LEADERSHIP

Presidential leadership is essential. The coordination of public assistance programs must be a top presidential domestic priority. Movement toward greater coordination will be nearly impossible without the president's prestige, visibility, and strong leadership. The president also needs to promote coordination as a top policy goal for his cabinet and subcabinet officials, for political appointees and career civil servants.

White House coordinating groups play a role as well, in part to lead the other agencies and, in part, to enforce the president's policies. The present White House structures most suited to play this role are the Economic Empowerment Task Force (EETF) and the Office of Management and Budget (OMB). The EETF's authority and mission should be expanded to resolve problems that affect the design and implementation of federal programs for the economically disadvantaged and to enhance the state role in assistance planning efforts. The management side has taken a back seat to budget at OMB, leaving it poorly suited to address coordination issues. OMB should move to develop its institutional capabilities for management and focus on such problems as differing eligibility criteria and documentation requirements.

ELEMENT 2: FEDERAL AGENCY REFORM

There are various ways to enhance coordination in federal agencies. Initially, it would be useful if agencies and agency heads could work together to develop common policy goals or program targets.

Administrative action is a second way to promote coordination. For example, the Departments of Education, Health and Human Services, and Labor entered into an interagency agreement in November 1989 to provide jointly technical assistance to states and localities to help them operate or improve their JOBS programs.

A third approach to improving coordination in federal agencies is by reorganizing agencies or programs to eliminate overlap or duplication or to provide more comprehensive services to clients. There is little enthusiasm in either the executive or legislative branches for combining either all federal assistance programs or selected aspects of these programs, such as all employment and training, under a more logical organizational structure, although President Bush's Job Training 2000 proposal did call for consolidation. Although the potential benefits of this approach are compelling, the time and costs involved in executive branch reorganization are great. In addition, the jurisdictional issues associated with congressional committees and executive departments, historical reasons, and the problems of responding to special interest groups present formidable obstacles to reorganization.

Despite these barriers, two potential targets for reorganization should be investigated. First, there is a great deal of overlap within the executive branch in providing job training services: the Departments of Agriculture (USDA), Health and Human Services (HHS), and Labor administer separate employment and training programs, serving essentially the same target groups. These and other relevant job training programs should be merged into one agency operating under the same policy leadership and direction. Ideally, that agency's operation should combine the best aspects of these programs, for example, state, local, and private sector participation and tying welfare to work. Several organizations have endorsed such an approach. In January 1991, the Carnegie Foundation for the Advancement of Teaching proposed consolidating all federal job training and vocational and adult education programs to improve coordination and the quality of the programs. The National Commission for Employment Policy made this type of recommendation to the president and the Congress in September 1991. The Congressional Office of Technology Assessment recommended in February 1992 the merger of the primary job training agencies.

Federal agencies can also learn from the example of local agencies. The Rural Coast Bend, Texas, Private Industry Council (PIC) administers an integrated employment and training system composed of the Food Stamps employment and training program, the Job Opportunities and Basic Skills (JOBS) program, and certain aspects of the Job Training Partnership Act (JTPA). Housing all three programs together has eased client processing. The PIC has also managed to keep track of the three separate funding streams, calendar-program years, and mandates. There is a lesson here for federal officials that these programs can be effectively administered by a single organization.

Second, greater efforts should be made to provide a seamless network of services to clients and design a program geared toward outputs and services rather than inputs. Ways to accomplish this are to move USDA's Food and Consumer Services programs (such as Food Stamps and the Women, Infants, and Children [WIC] food aid program) to HHS and merge these programs with the appropriate service agency (such as the Administration for Children and Families and its Aid to Families with Dependent Children [AFDC] program, the Public Health Service for maternal and child health, or the Health Care Financing Agency for Medicaid).

Reorganization or restructuring of agencies or programs is more feasible when the target agency or activity is under the same policy leadership and does not involve a shift in congressional jurisdiction. For example, Department of Health and Human Services (HHS) Secretary Louis Sullivan announced in April 1991 the merger of the HHS Office of Human Development Services and Family Support Administration into an Administration for Children and Families to bring together in one office under the same policy direction the department's many child and family programs. Congressional oversight remained with the Finance and Ways and Means committees.

A final administrative approach to coordination is through legislative direction. Congress has included provisions in some pieces of legislation that require certain agencies to coordinate with other agencies, provide funding for coordination, or mandate the joint preparation or review of certain programs. Examples of these approaches include Family Support Act requirements for the secretary of Health and Human Services to consult with the secretaries of Education and Labor on a continuing basis on education and training services, the provision for an 8 percent set-aside of each state's JTPA allocation to facilitate coordination of education and training services, and a mandate in the Carl D. Perkins Vocational and Applied Technology Act that requires the state plan for vocational education be furnished to the JTPA-created state job training coordinating council (SJTCC) for review and comment. Yet, a review of the literature on coordination suggests that these types of coordination provisions are helpful in promoting coordination, but are not sufficient by themselves to ensure maximum coordination.

ELEMENT 3: CONGRESSIONAL REFORM

Reform of the congressional committee system is integral to resolving many of the coordination problems faced at all levels of government. Congress represents the voice of widely divergent constituencies. State and local public assistance practitioners, public interest group representatives, and policy analysts who work in and observe the public assistance system have identified congressional action as necessary to solving the coordination problem. The problems associated with inconsistent programs and the lack of cohesion and coordination can only be solved by Congress. Undoubtedly, Congress has the power to do so and should exercise that power in order to see that many of its well-intended programs are melded into a more successful national effort to eradicate poverty.

Three options are available. One possibility is for each chamber to delegate the responsibility for legislation and oversight over public assistance programs to a single Committee on Public Assistance in each chamber. All food and nutrition, job training, housing, health, and income security programs targeted at the economically disadvantaged would be the responsibility of this committee. Issues relating to the tax treatment of the poor and the finance of these programs would still have to be directed through the Senate Finance and House Ways and Means committees, but much of the overlap and conflict within the current system would be eliminated.

A second option would be for Congress to establish a new Joint Committee on Public Assistance that would conduct oversight hearings and studies on the broad range of public assistance programs and provide staff resources for committees involved in public assistance programs. Although this proposed joint committee would not have the authority to draft legislation, it would be able to serve as a staff resource to committees that do have legislative authority for different public assistance programs, better enabling these committees to work out the details in statutory design that will facilitate, rather than hinder, the coordination of public assistance programs. Its role would be similar to that of the Joint Committee on Taxation on tax matters.

A third approach would be to require a Coordination Impact Statement to accompany all proposals dealing with public assistance programs. This impact statement would describe the relationship between the proposal and existing policies and programs, identify coordination issues that are raised by the proposal, and specify how the proposal addresses those issues. The Coordination Impact Statement would be prepared by the Congressional Budget Office in order to ensure its objectivity and freedom from committee jurisdictional concerns.

ELEMENT 4: STATE AND LOCAL PARTICIPATION

The critical feature of state involvement in programs for the economically disadvantaged is the policy linkage between the rules governing the distribution of benefits and the services designed to help welfare recipients become self-supporting. State and local governments have significant roles in delivering benefits and, in many cases, a great deal of flexibility in how they organize and manage the agencies that provide these benefits.

It is critical to retain state flexibility in the administration of programs that serve the economically disadvantaged. States can offer a wide range of services tailored to local needs. Also, the chances are much greater that the innovation needed for improved program performance will result from each individual state, better aware of its needs, experimenting with different approaches to these complex programs than from one federal agency.

Only a few states have attempted to coordinate public assistance at the policy or decision-making level. States should continue their efforts at the highest levels of government to improve policy coordination of the different federal and state public assistance programs that they currently administer. In these times of scarce dollars, governors must make coordination a top priority.

State governments usually rely on their health, welfare, and employment and training agencies to manage and implement these programs. Local governments utilize local agencies, county and district welfare offices, schools, food banks, and private organizations to implement most programs. Programs such as housing are administered by local governments or private landlords. State and local governments often strive for greater efficiency by using one local agency to administer many programs.

In recent years, considerable attention has been given to the question of how service delivery can be coordinated in a way that will enhance the system and reduce burdens on clients. These deliberations have given rise to proposals for administrative action; collocation of programs at the same geographical point of entry; one-stop eligibility determinations for determining eligibility, individual assessment, and referral to the appropriate public assistance program; integrated case management; and multipurpose or consolidated application forms. These techniques are used separately or in conjunction with each other, depending upon the state.

There are a variety of ways that administrative actions can be used to facilitate coordination of public assistance programs. For example, agencies may establish a contractual relationship or enter into a memorandum of understanding for one agency to administer the program of the other. Numerous cases discussed in this volume illustrate such arrangements.

Organizational change or reorganization is a second form of administrative action. As discussed in Chapter 7, New Jersey and Connecticut provide examples of reorganization efforts designed to enhance policy development and service delivery. Linda Harris demonstrates the benefits

of particular organizational arrangements when she points out in Chapter
13 that the development of the Lafayette Court Family Development
Center was made possible by the fact that the Housing Authority, the JTPA
system, and the Community Development Block Grant program operated
out of one agency.

A third form of administrative action brings disparate or multiple
funding streams together to provide an integrated, flexible service delivery
system. For example, the Lafayette Court Family Development Center in
Baltimore brings together numerous funding sources and provides an
integrated set of health, education, employment, and counseling services
for families in a high-rise public housing project.

Collocation is perhaps the simplest form of coordination. Without any
concessions in terms of changed eligibility criteria or lessened documentation requirements, collocation provides common office space for separately administered programs. Having one geographical point of entry
eases clients' access to a wide range of programs and improves service
delivery.

One-stop shopping for eligibility determination is another approach to
facilitating coordination at the local level. Some states have initiated
one-stop shopping systems for eligibility determinations, individual assessments, and referral to the appropriate public assistance program. Also
called co-eligibility determination for services, these systems provide a
single, centralized review of applications for two or more programs having
different eligibility requirements. These systems allow centralized collection of an applicant's financial data for all programs and determination of
financial eligibility for more than one program. The computer support that
generally accompanies centralization also ensures greater accuracy. One-
stop shopping brings diverse services together under one roof, making it
easier for clients to access multiple services offered by service producers.

Pennsylvania's Single Point of Contact (SPOC) program, discussed in
Chapter 12, places JTPA, JOBS, and Job Service staff in the county offices
of the state Public Welfare Department, which also administers the state's
welfare program. As the SPOC program was in place when JOBS was
enacted in 1988, Pennsylvania did not need to create a new job training
system for JOBS. The four programs also share an integrated intake
process.

One-stop shopping for eligibility determinations reduces administrative
costs and facilitates referral by service providers. Records are more
accessible, eligibility determination and verification needs to be done only
once, the likelihood of error is reduced, and eligibility redetermination can
be made to coincide. One-stop shopping minimizes travel inconveniences

for program recipients or beneficiaries, which is especially important for the elderly and the disabled, and uses less burdensome application procedures. This approach also encourages the use of a single purpose application form rather than many individual forms.

Integrated case management means that an applicant who applies for benefits under two or more programs would deal with only one case manager from the beginning of the application process through the provision or denial of benefits. The concept behind case management is that clients with multiple needs are often confronted by a fragmented system for addressing those needs. A case manager could see that the various needs of a client are met. This would include needs assessment, development of a service plan, and oversight of the delivery of the various components of the plan. The difficulty, of course, is to create a system or set of procedures that allows the services of various producers and providers to be coordinated in this manner. Many of the JOBS programs discussed in this volume have created such systems, as has the Baltimore Lafayette Court Family Development Center.

In support of case management or other efforts at coordinated service delivery, managers often recommend integrated data systems that allow partners in the service delivery system to provide and access data about clients. Information systems of this type facilitate eligibility determination and make it possible to track the progress of clients through the system. They also provide a data base for planning and evaluation. Integrated case management is also a first step toward integrating the eligibility criteria, rules, and regulations of some programs, although this level of integration often requires federal action to change the rules for programs such as AFDC and Food Stamps. A 1980 U.S. government interagency report, the *Eligibility Simplification Project*, found that implementing integrated case management with automated eligibility features would save substantial administrative costs and lead to reduced error rates, improved services to clients, and reduced administrative workloads (U.S. Office of Management and Budget, 1980).

If none of the more aggressive coordination approaches are acceptable or feasible, agencies can still turn to efforts to develop consolidated application forms. Multipurpose application forms provide an applicant the opportunity to record sufficient data on one form to permit the determination of his or her eligibility for several programs. Some questions on the form may apply to all programs, while others may apply to specific programs with specific requirements. This way, clients do not have to repeatedly provide the same or similar information to different service providers. The uniform use of a multipurpose application form is facilitated by generally standardized definitions among the programs using the form, simplified or standardized policy requirements, and reasonable, under-standable data requests of applicants.

One-stop shopping often involves the use of a multipurpose application form. For example, the North Dakota Job Service (which administers job service, unemployment insurance, and some JTPA programs) imple-mented an intake system in 1989 that allows clients to register for work, file a claim for unemployment insurance, and apply for JTPA benefits in one visit. This new system replaced three different intake points and three sets of application procedures. A major factor in consolidation of intake services was that the three programs were administered by the same state agency. The three programs also shared a common computer system that increased efficiency and cut costs. Administration of the JOBS programs was integrated into this system.

A 1977 study by the Federal Paperwork Commission found that the use of multipurpose application forms reduces cross-program eligibility deter-mination costs, application time, paperwork, and administrative costs (U.S. General Accounting Office, 1987). Some have found, however, that diverse eligibility criteria and rules can make such forms overly long and cumbersome.

These local efforts at improved service delivery, whatever their focus and range, must address a common set of issues involving planning, communication, decision making, management, and operational relation-ships. To successfully address these issues, local officials must develop strategies for building cooperation and overcoming significant barriers to joint action.

ELEMENT 5: ELIGIBILITY CRITERIA

Congress and the executive branch agencies should work together to develop a framework for streamlining eligibility requirements, formulating standard definitions and poverty measures, and easing administrative and documentation requirements in programs that serve the disadvantaged. Re-lated issues that need to be addressed include varying planning and operating timetables, conflicting federal and state regulations and reporting require-ments governing different programs, overlapping but not identical goals and performance measures, and administrative differences in operating proce-dures for processing clients, contracting, and reporting.

Standard or common definitions, usable by all programs, must serve two purposes. First, the definitions must identify what constitutes income and assets. Second, common definitions should indicate whether the income or asset is to be counted or included in determining eligibility.

Standard definitions relating to income and assets, when combined with common verification standards among agencies, would allow for (1) an applicant's financial information to be collected and recorded in an identical manner for all programs, thereby reducing the need for multiple forms; (2) a single verification by one program that should suffice for others; and (3) centralized determination of financial eligibility for all programs. Standard definitions and data collection would help in the implementation and monitoring of programs in the future. Michigan and other states have developed common definitions of terms and quantifiable outcomes across human investment programs.

The different income eligibility standards used in these programs increase the administrative burden upon both recipients and program staff and have a deleterious effect upon coordination. Congress should seek to unify and, thereby, simplify the income eligibility levels used in public assistance programs. This entails the establishment of a national standard for welfare, including both AFDC and Food Stamps. A national welfare standard would eliminate the current system of state-developed need and payment standards for AFDC that give rise to wide interstate variations in support and, some argue, resulting distortions in locational and labor market decisions. The national standard could be adjusted to reflect cost-of-living differences.

CONCLUSION

This book provides food for thought. The chapters address the institutions and processes of federal, state, and local assistance programs and discuss a wide range of coordination problems and possible solutions. In our introduction and this concluding chapter, we provide strategies for improving coordination in the existing public assistance system. What this demonstrates, and what we hope the reader will appreciate, is that there are a great many solutions to current problems in public assistance programs. In the end, however, it is up to the policymakers, the service providers, and the participants in the system to improve coordination and the quality and efficiency of public assistance programs.

REFERENCES

U.S. General Accounting Office. 1987. "Welfare Issues to Consider in Assessing Proposals for Reform." Washington, D.C. February.

U.S. Office of Management and Budget. 1980. *Eligibility Simplification Project*. Washington, D.C. October.

Index

About the Contributors

ROBERT G. AINSWORTH is an Associate Director of Research at the National Commission for Employment Policy. He was formerly Director of the Office of Resource Requirement, Federal Energy Administration.

LAWRENCE NEIL BAILIS is a Senior Research Associate at the Center for Human Resources at the Heller Graduate School of Brandeis University. He has conducted research on the administration of human service programs for several federal agencies, states, cities, and other organizations. He has a Ph.D. in government from Harvard University.

THOMAS J. CORBETT, a research affiliate with the Institute for Research on Poverty and member of the faculty of the Department of Governmental Affairs of the University of Wisconsin-Madison, works closely with the UW School of Social Work and the Robert LaFollette School of Public Affairs. He has worked extensively in government and has a Ph.D. in social welfare from the University of Wisconsin.

DAVID FARLEY is the Government Affairs Officer of the Office of the Mayor, City of Pittsburgh. He is former manager of Pittsburgh Partnership, the city's job training organization, and past chair of the Pennsylvania Service Delivery Areas Association. He has managed and operated employment and training programs for targeted urban populations for more than ten years.

JAMES GIMPEL is Assistant Professor of Government at the University of Maryland in College Park. He served on the Republican staff of the U.S. Senate Committee on Labor and Human Resources from 1989 to 1991.

LINDA A. HARRIS is Director of the Baltimore City Office of Employment Development. She is Vice President of the Maryland Association of Service Delivery Areas and serves as board member or advisor to numerous public organizations. She has more than eighteen years experience in the employment and training field and holds a master's degree in urban and public affairs from Carnegie-Mellon University.

KEVIN R. HOPKINS is an adjunct senior fellow at the Hudson Institute in Washington, D.C., and a former Special Assistant to President Reagan for policy development. He is the author of "Welfare Dependency: Behavior, Culture, and Public Policy."

EDWARD T. JENNINGS, JR., is Associate Professor of Public Administration and Political Science at the University of Kentucky. He has written extensively about policy making and administration and served as a consultant to national, state, and local agencies. He has a Ph.D. in political science from Washington University in St. Louis.

CHRISTOPHER T. KING, Associate Director of the Center for the Study of Human Resources at the Lyndon B. Johnson School of Public Affairs at the University of Texas, has conducted research on education, employment, training, and welfare programs. He was principal editor for the U.S. Department of Labor's JTPA Advisory Committee report, *Working Capital*. He has a Ph.D. in economics from Michigan State University.

DALE KRANE is Associate Professor of Public Administration at the University of Nebraska-Omaha. He has written extensively on public policy, intergovernmental management, and state and local politics. He is coeditor of *From Nation to States: the Small Cities Community Development Block Grant Program*. He has a Ph.D. in political science from the University of Minnesota.

BARBARA KING MISECHOK is a planning supervisor in the Pittsburgh Partnership. She was previously Assistant to the Executive Director, Turtle Creek Valley Mental Health Retardation, Inc. She received an M.P.A. from West Virginia University.

BARBARA B. OAKLEY is a Special Assistant at the National Commission for Employment Policy. She worked for ten years with the Iowa State Employment Service where she held the positions of Program Administrator, District Supervisor, and Des Moines Metro Manager.

KATHY R. THORNBURG is Professor of Human Development and Family Studies, University of Missouri. She is Director of the Child Development Laboratory and Coordinator of the Missouri Youth Data Base Project. She has a Ph.D. in Child and Family Development from the University of Missouri.

WILLIAM TRACY is Executive Director of the New Jersey State Employment and Training Commission. He has been involved in the design, operation, and evaluation of work-force investment system components for the past twenty years.

KATHLEEN WIMER is Director of the Connecticut Employment and Training Commission. She manages program and policy planning and development with the Connecticut Department of Labor and has a Master's of Public Administration degree.

NEAL S. ZANK is Associate Director of the National Commission for Employment Policy. He served previously as Senior Private Enterprise Policy Advisor at the U.S. Agency for International Development. He is coauthor of *Reforming Financial Systems: Policy Change and Privatization* (Greenwood Press, 1991) and has written extensively on privatization in the banking industry and foreign aid programs. He earned an M.B.A. at George Washington University.